DRUGS

A Healthy Understanding

LARRY W. LATTERMAN

Kendall Hunt
publishing company

Cover image © Shutterstock

Kendall Hunt
publishing company

www.kendallhunt.com
Send all inquiries to:
4050 Westmark Drive
Dubuque, IA 52004-1840

ISBN 978-1-4652-0975-7

Printed in the United States of America
10 9 8 7 6 5 4

DEDICATION

This textbook is dedicated to my wife Kim, my daughter Ladonna, and my son Christopher. Your love and encouragement have always meant more to me than you will ever know.
To my teachers, who encouraged me to pursue academic endeavors.
To our readers as they make good decisions for a complete healthier, happier life.

BRIEF CONTENTS

CONTENTS

Section One

Section Two

Section Four

Section Five

PREFACE

No matter where you are, drug use and abuse is in the headlines. Media sources ranging from Internet news to blogs and from talk shows and major news networks to special television segments bring us a daily dose of drug use and abuse information.

Today's tech savvy, media-oriented college students are well aware of the many issues relating to drug use and abuse. Just about every day you hear the concerns about tobacco, alcohol, club drugs, over-the-counter medications, and illicit drugs like methamphetamines.

Drug abuse is a major public health problem that impacts society on multiple levels. Directly or indirectly, every community is affected by drug abuse and addiction, as is every family. Drugs take a tremendous toll on our society at many levels.

A person's environment includes many different influences from family and friends to socioeconomic status and quality of life in general. Factors such as peer pressure, physical and sexual abuse, stress and parental involvement can greatly influence the course of drug abuse and addiction in a person's life.

The goal of *Drugs, a Healthy Understanding* is to transmit to students a healthier understanding of drug use and abuse and to give them a definite knowledge of the consequences of drug abuse.

To achieve this goal and encourage student education, I have compiled the data and information in an easy-to-understand and user-friendly manner.

ACKNOWLEDGEMENTS

An author's work is only one part of the effort that went into the development and production of this textbook. Many other people worked long hours to produce a visually appealing, high quality textbook for students. I would like to acknowledge their dedication and hard work.

First and foremost I would like to give thanks to God who has given me this opportunity; through him all things are possible.

Second, this first edition of *Drugs, a Healthy Understanding* could not have been completed without the many dedicated people at Kendall/Hunt Publishing Company. From Acquisitions Editor Stephanie Ramirez to Senior Project Coordinator Linda Chapman and Regional Project Coordinator Ryan Schrodt, they are truly first rate, and my interaction with them is always delightful.

Third, I am deeply grateful to those who continue to teach me: my students. They provide a feedback loop that helps to keep me focused on investigating the latest findings in drug research to be a better professor.

Fourth, I would like to express my appreciation to Dr. Rosemary Degner, Dr. Amanda Chau, Dr. Donald M Bailey and Mr. Bill Nix for their time and encouragement.

Finally, I wish to thank all my family and friends for their continued support and love.

ABOUT THE AUTHOR

Larry Latterman, M.A.

Larry Latterman is currently teaching Drug Use and Abuse, Personal Health, Foundations of Kinesiology and First Aid courses for the Health and Kinesiology Department at Blinn College, Bryan, TX. Prior to his time at Blinn College he taught for Region Six Educational Service Center in Huntsville, TX, and at Southwest Texas Junior College, Uvalde, TX. Larry earned both his undergraduate degree and his M.A. in Physical Education and Health from Sam Houston State University in Huntsville, TX. Outside of the classroom, Larry enjoys spending time with his family, camping, hiking and bicycling.

"The human mind is capable of excitement without the application of gross and violent stimulants; and he must have a very faint perception of its beauty and dignity who does not know this."

-William Wordsworth

CHAPTER 1

Drugs: An Introduction

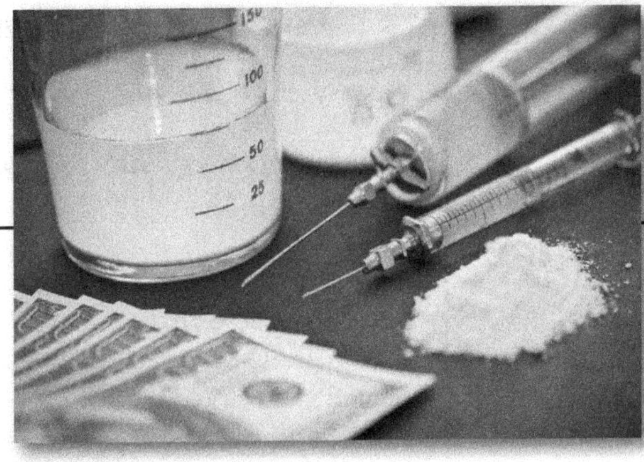
Shutterstock © kola-kola, 2011. Under license from Shutterstock, Inc.

OBJECTIVES

After you have finished this chapter, you should be able to:

- list the reasons why people take drugs;
- define and explain what drug addiction is;
- explain why some people become addicted but others do not;
- explain what factors increase the risk of addiction;
- explain if drug addiction can be treated successfully;
- explain why drug abuse is costly;
- explain why drug abuse is a major public health problem;
- describe how drug abuse affects us all;
- describe the trends in drug abuse;
- explain why drug abuse continues.

"I tried sniffing Coke once, but the ice cubes got stuck in my nose."

-Unknown

WHY DO PEOPLE TAKE DRUGS?[1]

In general, people begin taking drugs for a variety of reasons:[1]

- **To feel good.** Most abused drugs produce intense feelings of pleasure. This initial sensation of euphoria is followed by other effects, which differ with the type of drug used. For example, with stimulants such as cocaine, the "high" is followed by feelings of power, self-confidence, and increased energy. In contrast, the euphoria caused by opiates such as heroin is followed by feelings of relaxation and satisfaction.
- **To feel better.** Some people who suffer from social anxiety, stress-related disorders, and depression begin abusing drugs in an attempt to lessen feelings of distress. Stress can play a major role in beginning drug use, continuing drug abuse, or relapse in patients recovering from addiction.
- **To do better.** The increasing pressure that some individuals feel to chemically enhance or improve their athletic or cognitive performance can similarly play a role in initial experimentation and continued drug abuse.
- **Curiosity and "because others are doing it."** In this respect adolescents are particularly vulnerable because of the strong influence of peer pressure; they are more likely, for example, to engage in "thrilling" and "daring" behaviors such as drug use.

Fact

Stress can play a major role in beginning drug use, continuing drug abuse, or relapse in patients recovering from addiction.

If Taking Drugs Makes People Feel Good or Better, What's the Problem?[1]

At first, people may perceive what seem to be positive effects with drug use. They also may believe that they can control their use; however, drugs can quickly take over their lives. Consider how a social drinker can become intoxicated, put himself behind a wheel, and quickly turn a pleasurable activity into a tragedy for himself and others. Over time, if drug use continues, pleasurable activities become less pleasurable, and drug abuse becomes necessary for abusers to simply feel "normal." Drug abusers reach a point where they seek out and take drugs, despite the tremendous problems caused for themselves and their loved ones. Some individuals may start to feel the need to take higher or more frequent doses, even in the early stages of their drug use.

Is Continued Drug Abuse a Voluntary Behavior?[1]

The initial decision to take drugs is mostly voluntary. However, when drug addiction takes over, a person's ability to exert self control can become seriously impaired. Brain imaging studies from drug-addicted individuals show physical changes in areas of the brain that are critical to judgment, decision making, learning and memory, and behavior control. Scientists believe that these changes alter the way the brain works and may help explain the compulsive and destructive behaviors of addiction.

WHAT IS DRUG ADDICTION?[2]

Shutterstock © bitt24, 2011. Under license from Shutterstock, Inc.

Addiction is a chronic often relapsing brain disease that causes compulsive drug seeking and use despite harmful consequences to the individual who is addicted and to those around him or her. Drug addiction is a brain disease because the abuse of drugs leads to changes in the structure and function of the brain. Although it is true that for most people the initial decision to take drugs is voluntary, over time the changes in the brain caused by repeated drug abuse can affect a person's self control and ability to make sound decisions, and at the same time send intense impulses to take drugs.

No single factor can predict whether or not a person will become addicted to drugs.

It is because of these changes in the brain that it is so challenging for a person who is addicted to stop abusing drugs. Fortunately, there are treatments that help people counteract the powerful and disruptive effects of addiction and regain control.

Similar to other chronic and/or relapsing diseases, such as diabetes, asthma, or heart disease, drug addiction can be managed successfully. Additionally, like those afflicted with other chronic diseases, it is not uncommon for a drug addict to relapse and begin abusing drugs again. Relapse, however, does not signal failure; rather, it indicates that treatment should be reinstated or adjusted, or that alternate treatment is needed to help the individual regain control and recover.

Why Do Some People Become Addicted While Others Do Not?[2]

No single factor can predict whether a person will become addicted to drugs. The risk of addiction is influenced by a person's biology, social environment, and stage of development. The more risk factors an individual has, the greater the chance that taking drugs can lead to addiction:

- **Biology.** A person's genes in combination with environmental influences account for about half of their addiction vulnerability. Additionally, gender, ethnicity, and the presence of other mental disorders may influence the risk for drug abuse and addiction.

KEY TERMS

Addiction - A chronic, often relapsing brain disease that causes compulsive drug seeking and use despite harmful consequences to the individual who is addicted and to those around them.

- **Social environment.** A person's environment includes many different influences, from family and friends to socioeconomic status and quality of life in general. Factors such as peer pressure, physical and sexual abuse, stress, and the amount of parental interaction can greatly influence the course of drug abuse and addiction in a person's life.
- **Development.** Genetic and environmental factors interact with critical developmental stages in a person's life to affect addiction vulnerability, causing adolescents to experience a double challenge. Because adolescents' brains are still developing in the areas that govern decision making, judgment, and self-control, they are especially prone to risk-taking behaviors including trying drugs of abuse.

What Other Factors Increase the Risk of Addiction?[1]

- **Early use.** Although taking drugs at any age can lead to addiction, research shows that the earlier a person begins to use drugs the more likely he or she is to progress to more serious abuse. This may reflect the harmful effect that drugs can have on the developing brain. It also may result from a constellation of early biological and social vulnerability factors, including genetic susceptibility, mental illness, unstable family relationships, and exposure to physical or sexual abuse. The fact remains that early use is a strong indicator of problems ahead, such as substance abuse and addiction.
- **Method of administration.** Smoking a drug or injecting it into a vein increases its addictive potential. Both smoked and injected drugs enter the brain within seconds, producing a powerful rush of pleasure. However, this intense "high" can fade within a few minutes, taking the abuser down to lower, more normal levels. It is a starkly felt contrast and scientists believe that this low feeling drives individuals to repeated drug abuse in an attempt to recapture the high, pleasurable state.

One of the brain's areas still maturing during adolescence is the **prefrontal cortex**, which is the part of the brain that enables us to assess situations, make sound decisions, and keep our emotions and desires under control. The fact that this critical part of an adolescent's brain is still a work in progress puts him or her at increased risk for poor decisions, such as trying drugs and continued abuse. Introducing drugs while the brain is still developing may have profound and long-lasting consequences.

Addiction is a treatable, chronic disease that can be managed successfully.

Can Addiction Be Treated Successfully?[3]

Yes, addiction is a treatable, chronic disease that can be managed successfully. Research shows that combining behavioral therapy with medications is the best way

KEY TERMS

Prefrontal cortex - The part of the brain that enables us to assess situations, make sound decisions and keep our emotions and desires under control.

to ensure success for most patients. Treatment approaches must be tailored to address each patient's drug abuse patterns and drug-related medical, psychiatric, and social problems.

Does Relapse To Drug Abuse Mean Treatment Has Failed?[3]

No. The chronic nature of the disease means that relapsing to drug abuse is not only possible but also likely. Relapse rates are similar to those for other well-characterized chronic medical illnesses, such as diabetes, hypertension, and asthma, which also have both physiological and behavioral components. Treatment of chronic diseases involves changing deeply imbedded behaviors. For the addicted patient, lapses back to drug abuse indicate that treatment needs to be reinstated or adjusted, or that alternate treatment is needed.

Why Study Drug Abuse and Addiction?[4]

Abuse and addiction to alcohol, nicotine, and illegal substances cost Americans upwards of half a trillion dollars a year, considering their combined medical, economic, criminal, and social impact. Every year, abuse of illicit drugs and alcohol contributes to the death of more than 100,000 Americans, as compared to tobacco, which is linked to an estimated 440,000 deaths per year.

People of All Ages Suffer the Harmful Consequences of Drug Abuse and Addiction[4]

- **Babies** exposed to legal and illegal drugs in the womb may be born prematurely or underweight. Prenatal drug exposure can slow a child's intellectual development and affect behavior later in life.
- **Adolescents** who abuse drugs often act out, do poorly academically, and drop out of school. They are at risk of unplanned pregnancies, violence, and infectious diseases.
- **Adults** who abuse drugs often have problems thinking clearly, remembering, and paying attention. They often develop poor social behaviors as a result of their drug abuse, and their work performance and personal relationships suffer.
- **Parental** drug abuse often means chaotic, stress-filled homes, child abuse, and neglect. Such conditions harm the well-being and development of children in the home and may set the stage for drug abuse in the next generation.

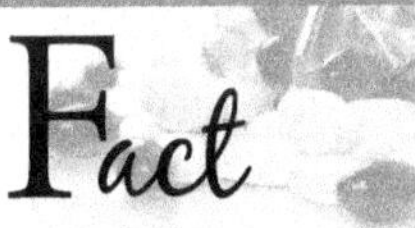

Babies exposed to legal and illegal drugs in the womb may be born premature and underweight.

How Does Science Provide Solutions for Drug Abuse and Addiction?[4]

Scientists study the effects that drugs have on the brain and on people's behavior. They use this information to develop programs for preventing drug abuse and for helping people recover from addiction. Further research helps transfer these ideas into practice in our communities.

DRUG ABUSE IS COSTLY[5]

Drug abuse is a major public health problem that impacts society on multiple levels. Directly or indirectly, every community is affected by drug abuse and addiction, as is every family. Drugs take a tremendous toll on U.S. society at many levels. Drug abuse costs the United States economy more than $600 billion annually in increased health care costs, crime, and lost productivity.

The costs of drug abuse are as substantial as those of other chronic conditions:

- Diabetes costs society $131.7 billion annually
- Cancer costs society $171.6 billion annually

These costs comprise health care expenditures, lost earnings, and financial effects associated with crime and accidents. This is an enormous burden that affects all of society including those who abuse these substances and those who do not.

DRUG ABUSE IS A MAJOR PUBLIC HEALTH PROBLEM[5]

Americans perceive drug abuse as a major public health problem. Many of America's top medical problems can be directly linked to drug abuse:

- **Cancer.** Tobacco contributes to 30 percent of cancer deaths each year.
- **Heart Disease.** Researchers have found a connection between the abuse of tobacco, cocaine, 3,4-Methylenedioxymethamphetamine **MDMA** (ecstasy), amphetamines, and steroids and the development of cardiovascular diseases. Tobacco is responsible for approximately 30 percent of all heart disease related deaths each year.

HIV/AIDS[8]

An estimated 1 million people in the U.S. are living with HIV/AIDS; about one-third of these cases are linked directly or indirectly to injection drug use. In 2003, more than one quarter (11,326) of the 43,171 AIDS cases reported in the U.S. involved injection drug use.

Fact

Injection drug use (IDU) is an important contributor to the HIV pandemic worldwide.

Many of America's Top Social Problems also Relate to or Affect Drug Abuse[5]

- **Drugged driving.** The National Highway Traffic Safety Administration estimates that drugs are used by approximately 10-22 percent of drivers involved in crashes, often in combination with alcohol.

KEY TERMS

MDMA - Commonly known as Ecstasy, it's a synthetic, psychoactive drug with both stimulant (amphetamine-like) and hallucinogenic (LSD-like) properties.

- **Violence.** At least half of the individuals arrested for major crimes including homicide, theft, assault, and domestic violence were under the influence of illicit drugs around the time of their arrest.
- **Stress.** Exposure to stress is one of the most powerful triggers of substance abuse in vulnerable individuals and of relapse in former addicts.
- **Child abuse.** At least two-thirds of patients in drug abuse treatment centers say they were physically or sexually abused as children.

Shutterstock © Phase4Photography, 2011. Under license from Shutterstock, Inc.

Individual Effects[5]

- **Adolescence.** This is a time period of high vulnerability to drug abuse and other risk-taking behaviors.
- **Mental illness.** People with mental illness are particularly at risk for problems related to substance abuse.
- **Consequences of substance abuse.** These can include illness, injuries, and death. Each year approximately 40 million debilitating illnesses or injuries occur among Americans as the result of their use of tobacco, alcohol, or another addictive drugs.
- **Deaths.** In 2006, approximately 2.4 million deaths were attributable to illicit drug abuse. Data on drug-induced deaths are based on information from all death certificates filed in the 50 States and the District of Columbia. Information from the states is provided to the National Center for Health Statistics, a component of the Center for Disease Control.

At least half of the individuals arrested for major crimes including homicide, theft, assault, and domestic violence were under the influence of illicit drugs around the time of their arrest.

Family Effects[5]

- **Prenatal:**
    - **Smoking.** Infants born to women who smoke during pregnancy have a lower average birth weight and may be at increased risk for attention deficit hyperactivity disorder (**ADHD**), conduct disorders, and childhood obesity.
    - **Cocaine.** Babies born to mothers who abuse cocaine during pregnancy can be born prematurely and have low birth weights. There may be as many as 45,000 cocaine-exposed babies per year in the United States.

Fact

At least two-thirds of patients in drug abuse treatment centers say they were physically or sexually abused as children.

KEY TERMS

ADHD - Attention Deficit Hyperactivity Disorder.

Fact

Infants born to women who smoke during pregnancy have a lower average birth weight and may be at increased risk for attention deficit hyperactivity disorder (ADHD), conduct disorders, and childhood obesity.

- **Child abuse.** In the United Sates, approximately 50 percent to 80 percent of all child abuse and neglect cases substantiated by Child Protective Services involve some degree of substance abuse by the child's parents.

Community Effects[5]

- **Homelessness.** An estimated 31 percent of America's homeless suffer from drug abuse or alcoholism.
- **Crime.** As many as 60 percent of adults in federal prisons are there for drug-related crimes.
- **Education.** Children with prenatal cocaine exposure are more likely (1.5 times) to require special education services in school. Special education costs for this population are estimated at $23 million per year.
- **Workplace.** In 2008, nearly 75 percent of all adult illicit drug users were employed, as were most binge and heavy alcohol users. Studies show that when compared with non-substance abusers, substance-abusing employees are more likely to change jobs frequently, be late to or absent from work, be less productive, be involved in a workplace accident, or file a worker's compensation claim.

FACES OF ADDICTION[6]

Fact

Drug abuse is an "equal opportunity destroyer." The effects of addiction reach across the lifespan, across cultures, and across genders.

Drug abuse is an "equal opportunity destroyer." The effects of addiction reach across the lifespan, across cultures, and across genders. No population group is immune to substance abuse and its damage. Drug abuse affects those at all levels of society, including people we may admire.

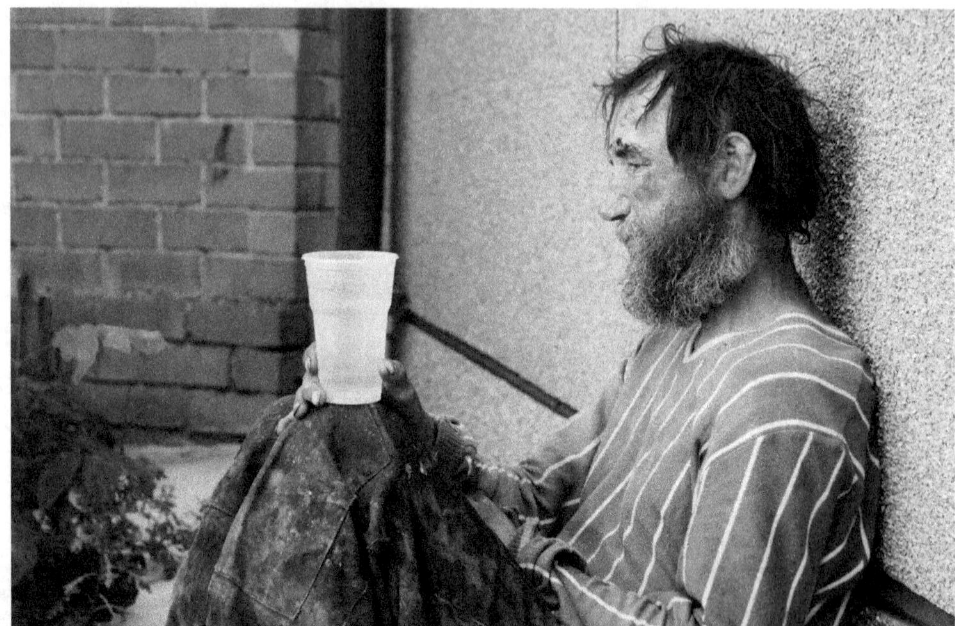

Shutterstock © wrangler, 2011. Under license from Shutterstock, Inc.

31% of America's homeless suffer from drug abuse or alcoholism.

TRENDS IN DRUG ABUSE[7]

The overall picture of drug abuse in the United States is constantly changing. A number of information sources are used to quantify America's drug problem and to monitor drug abuse trends. Foremost among these sources are the Monitoring the Future (MTF) survey and the National Survey on Drug Use and Health (**NSDUH**). Since 1975, the MTF survey has measured drug, alcohol, and cigarette use as well as related attitudes among adolescent students nationwide. For the 2009 survey, 46,097 students in eighth, tenth, and twelfth grades from 389 public and private schools participated. Funded by National Institute on Drug Abuse (**NIDA**), the MTF survey is conducted by investigators at the University of Michigan–Ann Arbor.

In the MTF and the NSDUH, there are three primary prevalence periods for which data are reported: lifetime, past year, and past month (also referred to as "current"). It is generally believed that past year and past month are the better indicators of actual use. However, some analyses are done for only one specific prevalence period; therefore, data for both past year and past month are reported here.

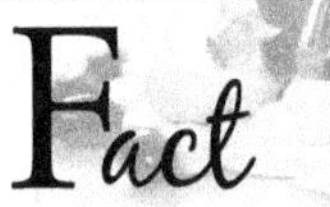

There are three primary prevalence periods for which data are reported: lifetime, past year, and past month (also referred to as "current"). It is generally believed that past year and past month are the better indicators of actual use.

According to the NSDUH, current **cocaine** use gradually declined between 2003 and 2008 among people aged twelve or older (from 2.3 million to 1.9 million). In 2009, significant declines from 2008 also were seen in past year use of cocaine among twelfth graders and in current cocaine use among tenth and twelfth graders in the MTF survey. Another positive long term decline (from 2004 to 2009) was seen in lifetime, past year, and current use of **crack cocaine** among tenth and twelfth graders.

Between 2004 and 2009, a drop in past year use of **methamphetamine** was reported for all grades. Among tenth and twelfth graders, five year declines were reported for past year use of **amphetamine**.

Both past year and past month use rates of **hallucinogens** among twelfth graders fell significantly between 2008 and 2009. Also during that time, lifetime use of heroin and current use of **inhalants** decreased significantly among tenth graders.

KEY TERMS

NSDUH - National Survey on Drug Use and Health, an information source used to quantify America's drug problem and to monitor drug abuse trends.
NIDA - National Institute on Drug Abuse, an information source used to quantify America's drug problem and to monitor drug abuse trends.
Cocaine - An illegal, addictive drug, cocaine produces feelings of euphoria and high energy by altering the regulation of neurotransmitters in the brain.
Crack cocaine - A purified and potent form of cocaine that is smoked rather than snorted; highly addictive.
Methamphetamine - Used as a stimulant to the nervous system and as an appetite suppressant and for the treatment of ADHD. Also know as speed and crank.
Amphetamines - A central nervous system stimulant that increases energy and decreases appetite; used to treat narcolepsy and some forms of depression. Also know as uppers.
Hallucinogens - A drug or substance that produces hallucinations, distortions in perception of sights and sounds, and disturbances in emotion, judgment, and memory.
Inhalants - Inhalants are a broad range of drugs in the forms of gases, aerosols, or solvents that are breathed in and absorbed through the lungs that cause drug-like effects.

The NSDUH showed that from 2002 to 2008, the rate of past month cigarette use fell from 13.0 percent to 9.1 percent among twelve-to seventeen-year-olds. Another encouraging trend is the decline in cigarette use by young adults aged eighteen to twenty-five years from 40.8 percent in 2002 to 35.7 percent in 2008.

Drug Abuse Continues Despite Positive Trends[7]

The NSDUH supported by the SAMHSA also tracks drug use in populations aged twelve and older. Both surveys (i.e, MTF, NSDUH) indicate that disturbing patterns in overall drug use are still evident:

- In 2006, 8.0 percent of Americans (that's more than 2 million) between the ages of twelve and seventeen met diagnostic criteria for abuse of or dependence on (i.e., addiction) illicit drugs.
- More than half (51 percent) of America's teenagers will have tried an illicit drug by the time they finish high school.
- Marijuana is the most widely used illicit substance in this country. In 2006, 6.8 percent of Americans had abused marijuana in the month prior to the survey.
- In 2008, an estimated 31 million people (12.4 percent) aged twelve or older reported driving under the influence of alcohol at least once in the previous year. Although this reflects a downward trend from 14.2 percent in 2002, it remains a cause for concern.

Fact

Marijuana is the most widely used illicit substance in this country.

According to the 2009 MTF survey, past year nonmedical use of **hydrocodone** and **oxycodone** increased during the preceding five years among tenth graders and remained unchanged among eighth and twelfth graders. The NSDUH showed that in 2008, the number of individuals age twelve or older who abused prescription pain relievers for the first time (2.2 million) was roughly even with that of marijuana. Many people do not understand why individuals become addicted to drugs or how drugs change the brain to foster compulsive drug abuse. They mistakenly view drug abuse and addiction as strictly a social problem and may characterize those who take drugs as morally weak. One very common belief is that drug abusers should be able to just stop taking drugs if they are only willing to change their behavior. What people often underestimate is the complexity of drug addiction, which is a disease that impacts the brain. It is because of this that stopping drug abuse is not simply a matter of willpower. We know that drug addiction can be successfully treated to help people stop abusing drugs and resume more productive lives.

KEY TERMS

Hydrocodone - Hydrocodone is an effective antitussive (anti-cough) agent.
Oxycodone - Oxycodone is an opioid analgesic medication synthesized from opium-derived thebaine.

REFERENCES

1. Drug abuse and addiction. National Institute on Drug Abuse (NIDA). 2010. http://www.nida.nih.gov/scienceofaddiction/addiction.html. Accessed April 19, 2011.
2. NIDA InfoFacts: understanding drug abuse and addiction. NIDA. http://www.nida.nih.gov/infofacts/understand.html. Accessed April 19, 2011.
3. Treatment and recovery. NIDA. http://www.nida.nih.gov/scienceofaddiction/treatment.html. Accessed April 19, 2011.
4. Introduction. NIDA. http://www.nida.nih.gov/scienceofaddiction/introduction.html. Accessed April 19, 2011.
5. Magnitude: Drug abuse is costly. NIDA. http://archives.drugabuse.gov/about/welcome/aboutdrugabuse/magnitude/. Accessed April 19, 2011.
6. Faces of addiction. NIDA. http://archives.drugabuse.gov/about/welcome/aboutdrugabuse/faces/. Accessed April 19, 2011.
7. Trends in drug abuse. NIDA. http://archives.drugabuse.gov/about/welcome/aboutdrugabuse/trends/. Accessed April 19, 2011.
8. National Institute on Drug Abuse (NIDA). Linked Epidemics: Drug Abuse and HIV/AIDS, 2005. http://drugabuse.gov/tib/drugs_hiv.html

CHAPTER 2

Drugs and Your Body

Shutterstock © Kiseley Andrey Valerevich, 2011. Under license from Shutterstock, Inc.

OBJECTIVES

After you have studied this chapter, you should be able to:

- define and explain what a drug is;
- describe how drugs are introduced into the body;
- explain how the method of administration influences rate of action;
- explain how the rate of action affects the brain;
- explain what makes a faster-acting psychoactive drug produce more euphoria than a slower-acting one;
- describe duration of action;
- explain how the brain basically communicates;
- describe how drugs work in the brain;
- list drugs that can cause neurological problems;
- describe the blood-brain barrier;

"Drugs are very much a part of professional sports today, but when you think about it, golf is the only sport where the players aren't penalized for being on grass."

-Bob Hope

- describe drug dependence;
- define and explain tolerance;
- describe withdrawal and how long it lasts;
- explain how drugs leave the body.

Fact

Drugs can be administered by oral ingestion, injection, inhalation, and through absorption.

Oral Ingestion, ingesting a drug by mouth, is the most common and simplest way of taking a drug.

A DRUG DEFINED[1]

A **drug** is a chemical compound or substance that can alter the structure and function of the body. Psychoactive drugs affect the function of the brain, and some of these may be illegal to use and possess.

HOW DRUGS ARE INTRODUCED INTO THE BODY[2]

Drugs can enter the body in different ways. Drugs can be administered by oral ingestion, injection, inhalation, and through absorption. How the drug is taken will determine how quickly it enters the bloodstream and the drug's rate of effect. Repeated use of any drug by any route of administration can lead to addiction and other adverse health consequences.

Shutterstock © RazoomGame, 2011. Under license from Shutterstock, Inc.

Oral Ingestion[2]

Oral ingestion, ingesting a drug by mouth, is the most common and simplest way of taking a drug. Drugs that are ingested include liquids, capsules, and tablets. Drugs that are commonly ingested or swallowed include alcohol, buprenorphine, opium, marijuana, sedatives, and heroin. This method is the most common and simplest, but it is also the slowest method of getting the drug into the bloodstream. Drugs are absorbed into the body when they travel from their point of entry into the blood. When a person takes drugs by mouth, they move through the digestive tract to the liver and enter the bloodstream as the body processes the chemicals.

Inhalation[3]

In recent years, smoking or inhalation of drugs has become a popular route of administration among drug users. Various drugs of different classes have been abused

KEY TERMS

Drug - Is a chemical compound or substance that can alter the structure and function of the body.

by inhalation or smoking, including phencyclidine (PCP), cocaine, heroin, methamphetamine, and marijuana. This increased popularity of smoking drugs has resulted from the fast onset of drug action and fears related to contracting acquired immunodeficiency syndrome (AIDS) or other infectious diseases from intravenous injections. Inhalation is a very potent route of drug administration and is characterized by fast absorption from the nasal mucosa and the extensive lung capillaries. Inhalation results in an immediate elevation of arterial blood drug concentration and a higher bioavailability by avoiding drug metabolism in the liver. The fact that smoking or inhalation provides rapid delivery of drugs to the brain may result in an immediate reinforcing effect of the drug and further contribute to its abuse liability or risk of dependency.

Fact

Oral Ingestion, ingesting a drug by mouth, is the most common and simplest way of taking a drug.

Injection[2]

A drug can be administered by injection (given parenterally) into a vein, into the skin, under the skin, or into a muscle using a hypodermic syringe and needle. For drugs given via any of these techniques, the absorption time is very fast. Drugs that are commonly injected include amphetamine-type stimulants, buprenorphine, heroin and sedatives.

Intravenous injection (IV).[2]

This method involves putting a drug through a needle directly into the vein. Drugs given intravenously enter the bloodstream directly and are absorbed faster. Therefore, drugs are given in this way when a rapid effect is needed. IV injection is the preferred route of administration with cocaine and heroin users. Because the drug is not significantly diluted, when a drug is injected into a vein, it reaches the brain by way of the lungs in a matter of seconds. For IV injecting, sometimes called

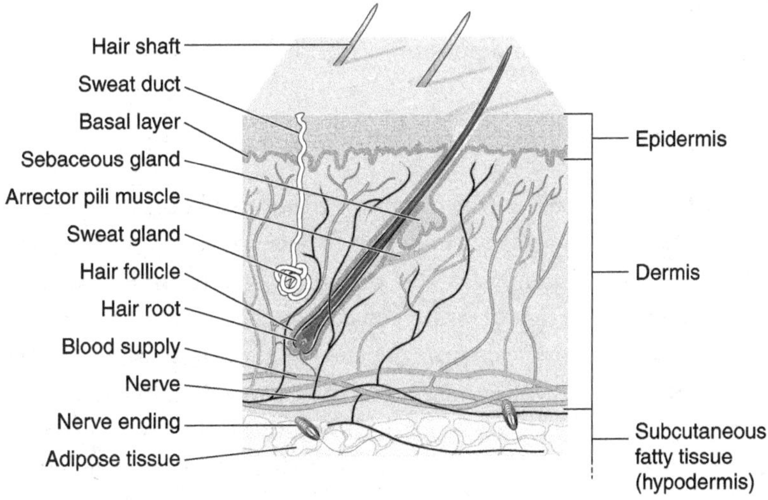

Shutterstock © Blamb, 2011. Under license from Shutterstock, Inc.

Subcutaneous injections (injections under the skin) go into the fatty tissue just below the skin. Many drugs are injected subcutaneously.

KEY TERMS

Intravenous injection - Putting a drug through a needle directly into the vein.

mainlining, the arms are the site of first choice. Other sites of the body used for injecting are the hands, fingers, legs, and feet.

Injections into the skin, sometimes called an **intradermal injection**, is given in the dermal layer of the skin just below the top layer, which is called the **epidermis**. The most common site for this type of injection is the lower arm.

Other methods of injection[4]

- Intramuscular injection (IM) - The drugs are injected by needle into the muscle.[4]
- Subcutaneous injection (SC) - The drugs are injected by needle just below the skin.[4]
- Intrathecal injection (IT) - The drugs are injected by needle into the spinal fluid.[4]

Absorption methods

Transdermal Patch[5]

The transdermal patch is an adhesive patch applied to the skin in order to administer a time-released dose of medication.

Intranasal[6]

Intranasal use, or snorting is the process of inhaling cocaine powder through the nostrils which leads to quicker absorption through the nasal tissue.

Suppositories[7]

- Rectal suppository is a suppository intended to be inserted into the rectum.
- Vaginal suppository is a suppository intended to be inserted into the vagina.

Fact

Smoked drugs that are delivered through a "crack" pipe or a cigarette and injected drugs that are administered through a hypodermic needle reach the brain very rapidly.

How Does Method of Administration Influence Rate of Action?[8]

The method of administering a drug can play a major role in the drug's rate of action, which in turn affects its abuse liability or potential as a treatment medication. Smoked drugs that are delivered through a "crack" pipe or a cigarette and injected drugs that are administered through a hypodermic needle reach the brain very rapidly. This rapid action is an important factor in the strong effect and high abuse liability of such drugs. Drug abuse treatment medications are often administered orally or through a patch affixed to the skin and take longer to reach the brain. This slower rate of action is an important factor in the milder effect and low abuse liability of treatment medications.

KEY TERMS

Mainlining - Injecting a drug of abuse intravenously.
Intradermal injection - Drug injection given in the dermal layer of the skin.
Epidermis - The top layer of skin.

Many complex factors affect a compound's rate of action in the human body. These factors include the compound's structure and properties, how quickly the body absorbs it and transports it to the brain, and how rapidly it crosses the blood-brain barrier and binds to a sufficient number of targeted brain sites called receptors to produce its effects. Because the method of administering a drug affects a number of these factors, method can play a major role in the drug's rate of action and abuse liability.

By using different methods of administering a compound, scientists can slow the rate of action and produce milder effects that may substitute for the stronger effects of an abused substance. Such a compound may be an effective medication for patients in treatment.

The effect that method of administration has on rate of action may be best illustrated by the transdermal nicotine patch, which uses the abused substance itself nicotine to ease withdrawal symptoms and aid smoking cessation. However, unlike smoking a cigarette, which delivers an almost instantaneous burst of nicotine-laden blood to the brain, administering nicotine through a patch affixed to the skin slows its rate of action and produces more sustained, lower peak levels of nicotine in the blood. This lower, slower dose of nicotine has proven to be effective in short-term treatment of nicotine dependence and aiding smoking cessation.

Why Does Rate of Action Affect the Brain?[28]

The rate at which a psycho-active drug occupies, or binds to, the receptors for that drug determines the intensity of its rewarding effects and its abuse liability, according to a hypothesis discussed at several scientific forums by Drs. George Uhl and David Gorelick of the National Institute of Drug Abuse (NIDA) Division of Intramural Research in Baltimore and Dr. Mary Jeanne Kreek of the Rockefeller University in New York. According to this rate hypothesis, the faster a drug such as heroin or cocaine occupies enough brain receptors to produce a psychoactive effect, the greater the euphoria users experience, the more they "like" the drug, and the more liable they are to abuse it.

What Makes a Faster-acting Psychoactive Drug Produce More Euphoria Than a Slower-acting One?[28]

"The brain has many adaptive mechanisms, and if you disturb the brain slowly, it often can catch up or compensate," explains Dr. George Uhl, who directs the Molecular Neurobiology Branch of the NIDA Division of Intramural Research in Baltimore. "But, if you do things rapidly, often it can't. For example, going suddenly from a dark room into bright sunlight will result in a temporary loss of vision because the light sensitivity mechanisms of the eye and the brain cannot adapt that quickly. But, if you proceed from dark to light slowly by stages, the mechanism works in a fairly automatic way, and you are able to see normally."

"If a drug acts slowly, the brain is able to compensate for the changes that the drug produces," Dr. Uhl says. "However, when a drug's onset of action is very rapid, it may be able to overwhelm the brain's adaptive mechanisms, thus producing a bigger boost in its pleasure circuits. Smoked and intravenous cocaine, for example, have fast rates of action. They reach the brain within seconds and rapidly flood the brain's 'pleasure pathway' with excess dopamine, a brain chemical that helps transmit pleasurable feelings. If the brain's adaptive mechanisms cannot respond quickly enough to the sudden excess of dopamine, the euphoric rush ensues."

DURATION OF ACTION[8]

Fact

Duration of action, or how long the drug occupies a receptor once it gets there, also plays an important role in drug abuse and treatment.

Duration of action, or how long the drug occupies a receptor once it gets there, also plays an important role in drug abuse and treatment. For example, cocaine has both a fast rate of action that produces euphoria and a rapid offset, or short duration of action, that allows frequent abuse.

Compounds with these traits may foster cravings for more drug and stronger conditioning of the drug-taking habit, according to a hypothesis proposed by Dr. Nora Volkow of Brookhaven National Laboratory in Upton, New York. Brain imaging studies conducted by Dr. Volkow indicate that while the fast rate at which cocaine acts on the brain plays a major role in its rewarding effects, it is cocaine's extremely rapid removal from the brain that both promotes and enables its frequent reuse and abuse.

Fact

The human brain is the most complex organ in the body.

THE CENTRAL NERVOUS SYSTEM[9]

The brain and spinal cord make up the **central nervous system**. The human brain is the most complex organ in the body. This three-pound mass of gray and white matter sits at the center of all human activity—you need it to drive a car, to enjoy a meal, to breathe, to create an artistic masterpiece, and to enjoy everyday activities. In brief, the brain regulates your basic body functions; enables you to interpret and respond to everything you experience; and shapes your thoughts, emotions, and behavior.

Fact

The **cerebellum** (Latin for little brain) is a region of the brain that plays an important role in motor control.

The brain consists of several large regions, each responsible for some of the activities vital for living. These include the brainstem, cerebellum, limbic system, diencephalon, and cerebral cortex. The **brainstem** is the part of the brain that connects the brain and the spinal cord. It controls many basic functions, such as heart rate, breathing, eating, and sleeping. The **cerebellum** (Latin for "little brain") is a region of the brain that plays an important role in motor control.

KEY TERMS

Brainstem - The part of the brain that connects the brain and the spinal cord.
Cerebellum - A region of the brain that plays an important role in motor control.

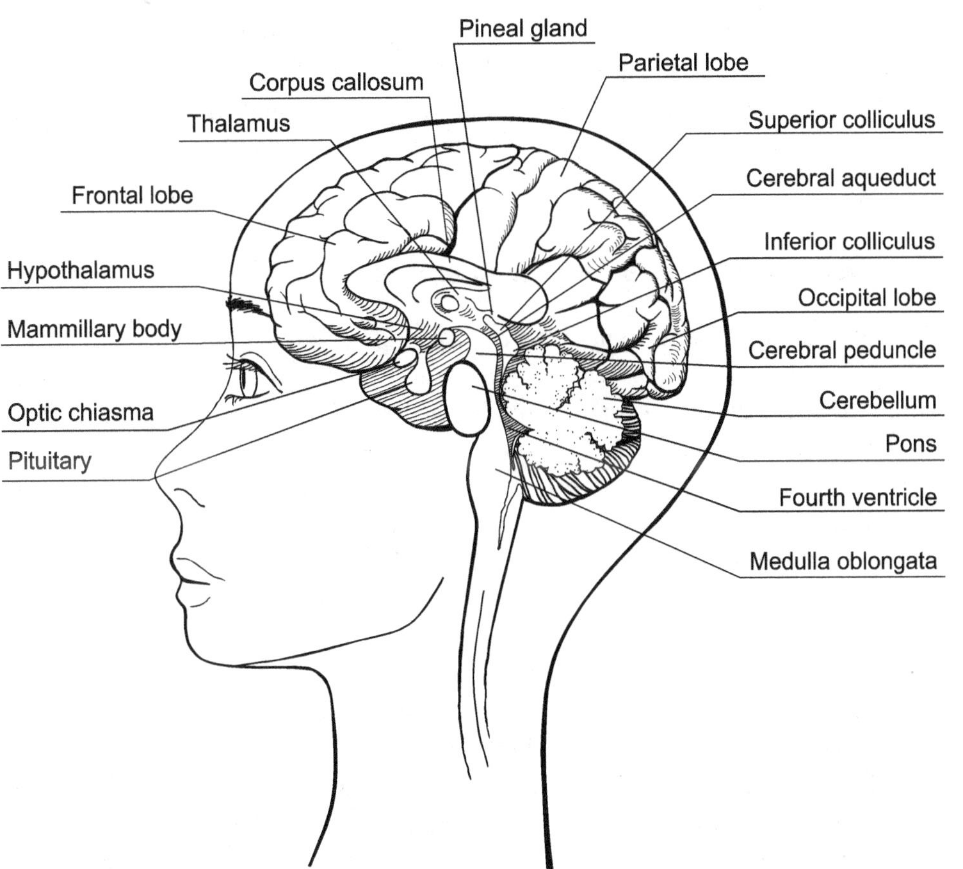

Shutterstock © yaskii, 2011. Under license from Shutterstock, Inc.

The brain consists of several large regions, each responsible for some of the activities vital for living. These include the brainstem, cerebellum, limbic system, diencephalon, and cerebral cortex.

On top of the brainstem and buried under the cortex, there is a set of more evolutionarily primitive brain structures called the **limbic system** (e.g., amygdala and hippocampus). The limbic system structures are involved in many of our emotions and motivations, particularly those that are related to survival, such as fear, anger, and sexual behavior. The limbic system also is involved in feelings of pleasure that are related to our survival, such as those experienced from eating and sex.

The **diencephalon**, which is also located beneath the cerebral hemispheres, contains the thalamus and hypothalamus. The **thalamus** is involved in sensory perception and regulation of motor functions (i.e., movement). The **hypothalamus** is a very small but important component of the diencephalon. It is a region of the brain that helps regulate hormone activity, directs autonomic nervous system functions, and influences or manages many critical functions including sleep.

KEY TERMS

Limbic system - The limbic system structures are involved in many of our emotions and motivations, particularly those that are related to survival, such as fear, anger, and sexual behavior.
Diencephalon - Located beneath the cerebral hemispheres, contains the thalamus and hypothalamus.
Thalamus - Is involved in sensory perception and regulation of motor functions (i.e., movement).
Hypothalamus - A region of the brain that helps regulate hormone activity, directs autonomic nervous system functions, and influences or manages many critical functions including sleep.

The **cerebral cortex**, which is divided into right and left hemispheres, encompasses about two-thirds of the human brain mass and lies over and around most of the remaining structures of the brain. It is the most highly developed part of the human brain and is responsible for thinking, perceiving, and producing and understanding language.

How Does the Brain Basically Communicate?[10]

Fact

The brain is a communications center consisting of billions of neurons, or nerve cells.

The brain is a communications center consisting of billions of neurons, or nerve cells. Networks of neurons pass messages back and forth to different structures within the brain, the spinal column, and the peripheral nervous system. These nerve networks coordinate and regulate everything we feel, think, and do.

- **Neuron to neuron.** Also called a "nerve cell," a neuron is a cell of the nervous system, which conducts nerve impulses. Neurons consist of an **axon** and several **dendrites**. Neurons are connected by **synapses**. Each nerve cell in the brain sends and receives messages in the form of electrical impulses. Once a cell receives and processes a message, it sends it on to other neurons.
- **Neurotransmitters.** Also known as the brain's chemical messengers, neurotransmitters are chemicals that carry, or transmit, messages between neurons.
- **Receptors.** Receptors are the brain's chemical receivers. The neurotransmitter attaches to a specialized site on the receiving cell called a receptor. A neurotransmitter and its receptor operate like a key and lock, an exquisitely specific mechanism that ensures that each receptor will forward the appropriate message only after interacting with the right kind of neurotransmitter.
- **Transporters.** The brain's chemical recyclers, transporters are located on the cell that releases the neurotransmitter. They recycle these neurotransmitters (i.e., bring them back into the cell that released them), thereby shutting off the signal between neurons.

How Do Drugs Work in the Brain?[10]

Drugs are chemicals that tap into the brain's communication system and disrupt the way nerve cells normally send, receive, and process information. There are at least two ways that drugs are able to do this: (1) by imitating the brain's natural chemical messengers, and/or (2) by over stimulating the "reward circuit" of the brain. Some

KEY TERMS

Cerebral cortex - Is divided into right and left hemispheres, encompasses about two-thirds of the human brain mass and lies over and around most of the remaining structures of the brain.
Neuron - Also called a "nerve cell," a neuron is a cell of the nervous system, which conducts nerve impulses and releases neurotransmitters.
Axon - The long, thread-like part of a neuron, or nerve cell, along which nerve signals are conducted.
Dendrites - Short fibers of a neuron that receive transmitter signals.
Synapse - The zone of junction between nerve cells through which they "communicate".
Neurotransmitter - A chemical substance that carries impulses from one nerve cell to another.
Receptor - A cell that detects different forms of energy and conveys it into the electrochemical signals used by the nervous system.
Transporters - A protein that recycles neurotransmitters.

drugs, such as marijuana and heroin, have a similar structure to neurotransmitters, which are naturally produced by the brain. Because of this similarity, these drugs are able to "fool" the brain's receptors and activate nerve cells to send abnormal messages. Generally, each neurotransmitter can bind only to a very specific matching receptor.

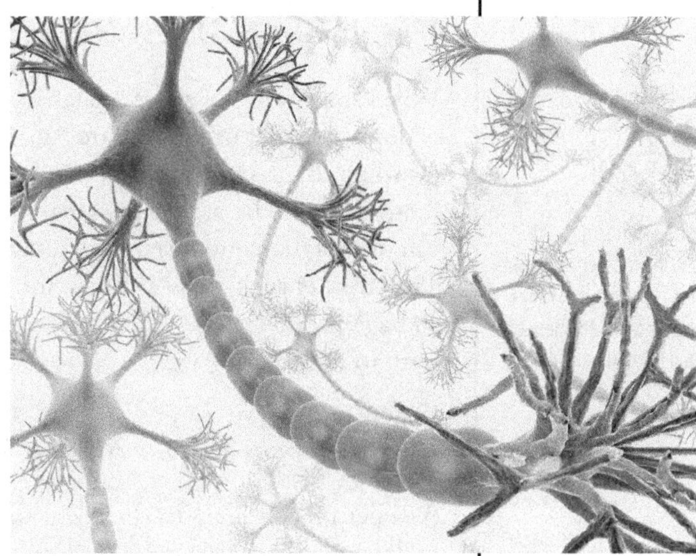

Shutterstock © iDesign, 2011. Under license from Shutterstock, Inc.

Also called a "nerve cell," a neuron is a cell of the nervous system, which conducts nerve impulses; consisting of an axon and several dendrites.

Other drugs, such as cocaine or methamphetamine, can cause the nerve cells to release abnormally large amounts of natural neurotransmitters, or prevent the normal recycling of these brain chemicals, which is needed to shut off the signal between neurons. This disruption produces a greatly amplified message that ultimately disrupts normal communication patterns. The difference in effect can be described as the difference between someone whispering into your ear and someone shouting into a microphone.

How Do Drugs Work in the Brain to Produce Pleasure?[10]

Nearly all drugs, directly or indirectly, target the brain's reward system by flooding the circuit with dopamine. **Dopamine** is a neurotransmitter present in regions of the brain that control movement, emotion, motivation, and feelings of pleasure. The overstimulation of this system, which normally responds to natural behaviors that are linked to survival (e.g., eating, spending time with loved ones), produces euphoric effects. This reaction sets in motion a pattern that "teaches" people to repeat the behavior of abusing drugs.

How Does Stimulating the Brain's Pleasure Circuit Teach Us to Keep Taking Drugs?[10]

Our brains are wired to ensure that we will repeat life-sustaining activities by associating those activities with pleasure or reward. Whenever this reward circuit is activated, the brain notes that something important is happening that needs to be remembered and teaches us to do it again and again without thinking about it. Because drugs of abuse stimulate the same circuit, we learn to abuse drugs in the same way.

KEY TERMS

Dopamine - A neurotransmitter present in regions of the brain that control movement, emotion, motivation, and feelings of pleasure.

When some drugs of abuse are taken, they can release two to ten times the amount of dopamine that natural rewards do.

Why Are Drugs More Addictive Than Natural Rewards?[10]

When some drugs of abuse are taken, they can release two to ten times the amount of dopamine that natural rewards do. In some cases, this occurs almost immediately (as when drugs are smoked or injected), and the effects can last much longer than those produced by natural rewards. The resulting effects on the brain's pleasure circuit dwarfs those produced by naturally rewarding behaviors such as eating and sex. The effect of such a powerful reward strongly motivates people to take drugs again and again. This is why scientists sometimes say that drug abuse is something we learn to do very, very well.

What Happens To Your Brain if You Keep Taking Drugs?[10]

As a person continues to abuse drugs, the brain adapts to the overwhelming surges in dopamine by producing less dopamine or by reducing the number of dopamine receptors in the reward circuit. As a result, dopamine's effect on the reward circuit is lessened, reducing the abuser's ability to enjoy the drugs and the things that previously brought pleasure. This decrease compels those addicted to drugs to keep abusing drugs in order to attempt to bring their dopamine function back to normal. Additionally, they may then require larger amounts of the drug than they first did to achieve the dopamine high, an effect known as tolerance.

How Does Long-Term Drug Abuse Affect Brain Circuits?[10]

Long-term abuse causes changes in other brain chemical systems and circuits as well. **Glutamate** is a neurotransmitter that influences the reward circuit and the ability to learn. When the optimal concentration of glutamate is altered by drug abuse, the brain attempts to compensate, which can impair cognitive function. Drugs of abuse facilitate nonconscious (i.e., conditioned) learning, which leads the user to experience uncontrollable cravings when they see a place or person they associate with the drug experience, even when the drug itself is not available. Brain imaging studies of drug-addicted individuals show changes in areas of the brain that are critical to judgment, decision making, learning and memory, and behavior control. Together, these changes can drive an abuser to seek out and take drugs compulsively despite adverse consequences. In other words, to become addicted to drugs.

What Other Brain Changes Occur with Abuse?[10]

Chronic exposure to drugs of abuse disrupts the way critical brain structures interact to control and inhibit behaviors related to drug abuse. Just as continued abuse may lead to tolerance or the need for higher drug dosages to produce an effect, it also

KEY TERMS

Glutamate - A neurotransmitter that influences the reward circuit and the ability to learn.

may lead to addiction, which can drive an abuser to seek out and take drugs compulsively. Drug addiction erodes a person's self-control and ability to make sound decisions, while sending intense impulses to take drugs.

All drugs of abuse act in the brain to produce their euphoric effects; however, some of them also have severe negative consequences in the brain such as seizures, stroke, and widespread brain damage that can affect all aspects of daily life. Drug use also can cause brain changes that lead to problems with memory, attention, and decision-making.

Fact

Drug use also can cause brain changes that lead to problems with memory, attention, and decision-making.

Drugs that can cause neurological problems include the following:

- Cocaine
- Gamma-hydroxybutyrate
- Inhalants
- Marijuana
- Methylenedioxymethamphetamine
- Methamphetamine
- Nicotine
- Prescription stimulants
- Rohypnol[11]

THE BLOOD BRAIN BARRIER[12]

The **blood-brain barrier** (BBB) is a thin layer of tightly packed cells that line the brain's blood vessels, shielding the organ from harmful chemical intruders while ushering in needed substances such as glucose, the molecular fuel used by all cells. The function of the BBB is to maintain the fluid level of the brain and spinal cord. Should there be a breakdown of the thin layer of the BBB, the fluid level is changed in the brain resulting in abnormalities. Brain cells and tissues are also at risk from the breakdown of the BBB leading to brain damage.

DRUG DEPENDENCE

Psychological dependence centers on the user's need of a drug to reach a level of functioning or feeling of well-being. Because this term is particularly subjective and almost impossible to quantify, it is of limited usefulness in making a diagnosis.

Physical dependence is not equivalent to dependence or addiction and may occur with the chronic use of any substance, legal or illegal, even when taken as prescribed.

KEY TERMS

Blood-brain barrier - A thin layer of tightly packed cells that line the brain's blood vessels.
Psychological dependence - The user's need of a drug to reach a level of functioning or feeling of well-being.
Physical dependence - Can lead to craving for the drug to relieve the withdrawal symptoms.

Physical dependence occurs because the body naturally adapts to chronic exposure to a substance (e.g., caffeine, a prescription drug), and when that substance is taken away, symptoms can emerge while the body readjusts to the loss of the substance. Physical dependence can lead to cravings for the drug to relieve the withdrawal symptoms. **Drug dependence** and addiction refer to drug or substance use disorders, which may include physical dependence but also must meet additional criteria. **Cross dependence** is dependence on a drug that can be relieved only by other similar drugs.[13]

What Is "Tolerance"?[14]

Tolerance occurs when the body changes in response to taking a drug causing the drug to no longer be affective at the same repeated dosage. A higher dosage of the drug is needed to maintain the level of response previously achieved. Tolerance may be a chief factor in drug addiction.

Cross-tolerance is defined as the development of tolerance to one substance that causes tolerance to related substances. A tolerance to morphine may cause a cross-tolerance to related drugs like heroin. For example, cross-tolerance between alcohol and nicotine has been well documented in animal models, though difficult to evaluate in humans.

What Is Withdrawal? How Long Does It Last?[13]

Withdrawal describes the various symptoms that occur after long-term use of a drug is reduced or stopped abruptly. Length of withdrawal and symptoms vary with the type of drug. For example, physical symptoms of heroin withdrawal may include restlessness, muscle and bone pain, insomnia, diarrhea, vomiting, and cold flashes. These physical symptoms may last for several days, but the general depression, or dysphoria (opposite of euphoria), that often accompanies heroin withdrawal may last for weeks. In many cases, withdrawal can be treated easily with medications to ease the symptoms, but treating withdrawal is not the same as treating addiction. For alcoholics, the onset of withdrawal symptoms is twenty-four to forty-eight hours after their blood alcohol level drops. Duration is five to seven days with characteristics of nausea, vomiting, and diarrhea; seizures; delirium; a rise in blood pressure and heart rate; and body temperature. The onset of withdrawal symptoms for the Cannabis (marijuana) user may be a few days. Duration may last up to several weeks with characteristics of irritability, appetite disturbance, sleep disturbance, nausea, concentration problems, and diarrhea.

Fact

For alcoholics, the onset of withdrawal symptoms is 24–48 hours after blood alcohol level drops.

KEY TERMS

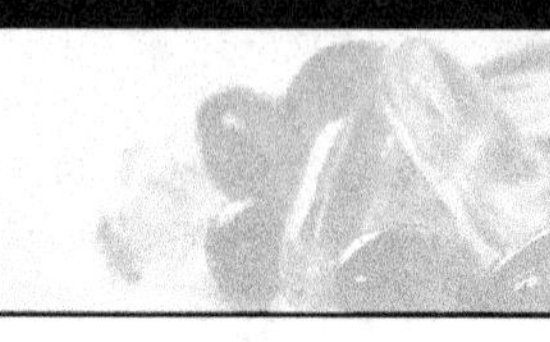

Drug dependence - A state in which the use of a drug is necessary for either physical or psychological well being.
Cross dependence - Dependence on a drug that can be relieved only by other similar drugs.
Tolerance - A reduction in the response to a drug after repeated exposure to the drug.
Cross-tolerance - The development of tolerance to one drug that causes tolerance to related drugs.

HOW DO DRUGS LEAVE THE BODY?[15]

Drug Elimination

Drugs can leave the body through different routes of elimination which can include:

- Skin (perspiration)
- Kidney's (urine)
- Lungs (exhalation)
- Bile (eliminated through feces)

Other forms of drug elimination are:

- Saliva
- Breast milk (which may affect the breastfeeding infant)

Drug Metabolism is the Chemical Alteration of a Drug by the Body[16]

As drugs are taken into the body, they are metabolized or chemically altered creating new substances called metabolites. The **metabolites** may be eliminated from the body by excretion or changed further through metabolism into another form and then used by the body. Many drugs are metabolized in the liver where they may be changed into active or inactive substances by particular enzymes. The group of **cytochrome P-450** enzymes is responsible for the majority of drug metabolism. These enzymes control how fast a drug may be metabolized by the body.

The metabolic enzyme systems are not fully developed in newborns, causing them to be unable to metabolize some drugs. In older adults, the enzyme systems no longer function as well causing them also to be unable to metabolize drugs as well as younger adults and children. Typically older adults and newborns must receive smaller doses of drugs.

REFERENCES

1. National Institute on Drug Abuse (NIDA). NIDA for Teens, Glossary. 2011. http://teens.drugabuse.gov/utilities/glossary.php
2. National Institute on Drug Abuse (NIDA). "Testimony at the United States Sentencing Commission Public Hearing." 2006. http://www.nida.nih.gov/testimony/11-14-06testimony.html
3. National Institute on Drug Abuse. NIDA Notes: Inhalation Studies With Drugs of Abuse [Monograph].1990; 173, pp. 201-224. http://archives.drugabuse.gov/pdf/Monographs/Monograph173/201-224_Meng.pdf

KEY TERMS

Metabolites - Substances that result from metabolism.
Cytochrome P-450 - A system of enzymes, located primarily in the liver, that participate in the break-down of drugs.

4. National Cancer Institute (NCI). Young People with Cancer: A Handbook for Parents. 2003. http://www.cancer.gov/cancertopics/coping/youngpeople/page5.
5. National Institute on Health (NIH), Appendix 2, Rx-Norm Dose Definitions. 2011.http://www.nlm.nih.gov/research/umls/rxnorm/docs/2010/appendix2.html
6. National Institute on Health (NIH), Appendix 2, Rx-Norm Dose Definitions. 2011.http://www.nlm.nih.gov/research/umls/rxnorm/docs/2010/appendix2.html
7. National Institute on Health (NIH), Appendix 2, Rx-Norm Dose Definitions. 2011.http://www.nlm.nih.gov/research/umls/rxnorm/docs/2010/appendix2.html
8. Mathias R. Rate and duration of drug activity play major roles in drug abuse, addiction, and treatment. NIDA Notes. 1997; 12 (2). http://archives.drugabuse.gov/nida_notes/nnvol12n2/NIDASupport.html. Accessed April 22, 2011.
9. Mind over matter: teacher's guide. NIDA for Teens. http://teens.drugabuse.gov/mom/tg_brain.php. Accessed April 22, 2011.
10. Drugs and the brain. National Institute on Drug Abuse (NIDA). 2010 http://www.nida.nih.gov/scienceofaddiction/brain.html. Accessed April 22, 2011.
11. National Institute on Drug Abuse (NIDA).Neurological Effects. 2010. http://www.nida.nih.gov/consequences/neurological/
12. National Institute on Drug Abuse. The blood brain barrier. NIDA Notes.2006;20(6).
13. Frequently asked questions. National Institute on Drug Abuse (NIDA). http://www.nida.nih.gov/tools/faq.html#Anchor-What-45736. Accessed April 22, 2011.
14. Funk D, Marinelli PW, Le AD. Biological processes underlying co-use of alcohol and nicotine: neuronal mechanisms, cross-tolerance, and genetic factors. National Institute on Alcohol Abuse and Alcoholism. http://pubs.niaaa.nih.gov/publications/arh293/186-192.htm. Accessed April 22, 2011.
15. Kopacek KB. Elimination. The Merck Manuals Online Medical Library. Revised November 2007. http://www.merckmanuals.com/home/sec02/ch011/ch011f.html. Accessed April 22, 2011.
16. Kopacek KB. Metabolism. The Merck Manuals Online Medical Library. Revised November 2007. http://www.merckmanuals.com/home/sec02/ch011/ch011e.html. Accessed April 22, 2011.

CHAPTER 3

Drugs and Regulations

Shutterstock © JustASC, 2011. Under license from Shutterstock, Inc.

OBJECTIVES

After you have studied this chapter, you should be able to:

- describe the history of drug laws;
- describe the Pure Food and Drug Act of 1906;
- describe the Harrison Narcotic Act of 1914;
- describe the Sherley Amendment of 1922;
- describe the Durham-Humphrey Amendment of 1951;
- describe the Kefauver-Harris Drug Amendments of 1962;
- list and describe the controlled substance schedules (I-V);
- describe the Orphan Drug Act of 1983;
- explain drug courts;
- explain testing for drugs.

"Sometimes I'm asked by kids why I condemn marijuana when I haven't tried it. The greatest obstetricians in the world have never been pregnant."

-Art Linkletter

THE HISTORY OF DRUG LAWS[1]

From the beginnings of civilization people have been concerned about the quality and safety of foods and medicines. In 1202, King John of England proclaimed the first English food law, the Assize of Bread, which prohibited adulteration of bread with such ingredients as ground peas or beans. Regulation of food in the United States dates from early colonial times. Federal controls over the drug supply began with inspection of imported drugs in 1848, although the first federal biologics law, which addressed the provision of reliable smallpox vaccine to citizens, was passed in 1813. The following chronology describes some of the milestones in the history of food and drug regulation in the United States.

In 1791 the **Whiskey Excise Tax** imposed a federal tax on the production of whiskey and required all stills to be registered. It eventually led to the Whiskey Rebellion of 1794. In 1820 eleven physicians met in Washington, DC to establish the U.S. Pharmacopeia, the first compendium of standard drugs for the United States. By 1848 the **Drug Importation Act** was passed by Congress that required the U.S. Customs Service inspection to stop entry of adulterated drugs from overseas.

President Lincoln appoints a chemist, Charles M. Wetherill, in 1862 to serve in the new Department of Agriculture. This was the beginning of the Bureau of Chemistry, the predecessor of the Food and Drug Administration. By 1880 Peter Collier, chief chemist, U.S. Department of Agriculture, recommended passage of a national food and drug law, following his own food adulteration investigations. The bill was defeated, but during the following twenty-five years, more than 100 food and drug bills were introduced in Congress.

Fact

Dr. Harvey W. Wiley was called the "Crusading Chemist" and "Father of the Pure Food and Drugs Act."

In 1883, Dr. Harvey W. Wiley became chief chemist, expanding the Bureau of Chemistry's food adulteration studies. Campaigning for a federal law, Dr. Wiley was called the "Crusading Chemist" and "Father of the Pure Food and Drugs Act." He retired from government service in 1912 and died in 1930. The Biologics Control Act was passed in 1902 to ensure purity and safety of serums, vaccines, and similar products used to prevent or treat diseases in humans. Congress appropriated $5,000 to the Bureau of Chemistry to study chemical preservatives and colors and their effects on digestion and health. Dr. Wiley's studies drew widespread attention to the problem of food adulteration.

The **Pure Food and Drugs Act of 1906** was passed by Congress on June 30 and signed by President Theodore Roosevelt. It prohibited interstate commerce in

KEY TERMS

Whiskey Excise Tax - A federal tax was imposed on the production of whiskey and required all stills to be registered.
Drug Importation Act - Passed by Congress that required the U.S. Customs Service inspection to stop entry of adulterated drugs from overseas.
Food and Drugs Act of 1906 - It prohibits interstate commerce in misbranded and adulterated foods, drinks and drugs.

misbranded and adulterated foods, drinks, and drugs. The **Meat Inspection Act** was passed the same day. It required the inspection of all cattle, sheep, goats, and horses when they were slaughtered and processed into products for human consumption. Shocking disclosures of unsanitary conditions in meat-packing plants, the use of poisonous preservatives and dyes in foods, and cure-all claims for worthless and dangerous patent medicines were the major problems that led to the enactment of these laws.

Beginning a new term in office in 1905, President Theodore "Teddy" Roosevelt pushed for programs to protect the food supply and address worker problems, and he promoted environmental conservation. President Roosevelt's second term, although continuing the goals of his first, resulted in further wide-reaching progressive legislation and stricter regulation of business practices. President Roosevelt, the "moral policeman," advocated for the 1906 Meat Inspection Act and the Pure Food and Drug Act of 1906, and he mediated an end to the 1905 Russo-Japanese War, for which he received a Nobel Peace Prize. Presient Roosevelt became the first man to assume the presidency upon the death of the president and win a new term on his own merits.

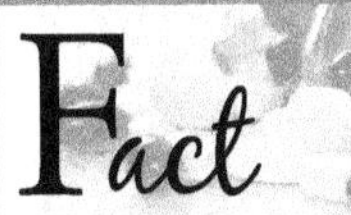

Theodore Roosevelt was called the "moral policeman.

In a period of investigative journalism, writers exposed the evils in American society, detailing corruption and unethical business practices. Roosevelt dubbed these men and women "muckrakers," a term taken from *Pilgrim's Progress.* It was one of these writers, Upton Sinclair, whose book *The Jungle* graphically illustrated conditions in Chicago's meat packing industry. Roosevelt, who had read the book, pushed for passage of the Meat Inspection Act and the Pure Food and Drug Act, both in 1906, to safeguard the nation's food supply.

Theodore Roosevelt dubbed the writers that exposed the evils in American society "muckrakers," a term taken from Pilgrim's Progress.

The United States was among the organizers of the 1909 International Opium Commission in Shanghai, China. This is the first federal law that banned the non-medical use of a substance.

By 1911, in *U.S. v. Johnson,* the Supreme Court ruled that the 1906 Food and Drugs Act did not prohibit false therapeutic claims but only false and misleading statements about the ingredients or identity of a drug. Congress enacted the **Sherley Amendment of 1912** to overcome the ruling in *U.S. v. Johnson.* The act prohibited labeling medicines with false therapeutic claims intended to defraud the purchaser, a standard difficult to prove, as shown in subsequent court cases. The United States was a signatory of the 1912 Hague Opium Convention, the first international treaty to make heroin a controlled substance.

KEY TERMS

Meat Inspection Act - It required the inspection of all cattle, sheep, goats, and horses when slaughtered and processed into products for human consumption.

Sherley Amendment of 1912 - It prohibits labeling medicines with false therapeutic claims intended to defraud the purchaser, a standard difficult to prove, as shown in subsequent court cases.

The **Harrison Narcotic Act of 1914** required prescriptions for products exceeding the allowable limit of narcotics and mandated increased record-keeping for physicians and pharmacists who dispensed narcotics. The Harrison Act limited opium availability to only small amounts as prescribed by physicians, who were required to register and pay taxes on the amounts they prescribed. It allowed physicians to prescribe narcotics only for the treatment of disease. At the time, narcotic addiction was not considered a disease.

In the United States, heroin was first placed under federal control by the 1914 Harrison Narcotic Act, which required anyone who sold or distributed narcotics–importers, manufacturers, wholesale and retail druggists, and physicians–to register with the federal government and pay an excise tax.

Addiction in the United States eventually fell to its lowest level during World War II, when the number of addicts is estimated to have been somewhere between 20,000 and 40,000. Many addicts, faced with disappearing supplies, were forced to give up their drug habits. What was virtually a drug-free society in the war years remained much the same way in the years that followed. In the mid-1950s, the Federal Bureau of Narcotics estimated the total number of addicts nationwide at somewhere between 50,000 to 60,000. The former chief medical examiner of New York City, Dr. Milton Halpern, said in 1970 that the number of New Yorkers who died from drug addiction in 1950 was 17. By comparison, in 1999, the New York City medical examiner reported 729 deaths involving drug abuse.

In 1930 the name of the Food, Drug, and Insecticide Administration was shortened to **Food and Drug Administration (FDA)** under an agricultural appropriations act. By 1933, the FDA recommended a complete revision of the obsolete 1906 Food and Drugs Act. The first bill is introduced into the Senate, launching a five-year legislative battle.

Elixir of Sulfanilamide, containing the poisonous solvent diethylene glycol, killed 107 people in 1937, many of whom were children, dramatizing the need to establish drug safety before marketing and to enact the pending food and drug law.

Fact

Elixir of Sulfanilamide, containing the poisonous solvent diethylene glycol, killed 107 people in 1937.

The Federal Food, Drug, and Cosmetic (FDC) Act of 1938 was passed by Congress. Provisions it contained included the following:

- Extending control to include cosmetics and therapeutic devices.
- Requiring new drugs to be shown safe before marketing—starting a new system of drug regulation.

KEY TERMS

Harrison Narcotic Act of 1914 - Required prescriptions for products exceeding the allowable limit of narcotics and mandates increased record keeping for physicians and pharmacists who dispense narcotics.
FDA - Food and Drug Administration.
The Federal Food, Drug, and Cosmetic (FDC) Act of 1938 - Extended control to cosmetics and therapeutic devices and required new drugs to be shown safe before marketing, starting a new system of drug regulation.

- Eliminating the Sherley Amendment requirement to prove intent to defraud in drug misbranding cases.
- Providing that safe tolerances be set for unavoidable poisonous substances.
- Authorizing standards of identity, quality, and fill-of-container for foods.
- Authorizing factory inspections.
- Adding the remedy of court injunctions to the previous penalties of seizures and prosecutions.

The FDC Act completely overhauled the public health system. Among other provisions, the law authorized the FDA to demand evidence of safety for new drugs, issue standards for food, and conduct factory inspections.

Under the **Wheeler-Lea Act,** the Federal Trade Commission was charged with overseeing advertising associated with products otherwise regulated by the FDA, with the exception of prescription drugs. By 1944, the **Public Health Service Act** was passed, covering a broad spectrum of health concerns, including regulation of biological products and control of communicable diseases.

In 1945 the Penicillin Amendment required FDA testing and certification of safety and effectiveness of all penicillin products. Later amendments extended this requirement to all antibiotics. However, this decision was reversed in 1903 and the amendments were abolished. By 1948, the Miller Amendment affirmed that the FDC Act applied to goods regulated by the FDA that had been transported from one state to another and had reached the consumer. The FDA published guidance to industry in 1949 for the first time. This guidance, "Procedures for the Appraisal of the Toxicity of Chemicals in Food," came to be known as the "black book."

By 1950, in *Alberty Food Products Co. v. U.S.*, a court of appeals ruled that the directions for use on a drug label must include the purpose for which the drug is offered. This decision prevented a worthless remedy from escaping the law by not stating the condition it is intended to treat.

The **Durham-Humphrey Amendment of 1951** defined the kinds of drugs that could not be safely used without medical supervision and restricted their sale to prescription by a licensed practitioner. The Durham-Humphrey Amendment explicitly defined two specific categories for medications: legend (prescription) and over-the-counter (OTC). This amendment was co-sponsored by former vice president and Senator Hubert H. Humphrey, Jr., who was a pharmacist in South Dakota

KEY TERMS

Wheeler-Lea Act - The Federal Trade Commission was charged with overseeing advertising associated with products otherwise regulated by FDA, with the exception of prescription drugs.
Public Health Service Act - Regulated biological products and control of communicable diseases.
Durham-Humphrey Amendment of 1951 - Defined the kinds of drugs that cannot be safely used without medical supervision and restricted their sale to prescription by a licensed practitioner.

before beginning his political career. The other sponsor of this amendment was Carl Durham, a pharmacist representing North Carolina in the House of Representatives.

The bill required any drug that was habit-forming or potentially harmful to be dispensed under the supervision of a health care practitioner as a prescription drug and required it to carry the statement, "Caution: Federal law prohibits dispensing without a prescription." This bill also required that all drugs have adequate directions for use. Until this law, there was no requirement that any drug be labeled for sale by prescription only. The amendment defined prescription drugs as those unsafe for self-medication and which should therefore be used only under a doctor's supervision.

After passage of this bill, legend drugs could only be dispensed with direct medical supervision whereas OTC drugs still could be purchased and used without a prescription. This law also allowed for new prescriptions and refill authorizations to be called in over the phone.

In 1958 the FDA published in the ***Federal Register*** the first list of substances generally recognized as safe. The list contained nearly 200 substances. The **Federal Hazardous Substances Labeling Act,** enforced by FDA in 1960, required prominent label warnings on hazardous household chemical products.

In 1962, Thalidomide, a new sleeping pill, was found to have caused birth defects in thousands of babies born in western Europe. News reports on the role of Dr. Frances Kelsey, FDA medical officer, in keeping the drug off the U.S. market aroused public support for stronger drug regulation.

Fact

In 1962, Thalidomide, a new sleeping pill, was found to have caused birth defects in thousands of babies born in western Europe.

The Kefauver-Harris Amendments of 1962, were passed to ensure drug efficacy and greater drug safety. For the first time, drug manufacturers were required to prove to the FDA the effectiveness of their products before marketing them. The Kefauver-Harris Amendments were inspired by the thalidomide tragedy in Europe (and the FDA's vigilance that prevented the drug from being marketed in the United States), and strengthened the rules for drug safety and required manufacturers to prove their drugs' effectiveness.

By 1965, the Drug Abuse Control Amendments were enacted to address problems caused by abuse of depressants, stimulants, and hallucinogens. The FDA contracted with the National Academy of Sciences/National Research Council in 1966 to evaluate the effectiveness of 4,000 drugs approved on the basis of safety alone between

KEY TERMS

Federal Register - In 1958 it published the first list of substances generally recognized as safe.
Federal Hazardous Substances Labeling Act - Required prominent label warnings on hazardous household chemical products.
The Kefauver-Harris Amendments of 1962 - Strengthened the rules for drug safety and required manufacturers to prove their drugs' effectiveness.

1938 and 1962. **The Child Protection Act** of 1966 enlarged the scope of the Federal Hazardous Substances Labeling Act to ban hazardous toys and other articles so hazardous that adequate label warnings could not be written. **The Fair Packaging and Labeling Act** of 1966 required all consumer products in interstate commerce to be honestly and informatively labeled, with FDA enforcing provisions on foods, drugs, cosmetics, and medical devices.

In 1968, the FDA Bureau of Drug Abuse Control and Treasury Department Bureau of Narcotics were transferred to the Department of Justice to form the Bureau of Narcotics and Dangerous Drugs (BNDD), consolidating efforts to police traffic in abused drugs. Reorganization of federal health programs placed the FDA in the Public Health Service. The FDA formed the Drug Efficacy Study Implementation to review recommendations of the National Academy of Sciences investigation on effectiveness of drugs first marketed between 1938 and 1962.

By 1970, in *Upjohn v. Finch,* the Court of Appeals upheld enforcement of the 1962 drug effectiveness amendments by ruling that commercial success alone did not constitute substantial evidence of drug safety and efficacy. The FDA required the first patient package insert: oral contraceptives were required to contain information for the patient about specific risks and benefits.

In response to America's growing drug problem, Congress passed the Controlled Substances Act, Title II of the **Comprehensive Drug Abuse Prevention and Control Act of 1970.** It replaced more than fifty pieces of drug legislation, went into effect on May 1, 1971, and was enforced by the BNDD, the predecessor agency of the Drug Enforcement Agency (DEA). This law, along with implementing regulations, established a single system of control for both narcotic and psychotropic drugs for the first time in U.S. history. It also established five schedules that classified controlled substances according to how dangerous they were, their potential for abuse and addiction, and whether they possessed legitimate medical value:

Schedule I - high abuse potential no accepted medical use.
Examples: marijuana, heroin, Lysergic acid diethylamide(LSD)

Schedule II - high abuse potential, severe psychological or physical dependence possible liability.
Examples: methadone, amphetamine, cocaine

Schedule III - abuse potential is less than those in Schedule II, but more than Schedule IV.

KEY TERMS

The Child Protection Act - Banned hazardous toys and other articles so hazardous that adequate label warnings could not be written.
The Fair Packaging and Labeling Act - Required all consumer products in interstate commerce to be honestly and informatively labeled, with FDA enforcing provisions on foods, drugs, cosmetics, and medical devices.
Comprehensive Drug Abuse Prevention and Control Act of 1970 - It established five schedules that classify controlled substances according to how dangerous they are, their potential for abuse and addiction, and whether they possess legitimate medical value.

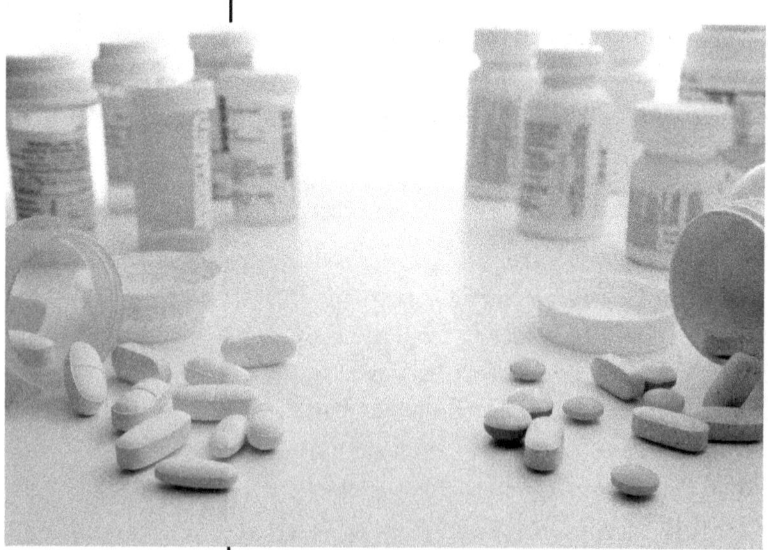

Shutterstock © Christopher Ewing, 2011. Under license from Shutterstock, Inc.

Examples: anabolic steroids, ketamine.

Schedule IV - abuse potential less than those listed in Schedule III and more than substances in Schedule V.

Examples: benzodiazepines, barbital, phenobarbital, chloral hydrate.

Schedule V - abuse potential less than those listed in Schedule IV.

Example: codeine.[2]

The Over-the-Counter Drug Review in 1972 started to enhance the safety, effectiveness, and appropriate labeling of drugs sold without a prescription. Regulation of Biologics—including serums, vaccines, and blood products—were transferred from National Institutes of Health to FDA. In 1973, the U.S. Supreme Court upheld the 1962 drug effectiveness law and endorsed FDA action to control entire classes of products by regulations rather than to rely only on time-consuming litigation.[1]

The year 1976 saw the Vitamins and Minerals Amendments ("Proxmire Amendments") stop the FDA from establishing standards that limited potency of vitamins and minerals in food supplements or regulating them as drugs based solely on potency. The Saccharin Study and Labeling Act of 1977 was passed by Congress to stop the FDA from banning the chemical sweetener but required a warning label stating that it had been found to cause cancer in laboratory animals.[1]

In 1981, the FDA and the Department of Health and Human Services (HHS) revised regulations for human subject protections based on the 1979 Belmont Report, which had been issued by the National Commission for the Protection of Human Subjects of Biomedical and Behavioral Research. The revised rules provided for wider representation on institutional review boards and they detailed elements of what constituted informed consent, among other provisions.[1]

By 1982, tamper-resistant packing regulations were issued by the FDA to prevent poisonings such as deaths from cyanide placed in acetaminophen capsules. The Federal Anti-Tampering Act passed in 1983, making it a crime to tamper with packaged consumer products. The FDA published the first "red book" (the successor to the 1949 "black book"), officially known as *Toxicological Principles for the Safety Assessment of Direct Food Additives and Color Additives Used in Food.*[1]

The Orphan Drug Act was passed in 1983, enabling the FDA to promote research and marketing of drugs needed for treating rare diseases. Fines Enhancement Laws of 1984 and 1987 amended the U.S. Code to greatly increase penalties for all federal

The Over-the-Counter Drug Review in 1972 had begun to enhance the safety, effectiveness and appropriate labeling of drugs sold without prescription.

Fact

The Over-the-Counter Drug Review in 1972 started to enhance the safety, effectiveness, and appropriate labeling of drugs sold without prescription.

Fact

FDA published the first Red Book (the successor to 1949 "black book"), officially known as Toxicological Principles for the Safety Assessment of Direct Food Additives and Color Additives Used in Food.

offenses. The maximum fine for individuals was set at $100,000 for each offense and $250,000 if the violation was a felony or caused death. For corporations, the amounts were doubled.[1]

The passage of **The Drug Price Competition and Patent Term Restoration Act** expedited the availability of less costly generic drugs by permitting the FDA to approve applications to market generic versions of brand-name drugs without repeating the research done to prove them safe and effective. At the same time, the brand-name companies could apply for up to five years additional patent protection for the new medicines they developed to make up for time lost while their products were going through the FDA's approval process.[1]

The AIDS test for blood was approved by the FDA in1985. This test saw its first major action to protect patients from infected donors. In 1987 there was action to amend the FDC to ban the re-importation of drugs produced in the United States, to place restrictions on the distribution of drug samples and ban certain re-sales of drugs by hospitals and other health care entities, among other purposes. Investigational drug regulations were revised to expand access to experimental drugs for patients with serious diseases with no alternative therapies.[1]

In 1988, The **Food and Drug Administration Act** officially established the FDA as an agency of HHS with a Commissioner of Food and Drugs appointed by the President with the advice and consent of the Senate, and broadly spelled out the responsibilities of the Secretary and the Commissioner for research, enforcement, education, and information. **The Prescription Drug Marketing Act of 1987** banned the diversion of prescription drugs from legitimate commercial channels. Congress found that the resale of such drugs led to the distribution of mislabeled, adulterated, sub-potent, and counterfeit drugs to the public. The new law required drug wholesalers to be licensed by the states; restricted re-importation from other countries; and banned sale, trade, or purchase of drug samples, as well as trafficking or counterfeiting of redeemable drug coupons.[1]

By 1989, the FDA issued a nationwide recall of all OTC dietary supplements containing 100 mg or more of L-tryptophan, due to a clear link between the consumption of L-tryptophan tablets and its association with a U.S. outbreak of eosinophilia-myalgia syndrome (EMS), characterized by fatigue, shortness of breath, and other symptoms. By 1990 the Centers for Disease Control and

KEY TERMS

The Orphan Drug Act - It enabled the FDA to promote the research and marketing of drugs needed for treating rare diseases.

Drug Price Competition and Patent Term Restoration Act - It expedites the availability of less costly generic drugs by permitting FDA to approve applications to market generic versions of brand-name drugs without repeating the research done to prove them safe and effective.

Food and Drug Administration Act - It officially established the FDA as an agency of the Department of Health and Human Services.

The Prescription Drug Marketing Act - Banned the diversion of prescription drugs from legitimate commercial channels.

Prevention confirmed more than 1,500 cases of EMS, including 38 deaths, and the FDA prohibited the importation of L-tryptophan.

Responding to increasing illicit traffic, Congress passes the **Anabolic Steroid Act of 1990,** which identified anabolic steroids as a class of drugs and specified more than two dozen items as controlled substances. In addition, a four-part definition of this class was established to permit new, black market compounds to be assigned to this category, and thus make them subject to regulation as controlled substances.[1]

Fact

Nutrition facts, basic per-serving nutritional information, were required on foods under the Nutrition Labeling and Education Act of 1990.

Nutrition facts, basic per-serving nutritional information, were required on foods under the Nutrition Labeling and Education Act of 1990. Based on the latest public health recommendations, the FDA and the Food Safety and Inspection Service of the Department of Agriculture recreated the food label to list the most important nutrients in an easy-to-follow format. The **Nutrition Labeling and Education Act** required all packaged foods to bear nutrition labeling and all health claims for foods to be consistent with terms defined by the HHS Secretary. The law preempted state requirements about food standards, nutrition labeling, and health claims and, for the first time, authorized some health claims for foods. The food ingredient panel, serving sizes, and terms such as "low fat" and "light" were standardized.[1]

Nutrition Facts
Serving Size 1/4 Cup (30g)
Servings Per Container About 38

Amount Per Serving	
Calories 200 Calories from Fat 150	
	% Daily Value*
Total Fat 17g	**26%**
Saturated Fat 2.5g	**13%**
Trans Fat 0g	
Cholesterol 0mg	**0%**
Sodium 120mg	**5%**
Total Carbohydrate 7g	**2%**
Dietary Fiber 2g	**8%**
Sugars 1g	
Protein 5g	
Vitamin A 0%	• Vitamin C 0%
Calcium 4%	• Iron 8%

*Percent Daily Values are based on a 2,000 calorie diet.

Shutterstock © XAOC, 2011. Under license from Shutterstock, Inc.

Nutrition facts, basic per-serving nutritional information, were required on foods under the Nutrition Labeling and Education Act of 1990.

The Safe Medical Devices Act was passed in 1990, requiring nursing homes, hospitals, and other facilities that used medical devices to report incidents to the FDA that suggested that a medical device probably caused or contributed to the death, serious illness, or serious injury of a patient. Manufacturers were required to conduct post-market surveillance on permanently implanted devices whose failure might cause serious harm or death, and to establish methods for tracing and locating patients depending on such devices. The act authorized the FDA to order device product recalls and other actions.[1]

In 1991, regulations were published to accelerate the review of drugs for life-threatening diseases. The policy for protection of human subjects in research, promulgated in 1981 by the FDA and HHS, was adopted by more than a dozen federal

KEY TERMS

Anabolic Steroid Act of 1990 - Identified anabolic steroids as a class of drugs and specifies over two dozen items as controlled substances.
Nutrition Labeling and Education Act - Required all packaged foods to bear nutrition labeling and all health claims for foods to be consistent with terms defined by the Secretary of Health and Human Services.
Safe Medical Devices Act - Required nursing homes, hospitals, and other facilities that use medical devices to report to the FDA incidents that suggest that a medical device probably caused or contributed to the death, serious illness, or serious injury of a patient.

entities involved in human subject research and became known as the common rule. This rule issued requirements for researchers who obtained and documented informed consent; secured special protection for children, women, and prisoners; elaborated on required procedures for institutional review boards; and ensured that research institutions comply with the regulations.[1]

The Generic Drug Enforcement Act of 1992 imposed debarment and other penalties for illegal acts involving abbreviated drug applications. The same year, the **Prescription Drug User Fee Act** required drug and biologics manufacturers to pay fees for product applications and supplements, as well as for other services. The act also required the FDA to use these funds to hire more reviewers to assess applications.[1]

By 1993, a consolidation of several adverse reaction reporting systems was launched as MedWatch, designed for voluntary reporting of problems associated with medical products to be filed with the FDA by health professionals. Revising a policy from 1977 that excluded women of childbearing potential from early drug studies, the FDA issued guidelines calling for improved assessments of medication responses as a function of gender. Companies were encouraged to include patients of both genders in their investigations of drugs and to analyze any gender-specific phenomena.[1]

In 1994, the **Dietary Supplement Health and Education Act** established specific labeling requirements, provided a regulatory framework, and authorized the FDA to promulgate good manufacturing practice regulations for dietary supplements. This act defined "dietary supplements" and "dietary ingredients" and classified them as food. The act also established a commission to recommend how to regulate claims.[1]

The FDA declared cigarettes to be "drug delivery devices" in 1995. Restrictions were proposed on marketing and sales to reduce smoking by young people. A series of proposed reforms to reduce regulatory burden on pharmaceutical manufacturers was announced, including expanding allowable promotional material on approved uses of drugs that firms could distribute to health professionals, streamlining certain elements in the documentation of investigational drug studies, and reducing both environmental impact filings and pre-approval requirements in tablet manufacturing.[1]

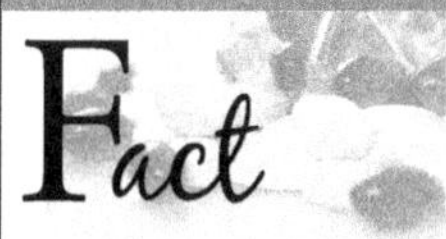

FDA declared cigarettes to be "drug delivery devices" in 1995.

The Food and Drug Administration Modernization Act of 1997 reauthorized the Prescription Drug User Fee Act of 1992 and mandated the most wide-ranging reforms in agency practices since 1938. Provisions included measures to accelerate

KEY TERMS

Generic Drug Enforcement Act of 1992 - Imposed debarment and other penalties for illegal acts involving abbreviated drug applications.
Prescription Drug User Fee Act - Required drug and biologics manufacturers to pay fees for product applications and supplements, and other services. The act also required the FDA to use these funds to hire more reviewers to assess applications.
Dietary Supplement Health and Education Act - Established specific labeling requirements, provides a regulatory framework, and authorizes the FDA to promulgate good manufacturing practice regulations for dietary supplements.
Food and Drug Administration Modernization Act of 1997 - Reauthorized the Prescription Drug User Fee Act of 1992 and mandates the most wide-ranging reforms in agency practices since 1938.

review of devices, regulate advertising of unapproved uses of approved drugs and devices, and regulate health claims for foods. The FDA promulgated the **Pediatric Rule in 1998,** a regulation that required manufacturers of selected new and extant drug and biological products to conduct studies to assess their safety and efficacy in children.[1]

In 1999, ClinicalTrials.gov was founded to provide the public with updated information on enrollment in federally and privately supported clinical research, thereby expanding patient access to studies of promising therapies. A final rule mandated that all OTC drug labels contain data in a standardized format. These drug facts were designed to provide the patient with easy-to-find information, analogous to the nutrition facts label for foods.[1]

In the year 2000, the U.S. Supreme Court upheld an earlier decision in *Food and Drug Administration v. Brown & Williamson Tobacco Corp. et al.* and ruled five to four that the FDA does not have authority to regulate tobacco as a drug. Within weeks of this ruling, the FDA revoked its final rule, issued in 1996, that restricted the sale and distribution of cigarettes and smokeless tobacco products to children and adolescents, and that determined cigarettes and smokeless tobacco products were combination products consisting of a drug (nicotine) and device components intended to deliver nicotine to the body.[1]

Under the Data Quality Act of 2001, federal agencies were required to issue guidelines to maximize the quality, objectivity, utility, and integrity of the information they generate, and to provide a mechanism whereby those affected can secure correction of information that does not meet these guidelines. Publication of a rule on dietary supplements defined the type of statement that could be labeled regarding the effect of supplements on the structure or function of the body.[1]

In 2002, the **Best Pharmaceuticals for Children Act** improved safety and efficacy of patented and off-patent medicines for children. It continued the exclusivity provisions for pediatric drugs as mandated under the FDA Modernization Act of 1997, in which market exclusivity of a drug was extended by six months, and in exchange the manufacturer carries out studies of the effects of drugs when they are taken by children. The provisions both clarified aspects of the exclusivity period and amended procedures for generic drug approval in cases when pediatric guidelines were added to the labeling.

In the wake of the events of September 11, 2001, the Public Health Security and Bioterrorism Preparedness and Response Act of 2002 was designed to improve the country's ability to prevent and respond to public health emergencies, and provisions

KEY TERMS

Pediatric Rule in 1998 - Required manufacturers of selected new and extant drug and biological products to conduct studies to assess their safety and efficacy in children.

Best Pharmaceuticals for Children Act - Improved safety and efficacy of patented and off-patent medicines for children.

included a requirement that FDA issue regulations to enhance controls over the imported and domestically produced commodities that it regulates.[1]

Under the Medical Device User Fee and Modernization Act of 2002, fees had been assessed to sponsors of medical device applications for evaluation, provisions were established for device establishment inspections by accredited third-parties, and new requirements emerged for reprocessed single-use devices.[1]

The Office of Combination Products was formed in 2002 within the Office of the Commissioner, as mandated under the Medical Device User Fee and Modernization Act, to oversee review of products that fell into multiple jurisdictions within the FDA.[1]

The current good manufacturing practice (cGMP) initiative, an effort to enhance and update the regulation of manufacturing processes and end-product quality of animal and human drugs and biological medicines, was announced in 2003. The goals of the initiative were to focus on the greatest risks to public health in manufacturing procedures, to ensure that process and product quality standards did not impede innovation, and to apply a consistent approach to these issues across the FDA.[1]

In 2003, the **Medicare Prescription Drug Improvement and Modernization Act** required, among other elements, that a study be made of how current and emerging technologies could be used to make essential information about prescription drugs available to the blind and visually impaired. To help consumers choose heart-healthy foods, HHS announced that the FDA would require food labels to include trans fat content, the first substantive change to the nutrition facts panel on foods since the label was changed in 1993.[1]

The Animal Drug User Fee Act of 2003, permitted the FDA to collect subsidies for the review of certain animal drug applications from sponsors, analogous to laws passed for the evaluation of other products the FDA regulated, ensuring the safety and effectiveness of drugs for animals and the safety of animals used as foodstuffs. The FDA was given clear authority under the **Pediatric Research Equity Act,** which required that sponsors conduct clinical research into pediatric applications for new drugs and biological products.[1]

A ban on over-the-counter steroid precursors; increased penalties for making, selling, or possessing illegal steroids precursors; and the assignment of dedicated funds for preventive children's education were features of the **Anabolic Steroid Control**

Fact

In the wake of the events of September 11, 2001, the Public Health Security and Bioterrorism Preparedness and Response Act of 2002 was designed to improve the country's ability to prevent and respond to public health emergencies, and provisions included a requirement that FDA issue regulations to enhance controls over the imported and domestically produced commodities that it regulates.

KEY TERMS

Medicare Prescription Drug Improvement and Modernization Act - Required, that a study be made of how current and emerging technologies can be utilized to make essential information about prescription drugs available to the blind and visually impaired.

Pediatric Research Equity Act - Required that sponsors conduct clinical research into pediatric applications for new drugs and biological products.

Act of 2004. The FDA published *Innovation or Stagnation: Challenge and Opportunity on the Critical Path to New Medical Products,* which examined the critical path needed to bring therapeutic products to fruition and how the FDA could collaborate in the process, from laboratory to production to end use, to make medical breakthroughs available to those in need as quickly as possible. Based on results from controlled clinical studies that indicated **Cox-2** selective inhibitor agents might be connected to an elevated risk of serious cardiovascular events, including heart attack and stroke, the FDA issued a public health advisory urging health professionals to limit the use of these drugs.[1]

The formation of the **Drug Safety Board** was announced in 2005 . The Board consisted of FDA staff members and representatives from the NIH and the Veterans Administration. The Board would advise the Director, Center for Drug Evaluation and Research, FDA, on drug safety issues and work with the agency in communicating safety information to health professionals and patients.[1]

The Drug Law Reform Act of 2009, signed by then-Governor Nelson Rockefeller, was designed to overhaul the Rockefeller Drug Laws that were enacted in 1973. The laws before provided some of the harshest drug sentences in the United States. They were brought about by the drug epidemic experienced in the early 1970s in New York City and elsewhere in the country. [1]

In recent history, President Barack Obama signed into law **The Fair Sentencing Act of 2010,** which narrowed the sentence disparities for crack and powder cocaine offenses. The former law, which went into effect in 1986, resulted in three-fourths of all persons in prison for drug offenses being people of color.[1]

TESTING FOR DRUGS[3]

Some schools, hospitals, or places of employment conduct drug testing. There are a number of ways this can be done, including pre-employment testing, random testing, reasonable suspicion or cause testing, post-accident testing, return to duty testing, and follow-up testing. This usually involves collecting urine samples to test for drugs such as marijuana, cocaine, amphetamines, phenylcyclohexyl piperidine (PCP), and opiates.

KEY TERMS

Anabolic Steroid Control Act of 2004 - Banned over-the-counter steroid precursors, increased penalties for making, selling, or possessing illegal steroids precursors.

COX-2 - A selective inhibitor that is a form of Non-steroidal anti-inflammatory drug that directly targets COX-2, an enzyme responsible for inflammation and pain.

Drug Safety Board in 2005 - Advise the Director on drug safety issues and work with the agency in communicating safety information to health professionals and patients.

Drug Law Reform Act of 2009 - Designed to overhaul the Rockefeller Drug Laws enacted in 1973. The laws before, provided some of the harshest drug sentences in the U.S. They were brought about by the drug epidemic experienced in the early 1970s in New York City and elsewhere in the U.S.

The Fair Sentencing Act of 2010 - Narrowed the sentence disparities for crack and powder cocaine offenses.

Testing Methods[3]

There are several testing methods available that use urine, hair, oral fluids, or sweat testing patches. These methods vary in cost, reliability, drugs detected, and detection period. Employers or institutions can determine their needs and choose the method that is most appropriate.

Accuracy of Drug Tests[3]

Tests are very accurate but not 100 percent accurate. Usually samples are divided, so if an initial test is positive, a confirmation test can be conducted. Federal guidelines are in place to ensure accuracy and fairness in drug testing programs.

"Beating" the Tests[3]

Many drug-using individuals are aware of techniques that supposedly detoxify their systems or mask their drug use. Popular magazines and Internet sites give advice on how to dilute urine samples, and there are even companies that sell clean urine or products designed to distort test results. A number of techniques and products are focused on urine tests for marijuana, but masking products increasingly are becoming available for tests of hair and oral fluids, as well as tests designed to detect multiple drugs.

Most of these products do not work, are very costly, are easily identified in the testing process, and need to be on hand constantly because of the very nature of random testing. Moreover, even if the specific drug is successfully masked, the product itself can be detected, in which case the person using it would become an obvious candidate for additional screening and attention. In fact, some testing programs label a test "positive" if a masking product is detected.

Legality of Random Drug Testing[3]

In June 2002, the U.S. Supreme Court broadened the authority of public schools to test students for illegal drugs. Voting five to four in *Pottawatomie County v. Earls,* the court ruled to allow random drug tests for all middle and high school students participating in competitive extracurricular activities. The ruling greatly expanded the scope of school drug testing, which previously had been allowed only for student athletes.

In June 2002, the U.S. Supreme Court broadened the authority of public schools to test students for illegal drugs.

The Cost of Drug Abuse[4]

Drug abuse is costly to Americans, tearing at the fabric of our society and taking a huge financial toll on our resources. Beyond its inextricable link to the spread of infectious diseases, such as HIV/AIDS and other sexually transmitted diseases

(**STDs**), tuberculosis, and hepatitis C, drug abuse often is implicated in family disintegration, loss of employment, failure in school, domestic violence, child abuse, and other crimes. The 2004 National Survey on Drug Use and Health puts the number of Americans dependent on illicit drugs at approximately 5 million. Placing dollar figures on the problem, smoking and illegal drugs cost this country about $338 billion a year, with illicit drug use alone accounting for about $180 billion in crime, productivity loss, health care, incarceration, and drug enforcement.

Effectiveness of Drug Polices[5]

According to Donnie R. Marshall, Administrator. U.S. Department of Justice, Drug Enforcement Administration:

America's drug policies work. Two things significantly contribute to that outcome. First, a strong program of public education; second, a strict program of law enforcement. Drug laws can work, if we have the national resolve to enforce them. America spends millions of dollars every year on researching the issue of drugs. We have crime statistics, opinion surveys, and biochemical research. However, the most important question is whether we can influence young people enough to keep them from taking the first step into the world of drugs, ruin their careers, destroy their relationships, and leave them in a cycle of drug dependency. If we as a society are unwilling to have the courage to say no to drug abuse, we will find that drugs will not only destroy the society we have built over 200 years, but ruin millions of people.

America's drug policies work. Two things significantly contribute to that outcome. First, a strong program of public education; second, a strict program of law enforcement.

REFERENCES

1. Milestones in food and drug law. Food and Drug Administration (FDA). http://www.fda.gov/AboutFDA/WhatWeDo/History/Milestones/default.htm. Accessed April 22, 2011.
2. Konnor DD, ed. Pharmacy Law Desk Reference. The Haworth Press, Inc; 2007:43-44.
3. Frequently asked questions about drug testing in schools. NIDA. September 2007. http://www.nida.nih.gov/drugpages/testingfaqs.html. Accessed April 22, 2011.
4. Fiscal Year 2007 Budget Information. NIDA. http://www.nida.nih.gov/funding/budget07.html. Accessed April 22, 2011.
5. Marshall D. DEA Congressional Testimony. June 16, 1999. http://www.justice. gov/dea/pubs/cngrtest/ct061699.htm. Accessed April 22, 2011.

KEY TERMS

STDs - Sexually transmitted diseases.

CHAPTER 4

Caffeine

OBJECTIVES

After you have finished this chapter, you should be able to

- describe the effects of caffeine;
- explain caffeine in the diet;
- list the side effects of caffeine;
- list the types of caffeinated drinks;
- list the ingredients of tea;
- define chocolate;
- define cocoa;
- define coffee;
- define tea;
- describe caffeine overdose.

Shutterstock © Anita Colic, 2011. Under license from Shutterstock, Inc.

Caffeine is the world's most widely consumed psychoactive substance.

"I have measured out my life with coffee spoons."

-T.S. Eliot

Chocolate has become one of the most popular food types and flavors in the world.

Shutterstock © LeahOAnne Thompson, 2011. Under license from Shutterstock, Inc.

CAFFEINE[1]

Some drugs may be helpful or harmful. Caffeine is one example. Although caffeine itself isn't a drug, it is an ingredient found in some medications. Caffeine is also found in coffee, tea, cocoa, chocolate, and soft drinks. It can be taken orally in pill form or consumed in food and drinks. **Caffeine** increases alertness, reduces fine motor coordination, alters sleep patterns, and can cause headaches, nervousness, and dizziness. Caffeine also stimulates the central nervous system by increasing the metabolism inside neurons, and increases wakefulness by blocking the neurotransmitter, adenosine. Caffeine in all forms should be used in moderation. Too much of this substance can make people feel uncomfortable and even sick.

Effects of Caffeine[2]

Caffeine's high incidence of use is significant because caffeine has both acute and chronic effects on measures of mood, cognitive performance, and physiology. Caffeine nonselectively antagonizes adenosine receptors, thereby acting as both a neurostimulant and vasoconstrictor. Acutely, caffeine improves mood and attention, and reduces resting cerebral blood flow. However, chronic caffeine use results in an upregulation of adenosine receptors. Among chronic users there is evidence that tolerance develops to the neurostimulant effects.

Psychological effects[3]

Fact

Caffeine is the most widely used psychoactive drug in the world.

Caffeine is the most widely used psychoactive drug in the world and its popularity is likely due to its subjective effects, including enhanced alertness and stimulation. Yet, there are large individual differences in acute response to caffeine, with some people experiencing increased stimulation whereas others experience anxiety, an undesirable effect. Although the mechanism underlying individual differences to caffeine is not known, some of this variability might have a genetic basis. One source of inherited variability might be in the variation in genes that code for the adenosine receptor, as activation of this central nervous system receptor gives rise to caffeine's psychological effects. Identifying the genetic basis for individual variation

KEY TERMS

Caffeine - Increases alertness, reduces fine motor coordination, alters sleep patterns, and can cause headaches, nervousness, and dizziness.

in quality or magnitude of response to addictive drugs may aid in understanding the vulnerability and resiliency for developing drug addiction.

CAFFEINE IN THE DIET[4]

Caffeine is a substance that exists naturally in certain plants. It can also be produced synthetically and used as an additive in food products. Not only does it act as a stimulant for the central nervous system, but it is also a diuretic.

Function[4]

Caffeine is absorbed and distributed very quickly. After absorption, it passes into the brain. Caffeine does not accumulate in the bloodstream nor is it stored in the body. It is excreted in the urine many hours after it has been consumed.

Caffeine will not reduce the effects of alcohol, although many people still believe a cup of coffee will "sober-up" an intoxicated person. Caffeine may be used as a treatment for migraine headaches and in relieving, for a short time, fatigue or drowsiness.

Food Sources[4]

Caffeine can be found naturally in the leaves, seeds, and fruits of more than 60 plants, including tea leaves, kola nuts, coffee beans, and cocoa beans.

Caffeine is frequently added to over-the-counter medications such as pain relievers, appetite suppressants, and cold medicines. Caffeine has no flavor and can be removed from a food by a chemical process called decaffeination.

Side Effects[4]

Excessive caffeine intake can lead to a fast heart rate, excessive urination, nausea, vomiting, restlessness, anxiety, depression, tremors, and difficulty sleeping.

Abrupt withdrawal of caffeine may cause headaches, drowsiness, irritability, nausea, vomiting, and other symptoms. Reduction of caffeine intake should be gradual to prevent any symptoms of withdrawal

Excessive caffeine intake can lead to a fast heart rate, excessive urination, nausea, vomiting, restlessness, anxiety, depression, tremors, and difficulty sleeping.

TYPES OF CAFFEINATED DRINKS

Caffeinated Energy Drinks

Since the introduction of Red Bull in Austria in 1987 and in the United States in 1997, the energy drink market has grown exponentially.[5] **Energy drinks** often pack in extra vitamins, along with caffeine, which delivers the eye-opening jolt of

Shutterstock © Fotonium, 2011.
Under license from Shutterstock, Inc.

Energy drinks may serve as a gateway to other forms of drug dependence.

energy, and is supposed to boost brain power. People, even teens, seek that extra kick from energy drinks to stay alert longer or perform better. These drinks are especially appealing to teens because they are busy with school, sports, a part-time job, and never-ending homework...finally sleep, then having to get up while it's still dark out to do it all over again. No wonder energy drinks are appealing![6]

Hundreds of different brands are now marketed, with caffeine content ranging from a modest 50 mg to an alarming 505 mg per can or bottle. Regulation of energy drinks, including content labeling and health warnings differs across countries, with some of the most lax regulatory requirements in the U.S. The absence of regulatory oversight has resulted in aggressive marketing of energy drinks, targeted primarily toward young males, for psychoactive, performance-enhancing and stimulant drug effects. There are increasing reports of caffeine intoxication from energy drinks, and it seems likely that problems with caffeine dependence and withdrawal will also increase. In children and adolescents who are not habitual caffeine users, vulnerability to caffeine intoxication may be markedly increased due to an absence of pharmacological tolerance. Genetic factors may also contribute to an individual's vulnerability to caffeine-related disorders including caffeine intoxication, dependence, and withdrawal. The combined use of caffeine and alcohol is increasing sharply, and studies suggest that such combined use may increase the rate of alcohol-related injury. Energy drinks may serve as a gateway to other forms of drug dependence.[5]

Chocolate and Cocoa[7]

Cocoa beans are not actually beans they are the seeds from the fruit of the cocoa tree (Theobroma cacao). These seeds (cocoa beans) are fermented, dried, roasted, and crushed to make a thick paste called liquor, which contains cocoa butter and cocoa solids. **Cocoa** is chocolate liquor minus the cocoa butter. **Chocolate** contains varying amounts of chocolate liquor, cocoa butter, sugar, and flavorings. Dark chocolate, also known as "bittersweet" and "semisweet", is highest in chocolate liquor with little or no added sugar.

KEY TERMS

Energy drinks - Often pack in extra vitamins, along with caffeine, which delivers the eye-opening jolt of energy, and is supposed to boost brain power.
Cocoa - Is chocolate liquor minus the cocoa butter.
Chocolate - Contains varying amounts of chocolate liquor, cocoa butter, sugar, and flavorings.

Chocolate and cocoa are naturally rich in free-radical-fighting antioxidants known as **flavanols**. In particular, they contain procyanidins and epicatechins, flavanols that are part of a group of antioxidants known as **polyphenols** found in a variety of foods including tea, red wine, and various fruits and vegetables. In choosing cocoa and chocolate products rich in flavanols, it is important to look for non-alkalized or lightly alkalized cocoas, also known as "dutched" cocoa. Natural cocoa is not alkalized. Because milk binds to the antioxidants in chocolate making them unavailable, milk chocolate is not an antioxidant source and is higher in fat. To get the maximum benefit of antioxidants, avoid drinking milk with dark chocolate.

Shutterstock © CREATISTA, 2011. Under license from Shutterstock, Inc.

Young coffee drinkers at a popular coffeehouse.

Coffee[8]

Caffeine is probably the most well-known compound in coffee. It can make one feel more awake and alert, which is why most people drink coffee in the first place. But too much can be harmful. Caffeine causes the most common problem reported by coffee drinkers: trouble sleeping. Caffeine can also blunt appetite and cause headaches, dizziness, nervous¬ness and irritability. A person who is sensitive to caffeine should simply drink less of it. If caffeine causes one to have trouble falling asleep at night, it should be avoided until later in the day. Caffeine is mildly addictive, and may cause headaches, drowsi¬ness, irritability, nausea and other symptoms if suddenly reduced. These effects can be avoided by gradually reducing caffeine intake.

Fact

Caffeine is probably the most well-known compound in coffee.

Carbonated drinks

In 1767, chemist **Joseph Priestley** stood in his laboratory one day with an idea to help English mariners stay healthy on long ocean voyages. He infused water with carbon dioxide to create an effervescent liquid that mimicked the finest mineral waters consumed at European health spas. Priestley's man-made tonic, which he urged his benefactors to test aboard His Majesty's ships, never prevented a scurvy outbreak. But, as the decades passed, his carbonated water became popular in cities and towns for its enjoyable taste and later as the main ingredient of sodas, sparkling

KEY TERMS

Flavanols - Are free-radical-fighting antioxidants.
Polyphenols - A group of antioxidants.
Joseph Priestley - He invented carbonation in 1767.

Tea is made from the leaf of the plant Camellia sinensis.

Shutterstock © Agphotographer, 2011. Under license from Shutterstock, Inc.

wines, and all variety of carbonated drinks.[9] Many carbonated drinks contained varying amounts of caffeine.

Tea[10]

Tea is one of the most ancient and popular beverages consumed around the world. Black tea accounts for about 75 percent of the world's tea consumption. In the United States, United Kingdom (UK), and Europe, black tea is the most common tea beverage consumed; green tea is the most popular tea in Japan and China. Oolong and white tea are consumed in much lesser amounts around the world.

Tea is made from the leaf of the plant Camellia sinensis. Shortly after harvesting, the tea leaves begin to wilt and oxidize. During oxidation, chemicals in the leaves are broken down by enzymes, resulting in darkening of the leaves and the well-recognized aroma of tea. This oxidation process can be stopped by heating, which inactivates the enzymes. The amount of oxidation and other aspects of processing determine a tea's type. **Black tea** is produced when tea leaves are wilted, bruised, rolled, and fully oxidized. In contrast, **green tea** is made from unwilted leaves that are not oxidized. Oolong tea is made from wilted, bruised, and partially oxidized leaves, creating an intermediate kind of tea. **White tea** is made from young leaves or growth buds that have undergone minimal oxidation. Dry heat or steam can be used to stop the oxidation process, and then the leaves are dried to prepare them for sale.

Tea is brewed from dried leaves and buds (either in tea bags or loose), prepared from dry instant tea mixes, or sold as ready-to-drink iced teas. So-called herbal teas are not really teas but infusions of boiled water with dried fruits, herbs, and/or flowers.

Fact

Tea is one of the most ancient and popular beverages consumed around the world.

What are the ingredients of tea?[10]

Tea is composed of **polyphenols**, alkaloids (caffeine, theophylline, and theobromine), amino acids, carbohydrates, proteins, chlorophyll, volatile organic compounds (chemicals that readily produce vapors and contribute to the odor of tea), fluoride, aluminum, minerals, and trace elements. The polyphenols, a large group of plant chemicals that includes the catechins, are thought to be responsible for the health benefits that have traditionally been attributed to tea, especially green tea.

KEY TERMS

Black tea - Is produced when tea leaves are wilted, bruised, rolled, and fully oxidized.
Green tea - Is made from unwilted leaves that are not oxidized.
White tea - Is made from young leaves or growth buds that have undergone minimal oxidation.
Polyphenols - Polyphenols are a group of chemicals found in tea leaves and are classified as antioxidants.

Black tea contains much lower concentrations of these catechins than green tea. The extended oxidation of black tea increases the concentrations of thearubigins and theaflavins, two types of complex polyphenols. **Oolong tea** contains a mixture of simple polyphenols, and complex polyphenols. White and green tea contains similar amounts of **Epigallocatechin gallate (EGCG)** but different amounts of other polyphenols.

Although iced and ready-to-drink teas are becoming popular worldwide, they may not have the same polyphenol content as an equal volume of brewed tea. The polyphenol concentration of any particular tea beverage depends on the type of tea, the amount used, the brew time, and the temperature. The highest polyphenol concentration is found in brewed hot tea, less in instant preparations, and lower amounts in iced and ready-to-drink teas. Ready-to-drink teas frequently have lower levels of tea solids and lower polyphenol contents because their base ingredient may not be brewed tea. The addition of other liquids, such as juice, will further dilute the tea solids. Decaffeination reduces the catechin content of teas.

Are there safety considerations regarding tea consumption?[10]

As with other caffeinated beverages, such as coffee and colas, the caffeine contained in many tea products could potentially cause adverse effects, including tachycardia, palpitations, insomnia, restlessness, nervousness, tremors, headache, abdominal pain, nausea, vomiting, diarrhea, and diuresis. However, there is little evidence of health risks for adults consuming moderate amounts.

The amount of caffeine present in tea varies by the type of tea; the caffeine content is higher in black teas, ranging from 64 to 112 mg per 8 fl oz serving, followed by oolong tea, which contains about 29 to 53 mg per 8 fl oz serving. Green and white teas contain slightly less caffeine, ranging from 24 to 39 mg per 8 fl oz serving and 32 to 37 mg per 8 fl oz serving, respectively. Decaffeinated teas contain less than 12 mg caffeine per 8 fl oz serving. Research on the effects of caffeine in children is limited. In general, caffeine doses of less than 3.0 mg per kg body weight have not resulted in adverse effects in children. Higher doses have resulted in some behavioral effects, such as increased nervousness or anxiety and sleep disturbances.

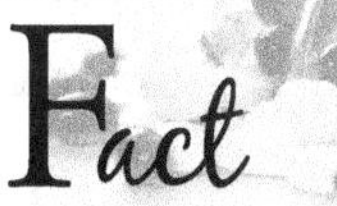

The amount of caffeine present in tea varies by the type of tea.

Black and green tea may inhibit iron bioavailability from the diet. The interaction between tea and iron can be mitigated by consuming, at the same meal, foods that enhance iron absorption, such as those that contain vitamin C (e.g., lemons), and animal foods that are sources of heme iron (e.g., red meat). Consuming tea between meals appears to have a minimal effect on iron absorption. Tea has long been regarded as an aid to good health, and many believe it can help reduce the risk of cancer.

KEY TERMS

Oolong tea - Contain a mixture of simple polyphenols, and complex polyphenols.
Epigallocatechin gallate (EGCG) - EGCG is found most notably in tea and is also a potent antioxidant.

LEGEND OF THE DANCING GOATS[11]

Why do we have coffee today? The "legend of the dancing goats" says that coffee beans were first discovered in a field in Ethiopia by a goat herder who noticed that his goats were acting strange at times, running around and dancing wildly. He could not determine the cause, so he decided to study them. He saw them eating small red berries on a certain shrub found in the area. These turned out to be coffee plants. After eating the berries with the coffee beans inside, the goats started their "dancing." Legend also has it that the goat herder also started eating the berries and dancing with them!

CAFFEINE OVERDOSE[12]

Caffeine overdose occurs when someone accidentally or intentionally takes more than the normal or recommended amount of this substance.
In the event of a caffeine overdose emergency, individuals should contact their local emergency number (such as 911) or the National Poison Control Center at 1-800-222-1222.

POISON CONTROL[12]

- The National Poison Control Center can be contacted from anywhere in the United States. This national hotline number will contact experts in poisoning situations who will be able to give further instructions.
- The National Poison Control Center is a free and confidential service. All local poison control centers in the United States use this national number. An individual should call for any questions about poisoning or poison prevention. It does NOT need to be an emergency. The center is available 24 hours a day, 7 days a week.

REFERENCES

1. National Institute on Drug Abuse (NIDA). Medicines and Drugs: What's Helpful, What's Harmful (Module 4), http://www.drugabuse.gov/JSP/MOD4/Mod4.PDF
2. National Institute on Drug Abuse (NIDA). Health Disparities Research Portfolio, 2008. http://www.drugabuse.gov/about/organization/healthdisparities/research/portfolio.html.

KEY TERMS

Caffeine overdose - occurs when someone accidentally or intentionally takes more than the normal or recommended amount of this substance.

3. National Institute on Drug Abuse (NIDA). Director's Report to the National Advisory Council on Drug Abuse - May, 2004. http://archives.drugabuse.gov/DirReports/DirRep504/DirectorReport2.html
4. National Institute on Health(NIH), Caffeine in the diet 2009. http://www.nlm.nih.gov/medlineplus/ency/article/002445.htm
5. National Institute on Drug Abuse (NIDA). 2009. Caffeinated Energy Drinks--A Growing Problem. http://www.drugabuse.gov/DirReports/DirRep509/DirectorReport8.html
6. National Institute on Drug Abuse (NIDA). NIDA for Teens, Energy drinks http://teens.drugabuse.gov/blog/tag/boost/
7. National Institute on Health (NIH). Dark Chocolate, 2009. http://dats.ors.od.nih.gov/eurest/superfoods/darkchocolate.pdf
8. National Institute on Health (NIH). Concerned About Coffee, 2009. http://newsinhealth.nih.gov/pdf/NIHNiH%20August09.pdf
9. National Institute on Health (NIH). Scientists Discover Protein Receptor for Carbonation Taste, 2009. http://www.nih.gov/news/health/oct2009/nidcr-15.htm
10. National Cancer Institute (NCI). Tea and Cancer Prevention: Strengths and Limits of the Evidence, 2010. http://www.cancer.gov/cancertopics/factsheet/prevention/tea
11. National Institute on Drug Abuse (NIDA). NIDA for Teens, "legend of the dancing goats" http://teens.drugabuse.gov/blog/so-why-do-people-like-drugs/
12. Caffeine overdose. National Institute on Health(NIH), 2010. http://www.nlm.nih.gov/medlineplus/ency/article/002579.htm

CHAPTER 5

Alcohol: How It Affects the Human Body

Shutterstock © kola-kola, 2011. Under license from Shutterstock, Inc.

OBJECTIVES

After you have finished this chapter, you should be able to

- explain America's alcohol problem;
- define and explain ethyl alcohol, or ethanol;
- explain how alcohol is produced;
- explain the effects of alcohol on the brain;
- describe blackouts and memory lapses;
- explain Wernicke–Korsakoff syndrome;
- explain cirrhosis of the liver;
- list the physical effects of fetal alcohol spectrum disorders;
- describe alcohol poisoning;
- define alcoholism;
- describe how a person can get help for an alcohol problem.

"Alcohol is barren; the words a man speaks in the night of drunkenness fade like the darkness itself at the coming of day"

-Marguerite Duras (French Novelist)

AMERICA'S ALCOHOL PROBLEM[1]

From the time the first colonists arrived in the New World bringing alcoholic beverages with them, Americans have had a problem. That problem is a historic inability to reach any kind of a national consensus about the role of alcohol in American society. Americans' inability to reach such a consensus, in turn, has led to shifts and changes in public perception and, consequently, has affected policy concerning how best to deal with the difficulties caused by individuals who use alcohol and those individuals themselves. As observed by Selden E. Bacon, former director of the Center of Alcohol Studies at Rutgers University and eminent scholar on alcohol problems in America:

Several major shifts have occurred in the way Americans have perceived and responded to alcohol problems from the colonial era to the temperance era (including Prohibition) and from the **Temperance movement** and **Prohibition era** to the present.

The Colonial Era: Alcoholism Is a Sin[1]

During the colonial period in America, alcohol was very much a part of a community's social life. Alcohol was used widely as both a beverage and a medicine, generally being considered a substance that was enjoyable and healthful. Even drunkenness was tolerated so long as it did not interfere with a person's livelihood or religious observance. In the colonial view, the problem was not alcohol but the individual who used alcohol. Habitual drunkenness, which kept people from working and praying, represented a weakness of character and a sin against God and the church. Punishment was colonial America's response to such weakness, and the stocks (i.e., structures that confined the arms and legs of social miscreants for public chastisement) were the colonial era's equivalent of the alcoholism treatment facility.

The Temperance Era: The Demon Is Rum[1]

During the mid to late 19th century, attempts to respond to alcohol problems shifted from trying to control the individual to trying to control the substance. With the nation's population transforming from an agrarian to an industrial society, new social problems, such as poverty and crime, began to emerge. Each of these social ills was seen as being connected to alcohol use. In response, a social reform movement was born that began to focus on eliminating alcohol use as a means of eliminating social problems. Aggressive public information and legislative activities of anti-alcohol groups, such as the American Temperance Society, the Women's Christian Temperance Union, and the Anti-Saloon League, with their images of "demon rum" and ax-toting women, helped change Americans' perceptions of alcohol problems and

KEY TERMS

Temperance movement - A social movement against the use of alcoholic beverages.
Prohibition era - The period from 1920 to 1933 when the sale of alcoholic beverages was prohibited in the United States by a constitutional amendment

caused them, in response, to consider eliminating the substance. Otherwise decent people could be transformed by drink to become dissolute, violent, or degenerate. Moreover, because alcohol was an addicting substance, even the most moderate drinker flirted with danger at the rim of every cup.

Although alcohol-related health problems generally were not a major consideration during the temperance era, there is some historical evidence that even during the hey-day of the anti-saloon leagues, some attention was given to the social and health consequences of problem drinking. According to medical historian Phillip J. Pauly:

In the early 1890's, Seth Low, a wealthy businessman, president of Columbia University, and future mayor of New York City, led the Sociology Group, an informal discussion circle of academic, commercial, and religious liberals interested in urban problems. In 1893 the group began to discuss alcohol, and became so persuaded of the need for knowledgeable, moderate action that they expanded to become a formal organization. The resulting Committee of Fifty for the Investigation of the Liquor Problem proposed to sponsor fact finding reports on the legal, economic, ethical, and physiological aspects of alcohol use.

Not much came of the Committee's efforts as the national climate moved toward Prohibition, and 1919 saw the passage of the **Volstead Act,** ushering in the legal abolition of alcohol consumption.

Fact

American Temperance Society, the Women's Christian Temperance Union, and the Anti-Saloon League, with their images of "demon rum" and ax-toting women, helped change Americans' perceptions of alcohol problems

Reaction and Inaction[1]

Prohibition was both a success and a failure. According to the Cooperative Commission on the Study of Alcoholism, rates of problem drinking decreased substantially during the early years of Prohibition and reported deaths from liver cirrhosis also declined as did hospitalization for alcoholism. Arrests for public drunkenness were much lower than earlier.

Although Prohibition achieved the goal of reducing alcohol-related problems, Americans found the loss of personal autonomy in the matter of alcoholic beverages excessive and voted to repeal the Volstead Act in 1932.

What is alcohol?[2]

Ethyl alcohol, or **ethanol**, is an intoxicating ingredient found in beer, wine, and liquor. Ethanol is a consumable alcohol. **Methyl alcohol, ethylene glycol** and **isopropyl alcohol** are non consumable alcohols and are poisonous. Alcohol is produced

KEY TERMS

Volstead Act - Reinforced the prohibition of alcohol in the United States, was named for Andrew Volstead.
Ethanol - Also called grain alcohol. A consumable type of alcohol.
Methyl alcohol - Flammable poisonous liquid alcohol; known as wood alcohol.
Ethylene glycol - A sweet but poisonous syrupy liquid used as an antifreeze and solvent.
Isopropyl alcohol - Rubbing alcohol, also used as an antiseptic.

Wine Fermenting in huge vats in a famous wine cellar in Spain.

Shutterstock © David H Seymour, 2011. Under license from Shutterstock, Inc.

by the **fermentation** of yeast, sugars, and starches. It is a central nervous system depressant that is rapidly absorbed from the stomach and small intestine into the bloodstream.

Alcohol affects every organ in the drinker's body and can damage a developing fetus. Intoxication can impair brain function and motor skills while heavy use can increase the risk of certain cancers, stroke, and liver disease. Alcoholism or alcohol dependence is a diagnosable disease characterized by a strong craving for alcohol and/or continued use despite harm or personal injury. Alcohol abuse, which can lead to alcoholism, is a pattern of drinking that results in harm to one's health, interpersonal relationships, or ability to work.

The National Institute on Drug Abuse -funded 2008 Monitoring the Future Study showed that 15.9% of eighth graders, 28.8% of tenth graders, and 43.1% of twelfth graders had consumed at least one drink in the thirty days prior to being surveyed, and 5.4% of eighth graders, 14.4% of tenth graders, and 27.6% of twelfth graders had been drunk.

THE EFFECTS OF ALCOHOL ON THE BRAIN

Neuroscience: Pathways to Alcohol Dependence[3]

Why does drinking alcohol have such profound effects on thought, mood, and behavior? And why does alcohol dependence develop and persist in some people and not in others? Scientists are addressing these questions and others through neuroscience, the study of the brain, where both alcohol intoxication and dependence begin. Through neuroscience research, scientists are gaining a better understanding of how alcohol changes the brain and how those changes in turn influence certain behaviors.

To function normally, the brain must maintain a careful balance of chemicals called neurotransmitters. These are small molecules involved in the brain's communication system that ultimately help regulate the body's function and behavior. Just as a heavy

KEY TERMS

Fermentation - The process where yeast interacts with sugars to create ethyl alcohol, commonly known as ethanol.

weight can tip a scale, alcohol intoxication can alter the delicate balance among different types of neurotransmitter chemicals and can lead to drowsiness, loss of coordination, and euphoria—hallmarks of alcohol intoxication.

Remarkably, with ongoing exposure to alcohol, the brain starts to adapt to these chemical changes. When alcohol is present in the brain for long periods, as with long-term heavy drinking, the brain seeks to compensate for its effects. To restore a balanced state, the function of certain neurotransmitters begins to change so that the brain can perform more normally in the presence of alcohol. These long-term chemical changes are believed to be responsible for the harmful effects of alcohol, such as **alcohol dependence**.

Today, thanks to rapidly advancing technology, researchers know more than ever about how alcohol affects the brain and how the brain responds and adapts to these effects. Alcohol Alert No. 77 from the National Institute on Alcohol Abuse and Alcoholism summarizes some of what we know about alcohol's short- and long-term effects on the brain and how breakthroughs in neuroscience are leading to better treatments for alcohol-related problems.

How Alcohol Changes the Brain: Tolerance and Withdrawal[3]

As the brain adapts to alcohol's presence over time, a heavy drinker may begin to respond to alcohol differently than someone who drinks only moderately. Some of these changes may be behind alcohol's effects, including alcohol tolerance (i.e., having to drink more to become intoxicated) and alcohol withdrawal. These effects are associated with alcohol dependence.

When the brain is exposed to alcohol, it may become tolerant or insensitive to alcohol's effects. Thus, as a person continues to drink heavily, he or she may need more alcohol than before to become intoxicated. As **tolerance** increases, drinking may escalate, putting a heavy drinker at risk for a number of health problems, including alcohol dependence.

Even as the brain becomes tolerant to alcohol, other changes in the brain may increase some people's sensitivity to alcohol. Desire for alcohol may transition into a pathological craving for these effects. This craving is strongly associated with alcohol dependence.

Other changes in the brain increase a heavy drinker's risk for experiencing **alcohol withdrawal,** a collection of symptoms that can appear when a person with alcohol dependence suddenly stops drinking. Withdrawal symptoms can be severe,

KEY TERMS

Alcohol dependence - A chronic disease characterized by a strong craving for alcohol.
Tolerance - Need to consume large amounts in order to feel effects, which causes the liver to become less efficient.
Alcohol withdrawal - A collection of symptoms that can appear when a person with alcohol dependence suddenly stops drinking.

especially during the forty-eight hours immediately following a bout of drinking. Typical symptoms include profuse sweating, racing heart rate, and feelings of restlessness and anxiety. Research shows that alcohol-dependent people may continue drinking to avoid experiencing withdrawal. Feelings of anxiety associated with alcohol withdrawal can persist long after the initial withdrawal symptoms have ceased, and some researchers believe that over the long-term, this anxiety is a driving force behind alcohol use relapse.

The Brain's Unique Communication System[3]

Tolerance and withdrawal are tangible evidence of alcohol's influence on the brain. Scientists now understand some of the mechanisms that lead to these changes that begin with the brain's unique communication system.

The brain communicates through a complex system of electrical and chemical signals. These signals are vital to brain function, sending messages throughout the brain which in turn regulate every aspect of the body's function. Neurotransmitter chemicals play a key role in this signal transmission.

Under normal circumstances, the brain's balance of neurotransmitters allows the body and brain to function unimpaired. Alcohol can cause changes that upset this balance, impairing brain function. For example, the brain balances the activity of inhibitory neurotransmitters, which work to delay or stop nerve signals, with that of excitatory neurotransmitters, which work to speed up these signals. Alcohol can slow signal transmission in the brain, contributing to some of the effects associated with **alcohol intoxication**, including sleepiness and sedation.

As the brain grows used to alcohol, it compensates for alcohol's slowing effects by increasing the activity of excitatory neurotransmitters, speeding up signal transmission. In this way, the brain attempts to restore itself to a normal state in the presence of alcohol. If the influence of alcohol is suddenly removed (that is, if a long-term heavy drinker stops drinking suddenly), the brain may have to readjust once again: this may lead to the unpleasant feelings associated with alcohol withdrawal, such as experiencing **"the shakes"** or increased anxiety.

Neurons and Synaptic Transmission[3]

The brain transmits information through a system of interconnected nerve cells known as neurons. Signals travel rapidly along chains of neurons using a combi-

KEY TERMS

Alcohol intoxication - When ethanol otherwise causes the physiological effect known as drunkenness.
The shakes - A pattern of behavior including twitches, tics, and spasms typical of withdrawal from addiction; also known as Delirium tremens.

nation of electrical and chemical processes. These signals cause many of alcohol's effects on behaviors, such as tolerance, craving, and addiction.

Signals travel from one neuron to the next through a process known as synaptic transmission. Synaptic transmission is made possible by the neuron's unique structure. In addition to a main cell body, neurons have two types of specialized thin branches: axons and dendrites. Axons transmit messages from one neuron to the next, and dendrites receive those messages from nearby neurons. Individual neurons are separated by tiny gaps known as synapses.

Messages travel from one neuron to the next across synaptic gaps and bind to special docking molecules on the receiving neuron's dendrites. These docking molecules are known as neurotransmitter receptors. When a neurotransmitter binds to a receptor, it changes the activity of the receiving neuron.

Depending on the situation, these changes might make the neuron either more likely or less likely to pass on, or "fire," the signal to the next neuron. If the signal is fired, it travels down the axon, sparking the release of more neurotransmitters into the next synapse and passing the signal along to the dendrites of the next neuron. If a signal is not fired, the signal stops.

Neurotransmitters: A Key to Effective Medications for Alcoholism[3]

As researchers learn more about how neurotransmitters are involved in addiction, they can develop more effective medications that target specific neurotransmitter systems.

Unfortunately, there is no "magic bullet" for treating alcohol-related problems. It is unclear why some people respond well to certain medications but others do not. However, exciting new research is helping scientists learn more about how alcohol affects different people. A handful of medications are now available to treat alcohol problems, many of which aim to alter the short- or long-term effects of alcohol by either interfering with or imitating the actions of key neurotransmitters.

Food and Drug Administration Approved Medications[3]

Benzodiazepines (Valium and Xanax) are used in treating alcohol withdrawal. They increase GABA activity, curbing the brain's "excitability" during its withdrawal from alcohol, allowing the brain to restore its natural balance. **Disulfiram** (Antabuse) is used in preventing alcohol consumption. Its main effect is on alcohol metabolism rather than in the brain. It increases the concentration of acetaldehyde,

Benzodiazepines - Are used in treating alcohol withdrawal.
Disulfiram - Are used in preventing alcohol consumption.

a toxic byproduct that occurs when alcohol is broken down (i.e., metabolized) in the body. Excess amounts of this byproduct cause unpleasant symptoms, such as nausea and flushing of the skin. **Naltrexone** (ReVia®, Vivitrol®, Naltrel®) are used in reducing/stopping drinking. They block opioid receptors involved in the pleasant sensations associated with drinking. **Acamprosate** (Campral®) is used for enhancing abstinence. It is thought to dampen glutamate activity and may reduce some of the hyper excitability associated with alcohol withdrawal.

New Strategies for Studying Alcohol and the Brain[3]

Powerful imaging methods now allow researchers to study how alcohol affects different brain systems and structures. Some of these methods include **positron emission tomography (PET), event-related potentials (ERPs), magnetic resonance imaging and magnetic resonance spectroscopy (MRI/MRS).** These methods are especially useful because they allow researchers to see, in real time, how alcohol changes the human brain. These imaging techniques when used with alcoholics, nonalcoholics, and children of alcoholics may help identify genetic risk factors for alcoholism.

PET is being used to track the changes that alcohol use causes in specific neurotransmitter systems. Changes that are the cause of alcohol's short-term pleasurable effects (i.e., intoxication) and long-term detrimental effects (i.e., alcohol dependence). PET technology allows researchers to see how certain molecules behave. For example, researchers are using PET to track the activity of dopamine, a neurotransmitter believed to contribute to alcoholism. With this information, researchers can identify specific parts of the dopamine system that could be targeted for the development of medications to treat alcoholism.

Using ERP, researchers have identified markers that appear in the brains of alcoholics and in children of alcoholics (a population that is at high risk for developing alcoholism). A marker is a distinct characteristic that can be associated with a certain group of people. Such markers may be useful for identifying people who are at risk for alcoholism. For example, scientists have found that certain electrical currents in the brain (as measured by a brainwave called P300) are different in people who are at risk for alcoholism. Research shows that alcoholics have a blunted P300 brainwave; that is, the peak of the brainwave is much lower than in people without an alcohol use disorder. Moreover, this difference in P300 peak is evident in children of alcoholics even before they have taken their first drink. Certain markers linked to alcoholism also are found with other mental health disorders, including drug

KEY TERMS

Naltrexone - Are used in reducing/stopping drinking.
Acamprosate - Is used for enhancing abstinence.
Positron emission tomography (PET), Event-related potentials (ERPs), Magnetic resonance imaging and Magnetic resonance spectroscopy (MRI/MRS) - Powerful imaging methods that allow researchers to study how alcohol affects different brain systems and structures.

use disorders, antisocial personality disorder, conduct disorder, and attention deficit hyperactivity disorder, suggesting that there may be a genetic connection among all of these disorders.

New Technology to Map Alcohol's Effects[3]

With MRI/MRS, researchers use a powerful magnetic field to generate a highly detailed "map" of the brain. For example, one technique known as functional MRI allows researchers to "see" blood flow to specific regions in the brain and to identify which regions of the brain currently are active. Using this technique, researchers are exploring how alcohol affects brain function and how brain function changes as alcohol dependence develops over time.

In addition to imaging studies, researchers are using animals to study alcoholism. The results of these studies can help researchers better understand how to treat alcoholism in humans. In particular, animal models help scientists study the genetic links involved in alcoholism. Researchers can "turn off" genes that may be involved in alcohol addiction in laboratory animals, giving them insight into how these genes affect behavior. For example, an animal model could show whether an animal will still seek alcohol once a specific gene has been turned off. Researchers also are able to work with small clusters of cells from animal brains and to study alcohol's effects on a cellular level.

Animal studies allow researchers to explore how alcohol damages the brain and how the brain begins to recover from this damage with abstinence from drinking. Studies in rats show that heavy episodic drinking (i.e., binge drinking) can injure the brain by causing the death of neurons and other components. These brain injuries may cause some of the changes in thought and behavior that are associated with alcohol dependence in humans. Animal studies suggest that the brain can recover at least partially from this damage. One method being investigated is the use of neural stem cells which over time may help to rewire new neurons and repair damage to the brain's communication system.

Neuroscience is showing that the pathways of addiction are based in the brain. Using advanced techniques such as imaging methods and studies with animal models, researchers are learning more about how alcohol interacts with the brain's communication system in different people. Innovative technology also is helping identify the changes that occur in the brain's structure and function as a result of drinking, and how alcohol disrupts the brain's delicate chemical balance. This information may help scientists understand why and how alcoholism develops in different populations and ultimately result in more effective and targeted therapies for alcohol abuse and dependence.

Difficulty walking, blurred vision, slurred speech, slowed reaction times, impaired memory: Clearly, alcohol affects the brain.

How Alcohol Damages the Brain[4]

Difficulty walking, blurred vision, slurred speech, slowed reaction times, impaired memory: Clearly, alcohol affects the brain. Some of these impairments are detectable after only one or two drinks and quickly resolve when drinking stops. On the other hand, a person who drinks heavily over a long period of time may have brain deficits that persist well after he or she achieves sobriety. Exactly how alcohol affects the brain and the likelihood of reversing the effect of heavy drinking on the brain remain hot topics in alcohol research today.

We do know that heavy drinking may have extensive and far reaching effects on the brain, ranging from simple "slips" in memory to permanent and debilitating conditions that require lifetime custodial care. Even moderate drinking leads to short–term impairment, as shown by extensive research on the impact of drinking on driving.

A number of factors influence how and to what extent alcohol affects the brain, including how much and how often a person drinks; the age at which he or she first began drinking and how long he or she has been drinking; the person's age, level of education, gender, genetic background, and family history of alcoholism; whether he or she is at risk as a result of prenatal alcohol exposure; and his or her general health status.

Blackouts and Memory Lapses[4]

Blackouts are much more common among social drinkers than previously assumed and should be viewed as a potential consequence of acute intoxication regardless of age or whether the drinker is clinically dependent on alcohol. For one study, 772 college undergraduates were surveyed about their experiences with blackouts and were asked, "Have you ever awoken after a night of drinking not able to remember things that you did or places that you went?" Of the students who had ever consumed alcohol, 51 percent reported blacking out at some point in their lives, and 40 percent reported experiencing a blackout in the year before the survey. Of those who reported drinking in the two weeks before the survey, 9.4 percent said they blacked out during that time. The students reported learning later that they had participated in a wide range of potentially dangerous events they could not remember, including vandalism, unprotected sex, and driving.

Mental Disorders[4]

Up to 80 percent of alcoholics have a deficiency in thiamine (vitamin B1 or beriberi), and some of these people will go on to develop serious brain disorders such as

Wernicke–Korsakoff syndrome (WKS) (also called "wet brain"). WKS is a disease that consists of two separate syndromes, a short-lived and severe condition called Wernicke's encephalopathy and a long-lasting and debilitating condition known as Korsakoff's psychosis.

The symptoms of Wernicke's encephalopathy include mental confusion, paralysis of the nerves that move the eyes (i.e., oculomotor disturbances), and difficulty with muscle coordination. For example, patients with Wernicke's encephalopathy may be too confused to find their way out of a room or may not even be able to walk.

Approximately 80-90 percent of alcoholics with Wernicke's encephalopathy also develop Korsakoff's psychosis, a chronic and debilitating syndrome characterized by persistent learning and memory problems. Patients with Korsakoff's psychosis are forgetful and quickly frustrated and have difficulty with walking and coordination. Although these patients have problems remembering old information (i.e., retrograde amnesia), it is their difficulty in "lying down" new information (i.e., anterograde amnesia) that is the most striking. For example, these patients can discuss in detail an event in their lives, but an hour later might not remember ever having the conversation.

Liver Disease[4]

Most people realize that heavy, long-term drinking can damage the liver, the organ chiefly responsible for breaking down alcohol into harmless byproducts and clearing it from the body. But people may not be aware that prolonged liver disfunction, such as liver **cirrhosis** resulting from excessive alcohol consumption, can harm the brain, leading to a serious and potentially fatal brain disorder known as hepatic encephalopathy.

Hepatic encephalopathy can cause changes in sleep patterns, mood, and personality; psychiatric conditions such as anxiety and depression; severe cognitive effects such as shortened attention span; and problems with coordination such as a flapping or shaking of the hands (called asterixis). In the most serious cases, patients may slip into a coma (i.e., **hepatic coma**), which can be fatal.

New imaging techniques have enabled researchers to study specific brain regions in patients with alcoholic liver disease, giving them a better understanding of how hepatic encephalopathy develops. These studies have confirmed that at least two toxic

Fact

Wernicke–Korsakoff Syndrome is also called "wet brain".

KEY TERMS

Wernicke–Korsakoff Syndrome (WKS) - A deficiency in thiamine (vitamin B1), or beriberi.
Cirrhosis - A disease in which scar tissue replaces normal, healthy tissue in the liver caused by damage from toxins (including alcohol).
Hepatic encephalopathy - Brain disease that occurs when serious liver damage prevents toxic substances from being filtered out of the blood and they enter the brain.
Hepatic coma - Coma that can occur in severe cases of liver disease.

substances, ammonia and manganese, have a role in the development of hepatic encephalopathy. Alcohol damaged liver cells allow excess amounts of these harmful byproducts to enter the brain, thus harming brain cells.

The Physical Effects of Fetal Alcohol Spectrum Disorders[5]

Alcohol is a **teratogen**, a substance that can harm a fetus. When a pregnant woman drinks alcohol, it passes through her blood and enters the fetus through the placenta. Its harmful effects may be seen in virtually every part of the fetus, including the brain, face, heart, liver, kidneys, eyes, ears, and bones. These effects can affect the infant's health for a lifetime.

What Is FASD?[5]

"Fetal alcohol spectrum disorders" (FASD) is an umbrella term describing the range of effects that can occur in an individual whose mother drank alcohol during pregnancy. These effects may include physical, mental, behavioral, and/or learning disabilities with possible lifelong implications. The term FASD is not a clinical diagnosis. It refers to conditions such as fetal alcohol syndrome (FAS), alcohol-related neurodevelopmental disorder, and alcohol-related birth defects. In the United States, FASD occurs in about ten per 1,000 live births, or 40,000 babies per year.

How Does FASD Affect a Person's Health?[5]

The effects of FASD vary widely from person to person. Difficulties in an individual's ability to succeed at home, school, work, and in social situations may arise at different ages. For many people with an FASD, brain damage is the most serious effect. It may result in cognitive and behavior problems. One obvious sign of brain damage in some babies born with FAS is a small head. This condition is called microcephaly. Individuals with FAS may have facial anomalies such as small eye openings, a smooth philtrum (groove under the nose), and a thin upper lip. When a person has all three features together, this is a sign of FAS. Other features, sometimes seen in persons with FAS, include a short nose, a flat mid-face, or a small upper jaw. However, people who do not have FAS also can have these features, so they are not by themselves a sign of FAS.

Because of damage by exposure to alcohol in the womb, babies with an FASD may be born small and underweight. Some have difficulty nursing or eating and their growth continues to lag, resulting in failure to thrive. Some infants with an FASD

KEY TERMS

Teratogen - A substance that can harm a fetus.
Fetal alcohol spectrum disorders: (FASD) - An umbrella term describing the range of effects that can occur in an individual whose mother drank alcohol during pregnancy.
Fetal alcohol syndrome (FAS) - A congenital medical condition in which body deformation occurs or facial development or mental ability is impaired because the mother drank alcohol during pregnancy.

may also have tremors, seizures, excessive irritability, and sleep problems. Physical effects of FASD may include heart defects, such as a hole in the wall of the heart that separates its chambers. Other effects are skeletal defects, such as fused bones in the arms, fingers, hands, and toes. People with an FASD also may have vision and hearing problems, kidney and liver defects, and dental abnormalities. Alcohol can damage the developing fetus from the earliest weeks through the end of the pregnancy. Other factors associated with women who drink during pregnancy are poor nutrition and lack of prenatal care. These factors also may affect organ and skeletal development. Researchers still have many questions about the effects of prenatal alcohol exposure.

Fact

Alcohol can damage the developing fetus from the earliest weeks through the end of the pregnancy.

Possible Physical Effects of FASD[5]

- Brain damage
- Facial anomalies
- Growth deficiencies
- Defects of the heart, kidneys, and liver
- Vision and hearing problems
- Skeletal defects
- Dental abnormalities

ALCOHOL POISONING[6]

What Is It?

Alcohol depresses nerves that control involuntary actions such as breathing and the gag reflex, which prevents choking. Someone who drinks a fatal dose of alcohol will eventually stop breathing. Even if someone survives an alcohol overdose, he or she can suffer irreversible brain damage. Rapid binge drinking is especially dangerous because the victim can drink a fatal dose before losing consciousness.

A person's blood alcohol concentration can continue to rise even while he or she is passed out. Even after someone stops drinking, alcohol in the stomach and intestine continues to enter the bloodstream and circulate throughout the body. A person who appears to be sleeping it off may be in real danger.

Signs of Alcohol Poisoning[6]

Critical signs of **alcohol poisoning** include mental confusion, stupor, or coma; the inability to be roused; vomiting; seizures; slow (fewer than eight breaths per minute)

KEY TERMS

Alcohol poisoning - A severe and potentially fatal physical reaction to an alcohol overdose.

or irregular (ten seconds or more between breaths) breathing; and hypothermia (low body temperature), bluish skin color, and paleness. A person exhibiting these symptoms requires immediate medical attention.

WHAT IS ALCOHOLISM?[7]

Alcoholism, also known as alcohol dependence, is a disease that includes the following four symptoms:

- Craving—A strong need, or urge, to drink.
- Loss of control—Not being able to stop drinking once drinking has begun.
- Physical dependence—Withdrawal symptoms such as nausea, sweating, shakiness, and anxiety after stopping drinking.
- Tolerance—The need to drink greater amounts of alcohol to get "high."

Is Alcoholism a Disease?7

Yes, **alcoholism** is a disease. The craving that an alcoholic feels for alcohol can be as strong as the need for food or water. An alcoholic will continue to drink despite serious family, health, or legal problems.

Like many other diseases, alcoholism is chronic, meaning that it lasts a person's lifetime, it usually follows a predictable course, and it has symptoms. The risk for developing alcoholism is influenced both by a person's genes and by his or her lifestyle.

Is Alcoholism Inherited?[7]

Research shows that the risk for developing alcoholism does indeed run in families. The genes a person inherits partially explain this pattern, but lifestyle is also a factor. Currently, researchers are working to discover the actual genes that put people at risk for alcoholism. A person's friends, the amount of stress in his or her life, and how readily available alcohol is also are factors that may increase a person's risk for alcoholism. Risk is not destiny. Just because alcoholism tends to run in families doesn't mean that a child of an alcoholic parent will automatically become an alcoholic too.

Can Alcoholism Be Cured?[7]

No, alcoholism cannot be cured at this time. Even if an alcoholic hasn't been drinking for a long time, he or she can still suffer a relapse. Not drinking is the safest course for most people with alcoholism.

KEY TERMS

Alcoholism - A chronic illness evidenced by compulsive, repeated drinking that injures one's health and social and economic functioning.

Can Alcoholism Be Treated?[7]

Yes, alcoholism can be treated. Alcoholism treatment programs use both counseling and medications to help a person stop drinking. Treatment has helped many people stop drinking and rebuild their lives.

Does a Person Have To Be an Alcoholic To Experience Problems?[7]

No. Alcoholism is only one type of an alcohol problem. Alcohol abuse can be just as harmful. A person can abuse alcohol without actually being an alcoholic; that is, he or she may drink too much and too often but still not be dependent on alcohol. Some of the problems linked to alcohol abuse include not being able to meet work, school, or family responsibilities; drunk-driving arrests and car crashes; and drinking-related medical conditions. Under some circumstances, even social or moderate drinking is dangerous; for example, when driving, during pregnancy, or when taking certain medications.

Are Specific Groups of People More Likely To Have Problems?[7]

Alcohol abuse and alcoholism cut across gender, race, and nationality. In the United States, 17.6 million people, or about one in every twelve adults, abuse alcohol or are alcohol dependent. In general, more men than women are alcohol dependent or have alcohol problems. Alcohol problems are highest among young adults ages eighteen to twenty-nine and lowest among adults ages sixty-five and older. We also know that people who start drinking at an early age, for example at age fourteen or younger, are at much higher risk of developing alcohol problems at some point in their lives compared to someone who starts drinking at age twenty-one or after.

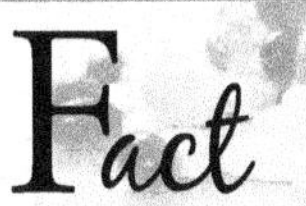

Alcohol problems are highest among young adults ages eighteen to twenty-nine and lowest among adults ages sixty-five and older.

Is It Safe To Drink During Pregnancy?[7]

No, alcohol can harm the baby of a mother who drinks during pregnancy. Although the highest risk is to babies whose mothers drink heavily, it is not clear yet whether there is any completely safe level of alcohol during pregnancy. For this reason, the U.S. Surgeon General released advisories in 1981 and again in 2005 urging women who are pregnant or may become pregnant to abstain from alcohol.

Does Alcohol Affect Older People Differently?[7]

Alcohol's effects do vary with age. Slower reaction times, problems with hearing and seeing, and a lower tolerance to alcohol's effects put older people at higher risk for falls, car crashes, and other types of injuries that may result from drinking.

Older people also tend to take more medicines than younger people. Mixing alcohol with over-the-counter (OTC) or prescription medications can be very dangerous, even fatal. In addition, alcohol can make many of the medical conditions common in older people, including high blood pressure and ulcers, more serious. Physical changes associated with aging can make older people feel "high" even after drinking only small amounts of alcohol.

Can a Person Drink When Taking Medication?[7]

Possibly. More than 150 medications interact harmfully with alcohol. These interactions may result in increased risk of illness, injury, and even death. Alcohol's effects are heightened by medicines that depress the central nervous system, such as sleeping pills, antihistamines, antidepressants, anti-anxiety drugs, and some painkillers. In addition, medicines for certain disorders, including diabetes, high blood pressure, and heart disease, can have harmful interactions with alcohol. People who are taking any OTC or prescription medications should ask their doctor or pharmacist if they can safely drink alcohol.

How Can a Person Get Help for an Alcohol Problem?[7]

There are many national and local resources that can help. The National Drug and Alcohol Treatment Referral Routing Service provides a toll-free telephone number, 1-800-662-HELP (4357), offering various resource information. Through this service, a person can speak directly to a representative concerning substance abuse treatment, request printed material on alcohol or other drugs, or obtain local substance abuse treatment referral information in his or her state.

ADDITIONAL INFORMATION

Contact the following organizations if you or someone you know needs help or more information about alcohol abuse or alcoholism:

Al–Anon Family Group Headquarters
Internet address: www.al–anon.alateen.org
Makes referrals to local Al–Anon groups, which are support groups for spouses and other significant adults in an alcoholic person's life. Also makes referrals to Alateen groups, which offer support to children of alcoholics.

- Locations of Al–Anon or Alateen meetings worldwide can be obtained by calling (888) 4AL–ANON (425–2666) Monday through Friday, 8 a.m.–6 p.m. (EST)
- Free informational materials can be obtained by calling (757) 563–1600, Monday through Friday, 8 a.m.–6 p.m.

Alcoholics Anonymous (AA) World Services
Phone: (212) 870–3400
Internet address: www.aa.org
Makes referrals to local AA groups and provides informational materials on the AA program. Many cities and towns also have a local AA office listed in the telephone book.

National Association for Children of Alcoholics (NACoA)
Phone: (888) 55–4COAS or (301) 468–0985
E–mail: nacoa@nacoa.org
Internet address: www.nacoa.net
Works on behalf of children of alcohol- and drug-dependent parents.

National Council on Alcoholism and Drug Dependence (NCADD)
Phone: (800) 622–2255
Internet address: www.ncadd.org
Provides telephone numbers of local NCADD affiliates who can provide information on local treatment resources and educational materials on alcoholism via the above toll–free number.

National Institute on Alcohol Abuse and Alcoholism (NIAAA)
Phone: (301) 443–3860
Internet address: www.niaaa.nih.gov
Makes available free publications on all aspects of alcohol abuse and alcoholism. Many are available in Spanish. Call, write, or search the NIAAA Web site for a list of publications and ordering information.

REFERENCES

1. America's alcohol problem. National Institute on Alcohol Abuse and Alcoholism (NIAAA). http://utakeitback.org/community/niaaa.html. Accessed April 22, 2011.
2. Alcohol. National Institute on Drug Abuse (NIDA). 2008. http://www.drugabuse.gov/drugpages/alcohol.html
3. Alcohol Alert Number 77: Neuroscience; Pathways to Alcohol Dependence. National Institute on Alcohol Abuse and Alcoholism (NIAAA). April 2009. http://pubs.niaaa.nih.gov/publications/AA77/AA77.htm. Accessed April 22, 2011.
4. Alcohol Alert Number 63: Alcohol's Damaging Effects on the Brain. NIAAA. October 2004. http://pubs.niaaa.nih.gov/publications/aa63/aa63.htm. Accessed April 22, 2011.
5. Substance Abuse and Mental Health Services Administration (SAMHSA). The Physical Effects of Fetal Alcohol Spectrum Disorders. 2007. http://www.fasdcenter.samhsa.gov/documents/WYNK_Physical_Effects.pdf. Accessed April 22, 2011.
6. Parents: help your teens party right at graduation. NIH Publication No. 07-5641. NIAAA. May 2009. http://pubs.niaaa.nih.gov/publications/GraduationFacts/NIAAA_graduation_flyer.pdf. Accessed April 22, 2011.
7. FAQs for the general public. NIAAA. February 2007. http://www.niaaa.nih.gov/FAQs/General-English/Pages/default.aspx#whatis. Accessed April 22, 2011.

CHAPTER 6

Alcohol and Our Behavior

Shutterstock © Liv friis-larsen, 2011. Under license from Shutterstock, Inc.

OBJECTIVES

After you have finished this chapter, you should be able to

- explain what is underage drinking;
- explain why underage drinking is a problem;
- explain why teens may choose to drink;
- explain what's a standard drink;
- explain binge drinking;
- explain blood alcohol concentration;
- list the alcohol treatment programs;
- explain the twelve-step facilitation approach;

"An intelligent man is sometimes forced to be drunk to spend time with his fools."

-Ernest Hemingway

A DRINKING CULTURE[1]

Too often today's headlines bring news of yet another alcohol-related tragedy involving a young person in a case of fatal alcohol poisoning on a college campus or a late-night drinking and driving crash. People ages eighteen to twenty-five often are in the news, but are they really at higher risk than anyone else for problems involving alcohol?

Some of the most important new data to emerge on young adult drinking were collected through a recent nationwide survey, the National Epidemiologic Survey on Alcohol and Related Conditions. According to these data, in 2001–2002 about 70 percent of young adults in the United States, or about 19 million people, consumed alcohol in the year preceding the survey.

It's not only that young people are drinking but the way they drink that puts them at such high risk for alcohol-related problems. Research consistently shows that people tend to drink the heaviest in their late teens and early to mid twenties. Young adults are especially likely to binge drink and to drink heavily. The recommended daily limits for moderate alcohol consumption are no more than two drinks for men or one drink for women per day. According to the National Institute on Alcohol Abuse and Alcoholism [**NIAAA**], men may be at risk for alcohol-related problems if their alcohol consumption exceeds fourteen standard drinks per week or four drinks per day, and women may be at risk if they have more than seven standard drinks per week or three drinks per day. A standard drink is defined as one 12-oz bottle of beer, one 5-oz glass of wine, or 1.5 oz of distilled spirits.

Such risky drinking often leads to tragic consequences, most notably alcohol-related traffic fatalities. Thirty-two percent of driver's ages sixteen to twenty who died in traffic crashes in 2008 had measurable alcohol in their blood, and 51 percent of drivers ages twenty-one to twenty-four who died tested positive for alcohol. Clearly, young adult drinkers pose a serious public health threat, putting themselves and others at risk.

Young adulthood is a stage of life marked by change and exploration. People move out of their parents' homes and into dormitories or houses with peers. They go to college, begin to work full-time, and form serious relationships. They explore their own identities and how they fit in the world. The roles of parents weaken and the influences of peers gain greater strength. Young adults are on their own for the first time, free to make their own decisions, including the decision to drink alcohol.

KEY TERMS

NIAAA - The National Institute on Alcohol Abuse and Alcoholism.

Young adulthood also is the time during which young people obtain the education and training they need for future careers. Mastery of these endeavors is vital to future success; problems with school and work can produce frustration and stress, which can lead to a variety of unhealthy behaviors, including increased drinking. Conversely, alcohol use during this important time of transition can impede the successful mastery of these developmental tasks, also increasing stress.

Fact

According to the U.S. Surgeon General, today, nearly 10.8 million youths ages twelve to twenty are underage drinkers.

WHAT IS UNDERAGE DRINKING?[2]

According to the U.S. Surgeon General, today, nearly 10.8 million youths ages twelve to twenty are underage drinkers. Drinking alcohol can harm the growing body and brain. That's why it's important for young people to grow up alcohol free. And it takes every adult in the community to help young people choose not to drink alcohol.

When anyone under age twenty-one drinks alcohol, it is called underage drinking. Underage drinking is against the law, except in special cases, such as when it is part of a religious ceremony. Underage drinking is also dangerous. It can harm the mind and body of a growing teen in ways many people don't realize. Yet, children and teens still drink, even though it can harm them. Underage drinking is a serious problem, with roots deep in our culture. It is time to change that picture. It's time to take action. It's time to stop looking the other way. It's time to tell children and teens that underage drinking is not okay. It will take a lot of work over time to change how people think about underage drinking. It's a long-term project for parents, schools, local groups, community leaders, and other concerned adults. And it's a project that should start when children are young and continue through the teen years. In any month, more youths are drinking than are smoking cigarettes or using marijuana.

As they grow older, the chance that young people will use alcohol grows. Approximately ten percent of twelve-year-olds say they have used alcohol at least once. By age thirteen that number doubles. And by age fifteen, approximately 50 percent have had at least one drink. Alcohol dependence is a term doctors use when people have trouble controlling their drinking and when their consumption of, or preoccupation with, alcohol occurs to the extent that it interferes with normal personal, family, social, or work life. Alcohol dependence rates are highest among young people between ages eighteen and twenty. And they're not even old enough to drink legally.

The greatest influence on young people's decisions to begin drinking is the world they live in, which includes their families, friends, schools, the larger community, and society as a whole. Alcohol use by young people often is made possible by adults. After all, teens can't legally get alcohol on their own.

Most young people who start drinking before age twenty-one do so when they are about thirteen or fourteen years old. That's why it's important to start talking early and keep talking about underage drinking. And that's why all adults working with young people should send the same message that underage drinking is not okay.

Why Is Underage Drinking A Problem?[2]

- **So many young people drink.** Many more young people use alcohol than tobacco or illegal drugs. By age eighteen, more than 70 percent of teens have had at least one drink. When young people drink, they drink a lot at one time. Teens drink less often than adults. But when teens do drink, they drink more than adults. On average, young people have about five drinks on a single occasion. This is called "binge drinking," a very dangerous way of drinking that can lead to serious problems and even death.
- **Early drinking can cause later alcohol problems.** Of adults who started drinking before age fifteen, around 40 percent say they have the signs of alcohol dependence. That rate is four times higher than for adults who didn't drink until they were age twenty-one.
- **Alcohol may have a special appeal for young people.** The teen years are a time of adventure, challenges, and risk taking. Alcohol is often one of the risks young people take. But most people don't know how alcohol affects a teen's body and behavior. They don't realize that alcohol can affect young people in different ways from adults. And they don't realize that underage drinkers can also harm people other than themselves.

Facts that Many People Don't Know About Underage Alcohol Use[2]

Fact

Each year, approximately 5,000 people under the age of twenty-one die as a result of underage drinking.

- **It is a major cause of death from injuries among young people.** Each year, approximately 5,000 people under the age of twenty-one die as a result of underage drinking; this includes about 1,900 deaths from motor vehicle crashes, 1,600 as a result of homicides, and 300 from suicide, as well as hundreds from other injuries such as falls, burns, and drowning.
- **It increases the risk of carrying out, or being a victim of, a physical or sexual assault.**
- **It can affect the body in many ways.** The effects of alcohol range from hangovers to death from alcohol poisoning.
- **It can lead to other problems.** These may include bad grades in school, run-ins with the law, and drug use.
- **It affects how well a young person judges risk and makes sound decisions.** For example, after drinking, a teen may see nothing wrong with driving a car or riding with a driver who has been drinking.
- **It plays a role in risky sexual activity.** This can increase the chance of teen pregnancy and sexually transmitted diseases, including **HIV**, the virus that causes AIDS.

KEY TERMS

(HIV) Human Immunodeficiency Virus - The virus that causes AIDS.

- **It can harm the growing brain, especially when teens drink a lot.** Today we know that the brain continues to develop from birth through the teen years into the mid twenties.

Why Teens May Choose to Drink[2]

Many things affect a young person's decisions about drinking:

- The different "worlds" in which teens live, including family, friends, school, and community
- A greater desire to take risks
- Less connection to parents and more independence
- More time spent with friends and by themselves
- Increased stress
- Greater attention to what they see and hear about alcohol

Teens with behavior or family problems are at higher risk for alcohol use. If anyone in a teen's family has a drinking problem, it can affect the entire family. It also may affect a teen's choices about drinking.

Youths with histories of behavior problems (e.g., delinquent activity, impulsive actions, difficulty controlling responses) are more likely to use alcohol than are other young people. The same is true for youths who have an unusually strong desire for new experiences and sensations, and for those with histories of family conflict, stress, and/or alcohol problems.

Underage Drinking Can Affect Anyone, Including People Who Don't Drink[2]

Underage alcohol use can lead to dangerous behavior, property damage, and violence. The results can be injury and even death for the drinker and for other people nearby. About 45 percent of people who die in car crashes involving a drinking driver under age twenty-one are people other than the driver.

The effects of underage drinking can be felt by everyone. That makes underage alcohol use everyone's problem.

There Is a Role for Everyone in Stopping Underage Drinking[2]

Everyone can work together to create a community where young people can grow up and feel good about themselves without drinking. Everyone in the community should deliver the message that underage drinking is not okay. The message should be the same whether youths hear it in school, at home, in places of worship, on the sports field, in youth programs, or in other places where young people gather. Families can help prevent underage drinking by staying involved in their children's lives. It is important for families to pay attention to what's happening with their teens.

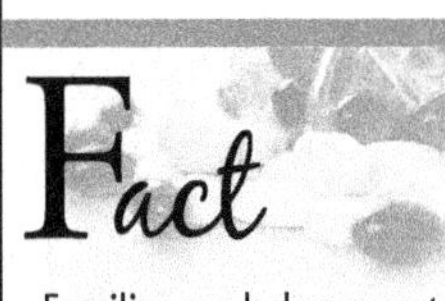

Families can help prevent underage drinking by staying involved in their children's lives.

Young people can learn about the dangers of alcohol use. They can change how they and others think about drinking.

The discussion concerning underage drinking needs to start long before young people start thinking about drinking. In order to help them understand that it is not okay to drink alcohol society should stop accepting and begin discouraging this behavior.

Underage Drinking Statistics[3]

The consequences of excessive and underage drinking affect virtually all college campuses, college communities, and college students, whether they choose to drink or not. The following information represents annual occurrences.

- **Death:** 1,825 college students between the ages of eighteen and twenty-four die from unintentional alcohol-related injuries, including motor vehicle crashes.
- **Injury:** 599,000 students between the ages of eighteen and twenty-four are unintentionally injured under the influence of alcohol.
- **Assault:** 696,000 students between the ages of eighteen and twenty-four are assaulted by another student who has been drinking.
- **Sexual Abuse:** 97,000 students between the ages of eighteen and twenty-four are victims of alcohol-related sexual assault or date rape .
- **Drunk Driving:** 3,360,000 students between the ages of eighteen and twenty-four drive under the influence of alcohol .

What's a Standard Drink?[4]

In the United States, **a standard drink** is any drink that contains about 14 grams of pure alcohol (about 0.6 fluid ounces or 1.2 tablespoons). Below are U.S. standard drink equivalents. These are approximate, since different brands and types of beverages vary in their actual alcohol content.

Beer or Cooler	Malt Liquor	Table Wine	80-proof Spirits (gin, vodka, whisky, etc.)
5% alcohol: 12 oz	7% alcohol: 8.5 oz	12% alcohol: 5 oz	40% alcohol: 1.5 oz

Many people don't know what counts as a standard drink and so don't realize how many standard drinks are in the containers in which alcoholic beverages are often sold.

KEY TERMS

A standard drink - Any drink that contains about 14 grams of pure alcohol (about 0.6 fluid ounces or 1.2 tablespoons).

Shutterstock © Quayside, 2011. Under license from Shutterstock, Inc.

Depending on factors such as the type of spirits and the recipe, a mixed drink can contain from one to three or more standard drinks.

For beer, the approximate number of standard drinks in relation to ounces are as follows:

- 12 oz = 1
- 16 oz = 1.3
- 22 oz = 2
- 40 oz = 3.3

For malt liquor, the approximate number of standard drinks in relation to ounces are as follows:

- 12 oz = 1.5
- 16 oz = 2
- 22 oz = 2.5
- 40 oz = 4.5

For table wine, the approximate number of standard drinks in relation to ounces is as follows:

- a standard 750-mL (25-oz) bottle = 5

For 80-proof spirits, or "hard liquor," the approximate number of standard drinks in relation to ounces are as follows:

- a mixed drink = 1 or more*
- a pint (16 oz) = 11
- a fifth (25 oz) = 17
- 1.75 L (59 oz) = 39

**Note: It can be difficult to estimate the number of standard drinks in a single mixed drink made with hard liquor. Depending on factors such as the type of spirits and the recipe, a mixed drink can contain from one to three or more standard drinks.*

DRINKING AND DRIVING[5,6]

"Have one [drink] for the road" was once a commonly used phrase in American culture. It has only been within the past twenty-five years that as a nation, we have begun to recognize the dangers associated with drunk driving. Through a multipronged and concerted effort involving many stakeholders, including educators, media, legislators, law enforcement, and community organizations such as Mothers Against Drunk Driving (**MADD**), the nation has seen a decline in the numbers of people killed or injured as a result of drunk driving.

KEY TERMS

MADD - Mothers Against Drunk Driving.

The principal concern regarding drugged driving is that driving under the influence of any drug that acts on the brain and could impair one's motor skills, reaction time, and judgment. Drugged driving is a public health concern because it puts not only the driver but also passengers and others who share the road at risk.

However, despite the knowledge about a drug's potentially lethal effects on driving performance and other concerns that have been acknowledged by some public health officials, policy officials, and constituent groups, drugged driving laws have lagged behind alcohol-related driving legislation, in part because of limitations in the current technology for determining drug levels and resulting impairment. For alcohol, detection of its blood alcohol concentration (BAC) is relatively simple, and concentrations greater than 0.08 percent have been shown to impair driving performance; thus, 0.08 percent is the legal limit in the United States.

In 2009, an estimated 12 percent of persons aged twelve or older (30.2 million persons) drove under the influence of alcohol at least once in the previous year. This percentage has dropped since 2002, when it was 14.2 percent. Driving under the influence of an illicit drug or alcohol was associated with age. In 2009, an estimated 6.3 percent of youths aged sixteen or seventeen drove under the influence. This percentage steadily increased with age to reach a peak of 24.8 percent among young adults aged twenty-one to twenty-five. Beyond the age of twenty-five, these rates showed a general decline with increasing age.

About one in three high school seniors has, in a two-week period, either driven a vehicle after drinking alcohol or taking illegal drugs or ridden as a passenger with a driver under the influence of those substances, a National Institute on Drug Abuse supported study suggests.

Researchers looked at data from six annual Monitoring the Future Surveys, 2001 to 2006, each of which asked approximately 2,500 high school seniors whether they had, in the two weeks prior to the survey, driven after drinking alcohol or using an illicit drug or ridden with a driver who had. Although the prevalence of alcohol or drug impaired driving and riding has declined over the six years, from 35 percent in 2001 to 30 percent in 2006, the problem remains serious and widespread.

The researchers focused on four categories of substance abuse: use of marijuana; use of any illicit drug other than marijuana; consumption of any amount of alcohol; and heavy drinking, defined as five or more alcoholic drinks in a row. The most prevalent single activity, reported by 21 percent of high school seniors in 2006, was riding with a driver who had used alcohol, closely followed by riding with a driver who had used marijuana (20 percent). Nearly a quarter of the students in the class of 2006 admitted to taking a ride with someone who had either used an illicit drug or had been drinking heavily. Fourteen percent admitted to driving after using alcohol, and 13 percent to doing so after marijuana use.

BINGE DRINKING DEFINED[7]

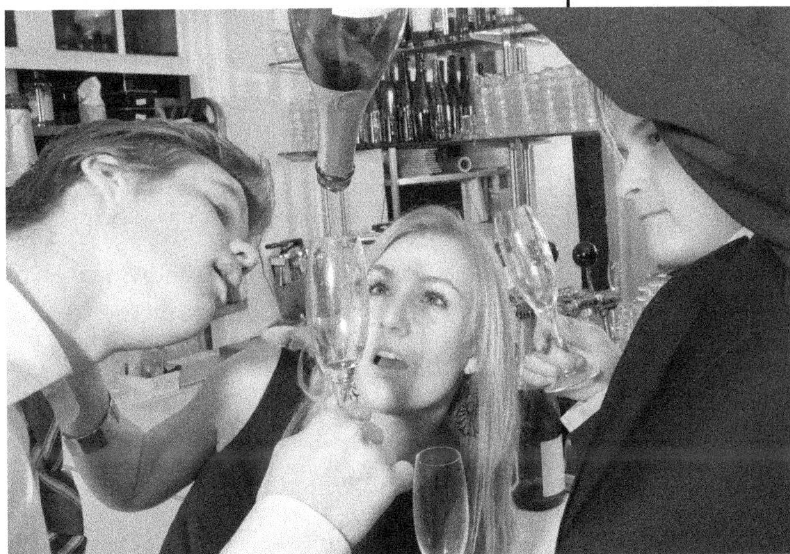
Shutterstock © corepics, 2011. Under license from Shutterstock, Inc.

College students abuse alcohol usually through binge drinking.

On February 5, 2004, the NIAAA National Advisory Council approved the following definition statement:

A **"binge"** is a pattern of drinking alcohol that brings blood alcohol concentration (BAC) to 0.08 grams percent or above. For the typical adult, this pattern corresponds to consuming five or more drinks (male), or four or more drinks (female), in about two hours. **Binge drinking** is clearly dangerous for the drinker and for society.

- In the above definition, a "drink" refers to half an ounce of alcohol (e.g., one 12-oz beer, one 5-oz glass of wine, or one 1.5-oz shot of distilled spirits).
- Binge drinking is distinct from "risky" drinking (reaching a peak BAC between 0.05 grams percent and 0.08 grams percent) and a "bender" (two or more days of sustained heavy drinking).
- For some individuals (e.g., older people or people taking other drugs or certain medications), the number of drinks needed to reach a binge level BAC is lower than for the typical adult.
- People with risk factors for the development of alcoholism have increased risk with any level of alcohol consumption, even that below a "risky" level.
- For pregnant women, any drinking presents risk to the fetus.
- Drinking by persons under the age of twenty-one is illegal.

BAC AND IMPAIRMENT[8]

Blood alcohol concentration (BAC) is the proportion of alcohol to blood in the body. In the field of traffic safety, BAC is expressed as a percentage reflecting grams of alcohol per deciliter of blood for example, 0.10 percent is equivalent to 0.10 grams per deciliter.

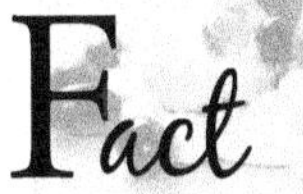

BAC is expressed as a percentage reflecting grams of alcohol per deciliter of blood.

Some skills are significantly impaired at 0.01 percent BAC, although other skills do not show impairment until 0.06 percent BAC. At BACs of 0.02 percent or lower, the

KEY TERMS

"Binge" - A pattern of drinking alcohol that brings blood alcohol concentration (BAC) to 0.08 gram percent or above.
Binge drinking - Consuming five or more drinks (male), or four or more drinks (female), in about two hours.
Blood alcohol concentration (BAC) - Is the proportion of alcohol to blood in the body.

ability to divide attention between two or more sources of visual information can be impaired. Starting at BACs of 0.05 percent, drivers show other types of impairment, including eye movement, glare resistance, visual perception, and reaction time.

FACTORS THAT INFLUENCE USE[1]

Outside influences as well as individual characteristics help determine whether a person will begin drinking and how much he or she will consume. Some of these factors increase a person's risk for problems with alcohol, whereas others serve to protect him or her from harm, as outlined below.

Gender

Men are much more likely than women to drink in ways that are harmful. As shown in a 2001–2002 national survey of nineteen- to thirty-year-olds, 45.0 percent of men and 26.7 percent of women reported heavy drinking (defined in that study as five or more drinks on one occasion) in the preceding two weeks, and 7.4 percent of men and 3.0 percent of women reported daily drinking.

Race and Ethnicity[1]

Racial, ethnic, and cultural differences in drinking and alcohol-related problems also have been documented. In general, white and Native American young adults drink more than African Americans and Asians, and drinking rates for Hispanics fall in the middle. In addition, while drinking among whites tends to peak around ages nineteen to twenty-two, heavy drinking among African Americans and Hispanics peaks later and persists longer into adulthood. Researchers suggest that these ethnic differences result, in part, from the fact that whites see heavy drinking as part of a youthful lifestyle, whereas Hispanics tend to see heavy drinking as a "right" they earn when they reach maturity.

College vs. Non-college Status[1]

Many people think that the college campus environment itself encourages heavy drinking. Alcohol use is present at most college social functions, and many students view college as a place to drink excessively. Yet several studies have shown that heavy drinking and related problems are pervasive among people in their early twenties, regardless of whether they attend college. In fact, a 2005 survey showed that college students drank less frequently than their non-college peers (that is, 3.7 percent of students reported daily drinking vs. 4.5 percent of non-students). However, when students do drink, such as at parties on the weekends, they tend to drink in greater quantities than non-students. On the other hand, students tend to stop these drinking practices more quickly than non-students, perhaps "maturing out" of harmful alcohol use before it becomes a long-term problem. Rates of alcohol dependence diagnosis appear lower for college students than for eighteen- to twenty-four-year olds in the general population. And people in their thirties who did not go to college reported a higher prevalence of heavy drinking than people who did go to college.

Military Service[1]

Young adults in the military are more likely to drink heavily (i.e., consume five or more drinks per typical drinking occasion at least once a week) than older enlistees. In 2002, 27 percent of adults ages eighteen to twenty-five in the military reported heavy drinking, compared with only 8.9 percent of those ages twenty-six to fifty-five. The reasons for heavy drinking rates in the military include a workplace culture that supports alcohol use and the increased availability of alcohol both in and around military bases.

Peer Influences[1]

People entering college or the workforce may be especially vulnerable to the influence of peers because of their need to make new friendships. They may increase their drinking to gain acceptance by peers.

The phenomenon of perceived social norms or the belief that "everyone" is drinking and drinking is acceptable is one of the strongest correlates of drinking among young adults, and the subject of considerable research. Many college students think campus attitudes are much more permissive toward drinking than they really are and believe other students drink much more than they actually do. Research published in 2001 has shown that addressing these misperceptions can help reduce drinking. Then again, the relationship between drinking practices and peer groups may not be so clear. That is, a young person may opt to join a peer group based on that group's drinking practices rather than change his or her drinking behavior to fit in with a particular peer group.

Marriage and Parenthood[1]

Just as the move to adulthood leads to greater exploration of the world and experimentation with alcohol, assuming adult roles and responsibilities consistently curbs alcohol use. This reduction in drinking may be a result of limitations that adult roles place on social activities in general or may reflect a change in these young adults' attitudes toward drinking.

Young married women have the greatest decreases in drinking behavior, and married men, compared with men in all other categories of living arrangements (i.e., living with parents, in a dormitory, alone, or in other arrangements), have the fewest increases. The data also indicate that becoming engaged (i.e., making a commitment to a relationship) has a similar but less powerful effect on drinking compared with marriage, whereas becoming divorced leads to increased drinking behavior.

Being a parent also is related to lower alcohol use for both men and women, although a large part of this effect may simply be a result of getting married. Most women who became pregnant eliminate their alcohol use, although most of their husbands do not.

Young adults with serious alcohol problems—that is, who fit the diagnostic criteria for alcohol dependence—may not be as likely to choose stable roles such as marriage and parenthood, or these milestones may not affect their drinking behavior to the same extent that they affect people with less problematic drinking practices.

Family Influences[1]

During young adulthood parents may have less direct influence on their children's drinking behavior, but they still play a major protective role. The example set by parents with their own drinking has been shown to affect children's drinking throughout their lifetime. Young people model their behavior after their parents' patterns of consumption (including quantity and frequency), situations and contexts of use, attitudes regarding use, and expectancies. The family's structure and aspects of the parent-child relationship (e.g., parenting style, attachment and bonding, nurturance, abuse or neglect, conflict, discipline, monitoring) also have been linked to young people's alcohol use.

Genetics[1]

Alcohol problems seem to run in some families. This family connection to alcoholism may be the result of a genetic link and/or may reflect the child's modeling of drinking behavior. Siblings also can influence drinking through modeling and by providing access to alcohol. It's unclear whether children of alcoholics have different drinking patterns and problems in young adulthood than those who do not have a family history of alcoholism. Research does show, however, that people with a family history of alcoholism are less likely than those with no family history to mature out of heavy drinking as they approach young adulthood.

DESIRE TO STOP DRINKING?[9]

If a person thinks they may be dependent on alcohol and decide to stop drinking completely, they should not go it alone. Sudden withdrawal from heavy drinking can be life-threatening. Medical help will ensure a plan for safe recovery.

Small changes can make a big difference in reducing the chances of having alcohol-related problems. Whatever strategies are chosen should be given a fair trial. If one approach doesn't work, another may succeed.

Here are some strategies to try:

- **Find alternatives.** Alternatives may include filling free time by developing new activities, hobbies, and relationships, or renewing old ones.
- **Avoid "triggers."** If certain activities, times of day, or feelings trigger the urge, plans can be made for something else to do instead of drinking. If drinking at home is a problem, little or no alcohol should be kept there.
- **Plan to handle urges.** When a trigger or an urge hits, these options may be considered: Remembering the reasons for changing (perhaps carry them in writing or store them in an electronic message easily accessible), talking things through with someone trusted, getting involved with a healthy, distracting activity, such as physical exercise or a hobby that doesn't involve drinking, or, instead of fighting the feeling, accepting it and riding it out without giving in, knowing that it will soon crest like a wave and pass.
- **Keep track.** Keeping track of the amount of drinks consumed by finding a way that works such as, carry drinking tracker cards in a wallet, make check marks on a kitchen calendar, or enter notes in a mobile phone notepad or personal digital assistant will help a person keep track of their drinking. Making note of each drink before consumed may help slow down drinking when needed.
- **Count and measure.** Knowing the standard drink sizes will help a person count drinks accurately as well as measuring drinks at home. Away from home, it can be hard to keep track, especially with mixed drinks, and at times, more alcohol may be consumed than realized.
- **Set goals.** A person can set goals by deciding how many days a week to drink and how many drinks will be consumed each day. There should be some days when no drinks are consumed. Drinkers with the lowest rates of alcohol use disorders stay within the low-risk limits.
- **Pace and space.** Drinks should be sipped slowly. No more than one standard drink with alcohol per hour should be consumed. It is a good idea to have **"drink spacers"**, by making every other drink a non-alcoholic one, such as water, soda, or juice.
- **Know how to say "no."** A person is likely to be offered a drink at times when they don't want one. By having a polite, convincing "no, thanks" ready, the less likely one is to give in. Hesitation allows a person time to think of excuses to go along.

Social Support to Stop Drinking[8]

One potential challenge when people stop drinking is rebuilding a life without alcohol. It may be important to

- educate family and friends,
- develop new interests and social groups,

KEY TERMS

Drink spacers - Making every other drink a non-alcoholic one, such as water, soda, or juice.

- find rewarding ways to spend your time that don't involve alcohol, or
- ask for help from others.

When asking for support from friends or significant others, be specific. This could include

- not offering you alcohol,
- not using alcohol around you,
- giving words of support and withholding criticism,
- not asking you to take on new demands right now, or
- going to a group like **Al-Anon**.

Consider joining **Alcoholics Anonymous (AA)** or another mutual support group. Recovering people who attend groups regularly do better than those who do not. Groups can vary widely, so shop around for one that's comfortable. You'll get more out of it if you become actively involved by having a sponsor and reaching out to other members for assistance.

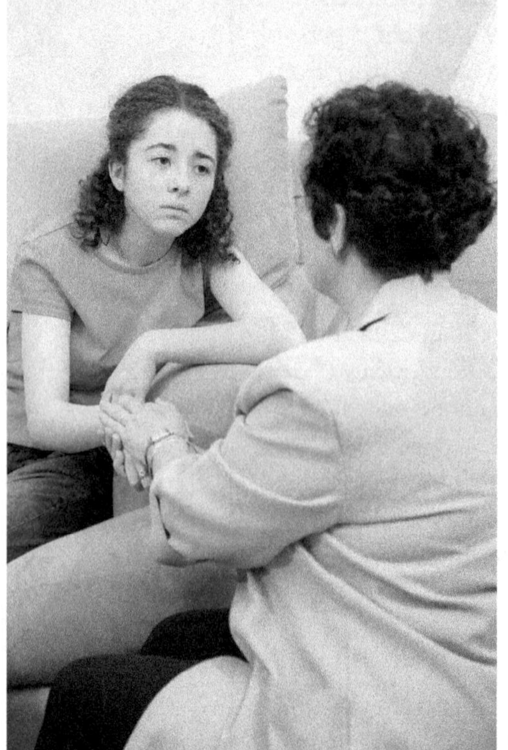

There are several counseling approaches including "Talk therapy".

Seek Professional Help[8]

Advances in alcoholism treatment in recent years have provided more choices for patients and health professionals.

Medications to treat alcoholism. Newer medications (e.g., naltrexone, topiramate, acamprosate) can make it easier to quit drinking by offsetting changes in the brain caused by alcoholism. They don't make you sick if you do drink, unlike an older medication (e.g., disulfiram). None of these medications are addictive. They also can be combined with support groups or alcohol counseling.

In addition to specialists, your regular physician can now treat alcohol problems using the new medications and several brief office visits for support.

Alcohol counseling. "Talk therapy" also works well. There are several counseling approaches that are about equally effective; 12-step, cognitive-behavioral, motivational enhancement, or a combination. Getting help in itself appears to be more important than the particular approach used, as long as it offers empathy, avoids heavy confrontation, strengthens motivation, and provides concrete ways to change drinking behavior.

KEY TERMS

Al-Anon - An International organization that provides a twelve-step program of recovery for friends and family members of alcoholics.

Specialized, intensive treatment programs. Some people will need more intensive programs. If you need a referral to a program, ask your physician.

ALCOHOL TREATMENT PROGRAMS

Detoxification, or "Detox"[10]

Detoxification is the process of allowing the body to rid itself of a drug while managing the symptoms of withdrawal. It is often the first step in a drug treatment program and should be followed by treatment with a behavioral-based therapy and/or a medication, if available. Detoxification alone with no follow-up is not treatment.

Outpatient Programs[11,12]

Cognitive-behavioral therapy. This therapy is based on the principles of social learning theory and views drinking behavior as functionally related to major problems in the person's life. This theory indicates that addressing this broad spectrum of problems will prove more effective than focusing on drinking alone. Emphasis is placed on overcoming skill deficits and increasing the person's ability to cope with high-risk situations that commonly precipitate relapse, including both interpersonal difficulties and intrapersonal discomfort, such as anger or depression. The program consists of twelve sessions with the goal of training the individual to use active behavioral or cognitive coping methods to deal with problems, rather than relying on alcohol as a maladaptive coping strategy. The skills also provide a means of obtaining social support critical to the maintenance of sobriety.

Twelve-step facilitation approach. This therapy is grounded in the concept of alcoholism as a spiritual and medical disease. The content of this intervention is consistent with the 12 Steps of AA, with primary emphasis given to Steps 1 through 5. In addition to abstinence from alcohol, a major goal of the treatment is to foster the patient's commitment to participation in AA. During the course of the program's twelve sessions, patients are actively encouraged to attend AA meetings and to maintain journals of their AA attendance and participation. Therapy sessions are highly structured, following a similar format each week that includes symptoms inquiry, review and reinforcement for AA participation, introduction and explication of the week's theme, and setting goals for AA participation for the next week. Material introduced during treatment sessions is complemented by reading assignments from AA literature.

KEY TERMS

Detoxification, or "Detox" - The process of allowing the body to rid itself of a drug while managing the symptoms of withdrawal.

Motivational enhancement therapy (MET). MET is based on principles of motivational psychology and is designed to produce rapid, internally motivated change. This treatment strategy does not attempt to guide and train the client, step by step, through recovery, but instead employs motivational strategies to mobilize the client's own resources. MET consists of four carefully planned and individualized treatment sessions. The first two sessions focus on structured feedback from the initial assessment, future plans, and motivation for change. The final two sessions at the midpoint and end of treatment provide opportunities for the therapist to reinforce progress, encourage reassessment, and provide an objective perspective on the process of change.

Couples therapy. Evidence indicates that involvement of a nonalcoholic spouse in a treatment program can improve patient participation rates and increase the likelihood that the patient will alter drinking behavior after treatment ends.
There are various approaches to marital family therapy. Behavioral marital therapy (BMT) combines a focus on drinking with efforts to strengthen the marital relationship through shared activities and the teaching of communication and conflict evaluation skills.

Inpatient Program

Residential treatment. This is a type of drug abuse rehabilitation program that allows the patient to stay in a housing facility. These alcohol treatment options provide the best care for severe addicts who have a physical dependency on the drug. Residential treatment programs can be short-term (i.e,. three to six weeks) or long-term (i.e., six to twelve months).

How can a person get help for an alcohol problem?

There are many national and local resources that can help. The National Drug and Alcohol Treatment Referral Routing Service provides a toll-free telephone number, 1-800-662-HELP (4357), offering various resource information. Through this service, callers can speak directly to a representative concerning substance abuse treatment, request printed material on alcohol or other drugs, or obtain local substance abuse treatment referral information in their state (See Additional Information) for organizations to help them find a psychiatrist, psychologist, social worker, or other substance abuse professional.

Many people also find support groups a helpful aid to recovery. The following list includes a variety of resources:

- Al-Anon/Alateen
- Alcoholics Anonymous (AA)
- National Association for Children of Alcoholics (NACOA)
- National Clearinghouse for Alcohol and Drug Information (NCADI)

ADDITIONAL INFORMATION

Several groups may be tried out before finding one that is comfortable.

Alcoholics Anonymous (AA)
http://www.aa.org
212-870-3400 (or check your local phone directory under "Alcoholism")

Moderation Management
http://www.moderation.org
212-871-0974

Secular Organizations for Sobriety
http://www.sossobriety.org
323-666-4295

SMART Recovery
http://www.smartrecovery.org
440-951-5357

Women for Sobriety
http://www.womenforsobriety.org
215-536-8026

Groups for family and friends

Al-Anon/Alateen
http://www.al-anon.alateen.org
888-425-2666 for meetings

Adult Children of Alcoholics
http://www.adultchildren.org
310-534-1815

National Institute on Alcohol Abuse and Alcoholism (NIAAA)
301-443–3860
www.niaaa.nih.gov
Makes available free publications on all aspects of alcohol abuse and alcoholism. Many are available in Spanish. Call, write, or search the NIAAA Web site for a list of publications and ordering information.

REFERENCES

1. Alcohol Alert Number 68: Young adult drinking. National Institute on Alcohol Abuse and Alcoholism (NIAAA). April 2006. http://pubs.niaaa.nih.gov/publications/aa68/aa68.htm
2. U.S. Department of Health and Human Services. The Surgeon General's Call to Action to Prevent and Reduce Underage Drinking: A Guide to Action for Communities. U.S. Department of Health and Human Services, Office of the Surgeon General, 2007.
3. A snapshot of annual high-risk college drinking consequences. NIAAA. Reviewed July 1, 2010. http://www.collegedrinkingprevention.gov/statssummaries/snapshot.aspx. Accessed April 22, 2011.
4. Patient education materials. NIAAA. http://pubs.niaaa.nih.gov/publications/practitioner/cliniciansguide2005/clinicians_guide13_p_mats.htm. Accessed April 22, 2011.
5. NIDA InfoFacts: drugged driving. National Institute on Drug Abuse (NIDA).. December 2010. http://www.drugabuse.gov/Infofacts/driving.html. Accessed April 22, 2011.
6. National Institute on Drug Abuse (NIDA). High School Seniors Report Alcohol or Drug-Impaired Driving Experiences. Vol. 22, No. 3 (April 2009).
7. NIAAA Council approves definition of binge drinking. NIAAA Newsletter. 2004;NIH Publication No. 04-5346:3. http://pubs.niaaa.nih.gov/publications/newsletter/winter2004/newsletter_number3.pdf. Accessed April 22, 2011.
8. Alcohol Alert Number 52:BAC and Impairment. National Institute on Alcohol Abuse and Alcoholism. (NIAAA) April 2001. http://pubs.niaaa.nih.gov/publications/aa52.htm.
9. Rethinking drinking; alcohol and your health. NIAAA. http://rethinkingdrinking.niaaa.nih.gov/default.asp. Accessed April 22, 2011.
10. Frequently asked questions. NIDA. http://www.nida.nih.gov/tools/faq.html#Anchor-What-16877. Accessed April 22, 2011.
11. Project MATCH. NIAAA. http://pubs.niaaa.nih.gov/publications/MATCHSeries3/preface.htm. Accessed April 22, 2011.
12. Alcohol Alert Number 49: New Advances in Alcoholism Treatment. NIAAA. http://pubs.niaaa.nih.gov/publications/aa49.htm. Accessed April 22, 2011.

CHAPTER 7

Tobacco: The Use and Regulation

Shutterstock © Laurentiu Nica, 2011. Under license from Shutterstock, Inc.

OBJECTIVES

After you have finished this chapter, you should be able to

- describe the extent and impact of tobacco use;
- describe the "light" cigarettes;
- describe smokeless tobacco;
- list alternative cigarettes;
- describe the new rules for cigarette companies;
- list some of the withdrawal symptoms associated with quitting smoking;

"The believing we do something when we do nothing is the first illusion of tobacco."

-Ralph Waldo Emerson

Shutterstock © gresei, 2011. Under license from Shutterstock, Inc.

Tobacco use is the leading preventable cause of death in the United States.

TOBACCO ADDICTION[1]

What Are the Extent and Impact of Tobacco Use?

An estimated 70.9 million Americans aged 12 or older reported current use of tobacco, 60.1 million (24.2 percent of the population) were current cigarette smokers, 13.3 million (5.4 percent) smoked cigars, 8.1 million (3.2 percent) used smokeless tobacco, and 2 million (0.8 percent) smoked pipes, confirming that tobacco is one of the most widely abused substances in the United States.

Tobacco use is the leading preventable cause of death in the United States. The impact of tobacco use in terms of morbidity and mortality to society is staggering.

Economically, more than $96 billion of total U.S. health care costs each year are attributable directly to smoking. However, this is well below the total cost to society because it does not include burn care from smoking-related fires, prenatal care for low-birth weight infants of mothers who smoke, and medical care costs associated with disease caused by secondhand smoke. In addition to health care costs, the costs of lost productivity due to smoking effects are estimated at $97 billion per year, bringing a conservative estimate of the economic burden of smoking to more than $193 billion per year.

Want To Look Your Best? Don't Smoke![2]

Many teens and their parents spend money on clothes, haircuts, braces, perfumes, athletic gear and sports memberships, all to try and look their best. But smoking cigarettes can cancel out all these hard-earned efforts.

Besides diseases like cancer and emphysema, smoking can cause:

- Yellow-brown teeth and bad breath
- Discolored skin on your fingers
- Smelly clothes and hair (Not good on a date!)
- Loss of sense of smell and taste (So much for your favorite foods)
- Lower stamina for exercise and sports
- Deeper wrinkles than average for a person's age
- Uncontrollable coughing fits and mucous overload

"LIGHT" CIGARETTES AND CANCER RISK[3]

When tar is measured with a smoking machine, the smoke from a so-called light cigarette has a lower yield of tar than smoke from a regular cigarette. However, people don't smoke cigarettes like a machine, so they may still get a high yield of tar with a light cigarette. The only way to reduce the risk of smoking-related diseases is to stop smoking completely.

When tar is measured with a smoking machine, the smoke from a so-called light cigarette has a lower yield of tar than smoke from a regular cigarette.

Tobacco manufacturers have been redesigning cigarettes since the 1950s. Certain redesigned cigarettes with the following features were marketed as **"light" cigarettes:**

- Cellulose acetate filters (to trap tar).
- Highly porous cigarette paper (to allow toxic chemicals to escape).
- Ventilation holes in the filter tip (to dilute smoke with air).
- Different blends of tobacco.

On June 22, 2009, President Barack Obama signed into law the **Family Smoking Prevention and Tobacco Control Act,** which granted the U.S. Food and Drug Administration the authority to regulate tobacco products. One provision of the new law bans tobacco manufacturers from using the terms "light," "low," and "mild" in product labeling and advertisements. This provision went into effect on June 22, 2010. However, some tobacco manufacturers are using color-coded packaging (such as gold or silver packaging) on previously marketed products and selling them to consumers who may continue to believe that these cigarettes are not as harmful as other cigarettes.

Are light cigarettes less hazardous than regular cigarettes?[3]

Many smokers chose so-called low-tar, mild, light, or ultra light cigarettes because they thought these cigarettes would expose them to less tar and would Be less harmful to their health than regular or full-flavor cigarettes. However, light cigarettes are no safer than regular cigarettes. Tar exposure from a light cigarette can be just as high as that from a regular cigarette if the smoker takes long, deep or frequent puffs. The bottom line is that light cigarettes do not reduce the health risks of smoking.

Moreover, there is no such thing as a safe cigarette. The only guaranteed way to reduce the risk to your health, as well as the risk to others, is to stop smoking completely.

KEY TERMS

Light cigarette - has a lower yield of tar than smoke from a regular cigarette.
Family Smoking Prevention and Tobacco Control Act - Granted the U.S. Food and Drug Administration the authority to regulate tobacco products.

Fact

People who smoke any kind of cigarette are at much greater risk of lung cancer than people who do not smoke.

Do light cigarettes cause cancer?[3]

Yes. People who smoke any kind of cigarette are at much greater risk of lung cancer than people who do not smoke. Smoking harms nearly every organ of the body and diminishes a person's overall health.

People who switched to light cigarettes from regular cigarettes are likely to have inhaled the same amount of toxic chemicals, and they remain at high risk of developing smoking-related cancers and other disease. Smoking causes cancers of the lung, esophagus, larynx (voice box), mouth, throat, kidney, bladder, pancreas, stomach, and cervix, as well as acute myeloid leukemia.

Shutterstock © RoJo Images, 2011. Under license from Shutterstock, Inc.

Regardless of their age, smokers can substantially reduce their risk of disease, including cancer, by quitting.

Because all tobacco products are harmful and cause cancer, the use of these products is strongly discouraged. There is no safe level of tobacco use. People who use any type of tobacco product should quit.

Because all tobacco products are harmful and cause cancer, the use of these products is strongly discouraged. There is no safe level of tobacco use. People who use any type of tobacco product should quit.

What is Smokeless Tobacco?[4]

There are two types snuff and chewing tobacco. **Snuff,** a finely ground or shredded tobacco, is packaged dry, moist, or in porous tea bag like pouches. Typically, the user places a pinch or "dip" between the cheek and gum. **Chewing tobacco** is available in loose leaf, plug, or twist forms, with the user putting a wad of tobacco inside the cheek. Smokeless tobacco is sometimes called "spit" or "spitting" tobacco because people spit out the juices and saliva that build up in the mouth.

Snus pouches are a new version of snuff, or chewing tobacco laced with nicotine. Instead of putting a loose wad of tobacco inside the upper lip or between the cheek and gums, snus pouches look like small tea bags. These products are "spitless", making their use easy to hide. Some tobacco companies even add flavors like vanilla, peppermint, or spearmint along with a sweetener.

KEY TERMS

Snuff - A finely ground or shredded tobacco, is packaged dry, moist, or in porous tea bag like pouches.
Chewing tobacco - The user putting a wad of tobacco inside the cheek. Smokeless tobacco is sometimes called "spit" or "spitting" tobacco because people spit out the juices and saliva that build up in the mouth.
Snus pouches - Are a new version of snuff, or chewing tobacco laced with nicotine. Snus pouches look like small tea bags.

Is Smokeless Tobacco Addictive?[4]

All tobacco, including smokeless tobacco, contains nicotine, which is addictive. The amount of nicotine absorbed from smokeless tobacco is 3-4 times greater than that delivered by a cigarette, and while nicotine is absorbed more slowly from smokeless tobacco, more nicotine per dose is absorbed and stays in the bloodstream longer. Furthermore, when smokeless tobacco users try to quit, they can experience an array of withdrawal symptoms, including craving, irritability and depressed mood, which can cause them to resume use.

Smokeless tobacco also has harmful effects. Chewing tobacco can cause damage to gum tissue and even loss of teeth. It also reduces a person's ability to taste and smell. Most importantly, smokeless tobacco contains cancer-causing chemicals that can cause cancers of the mouth, pharynx, larynx, and esophagus. This can even happen in very young users of chewing tobacco. In fact, most people who develop these cancers were users of chewing tobacco.[5]

ALTERNATIVE CIGARETTES[6]

Clove cigarettes, bidis, and additive-free cigarettes deliver at least as much nicotine as conventional cigarettes. Smokers who choose these cigarettes are as likely to become addicted to nicotine as are other smokers and are exposing themselves to the increased risk of cancers, respiratory disease, and heart disease associated with smoking.

Alternative Cigarettes and Young Smokers[6]

Clove cigarettes, made in Indonesia and exported worldwide, are composed of 60 to 80 percent tobacco and 20 to 40 percent ground clove buds. They are usually machine rolled, are available with or without filters, and usually are sold in brightly colored packages. Clove cigarettes are sometimes referred to as "trainer cigarettes" and may serve as "gateway" products that introduce young people to smoking.

Bidis are small, brown, hand-rolled cigarettes that are made primarily in India and other South Asian countries. They are available in many flavors, such as chocolate, raspberry, and strawberry, making them appealing to adolescent smokers.

Additive-free cigarettes are made with whole-leaf tobacco and contain no chemical additives, preservatives, or reconstituted tobacco.

KEY TERMS

Clove cigarettes - Made in Indonesia and exported worldwide, are composed of 60 to 80 percent tobacco and 20 to 40 percent ground clove buds.
Bidis - Are small, brown, hand-rolled cigarettes that are made primarily in India and other South Asian countries.
Additive-free cigarettes - Are made with whole-leaf tobacco and contain no chemical additives, preservatives, or reconstituted tobacco.

Shutterstock © Duard van der Westhuizen, 2011. Under license from Shutterstock, Inc.

Tobacco companies will no longer be allowed to sponsor cultural and sporting events, distribute logo clothing, give away free samples or sell cigarettes in packages of less than 20 what's known as "kiddy packs."

New Rules for Cigarette Companies[7]

As the 1-year anniversary of the signing of the Tobacco Control Act approaches, new rules that let the Government regulate tobacco products are going into effect. Starting on June 22, 2010 cigarette packs may no longer use labels that say "light," "low" and "mild." Also, tobacco companies will no longer be allowed to sponsor cultural and sporting events, distribute logo clothing, give away free samples or sell cigarettes in packages of less than 20, what's known as "kiddy packs."

HANDLING WITHDRAWAL SYMPTOMS AND TRIGGERS WHEN YOU DECIDE TO QUIT SMOKING[8]

Quitting is the only way that smokers can substantially reduce their risk of disease.

Although quitting is difficult, millions of people have quit smoking for good. Many tips are offered in this fact sheet, but everyone is different so choose the tips that will work best for you. In general, keeping busy and avoiding the things that tempt you to smoke will help you manage withdrawal symptoms and avoid your triggers to smoke.

- Common withdrawal symptoms associated with quitting include nicotine cravings, anger, frustration, irritability, anxiety, depression, and weight gain. It may help to know that withdrawal symptoms are usually worst during the first week after quitting. From that point, the intensity of the symptoms drops over the first month.
- Triggers are the moods, feelings, places, or things that you do in your daily life that make you want to smoke. Triggers for smoking may include being around other smokers, feeling stressed, drinking coffee or tea, and enjoying a meal.

What are some of the withdrawal symptoms associated with quitting smoking?[8]

Quitting smoking may cause short-term problems, especially for those who have smoked heavily for many years. These temporary changes can result in withdrawal symptoms.

Common withdrawal symptoms associated with quitting include the following:

- Nicotine cravings (nicotine is the substance in tobacco that causes addiction).
- Anger, frustration, and irritability.

- Anxiety.
- Depression.
- Weight gain.

What can I do about nicotine cravings?[2]

As a smoker, you get used to having a certain level of nicotine in your body. You control that level by how much you smoke, how deeply you inhale the smoke, and the kind of tobacco you use. When you quit, cravings develop when your body wants nicotine. It takes time to break free from nicotine addiction. Also, when you see people smoking or are around other triggers, you may get nicotine cravings. Cravings are real. They are not just in your imagination. At the same time, your mood may change, and your heart rate and blood pressure may go up.

The urge to smoke will come and go. Cravings usually last only a very brief period of time. Cravings usually begin within an hour or two after you have your last cigarette, peak for several days, and may last several weeks. As the days pass, the cravings will get farther apart. Occasional mild cravings may last for 6 months. Here are some tips for managing cravings:

- Remind yourself that they will pass.
- Avoid situations and activities that you used to associate with smoking.
- As a substitute for smoking, try chewing on carrots, pickles, apples, celery, sugarless gum, or hard candy. Keeping your mouth busy may stop the psychological need to smoke.
- Try this exercise: Take a deep breath through your nose and blow out slowly through your mouth. Repeat 10 times.
- Ask your doctor about nicotine replacement products or other medications.
- Engage in a physical activity, such as taking a walk.
- Reduce caffeine by limiting or avoiding coffee, soda, and tea.
- Try meditation or other relaxation techniques, such as getting a massage, soaking in a hot bath, or breathing deeply through your nose and out through your mouth for 10 breaths.

What can I do about anxiety?[8]

Within 24 hours of quitting smoking, you may feel tense and agitated. You may feel a tightness in your muscles—especially around the neck and shoulders. Studies have found that anxiety is one of the most common negative feelings associated with quitting. If anxiety occurs, it builds over the first 3 days after quitting and may last 2 weeks.

Here are some tips for managing anxiety:

- Remind yourself that anxiety will pass with time.
- Set aside some quiet time every morning and evening—a time when you can be alone in a quiet environment.

What can I do about depression?[28]

It is normal to feel sad for a period of time after you first quit smoking. If mild depression occurs, it will usually begin within the first day, continue for the first couple of weeks, and go away within a month.

Having a history of depression is associated with more severe withdrawal symptoms—including more severe depression. Some studies have found that many people with a history of major depression will have a new major depressive episode after quitting. However, in those with no history of depression, major depression after quitting is rare.

It is normal to feel sad for a period of time after you first quit smoking.

What can I do about weight gain?[28]

Gaining weight is common after quitting. Studies have shown that, on average, people who have never smoked weigh a few pounds more than smokers, and, when smokers quit, they attain the weight they would have had if they had never smoked. Although most smokers gain fewer than 10 pounds after they quit smoking, the weight gain can be troublesome for some people. However, the health benefits of quitting far outweigh the health risks of a small amount of extra weight.

HOW CAN I GET HELP TO QUIT SMOKING?[3]

For help with quitting, refer to the National Cancer Institute (NCI) fact sheet *Where To Get Help When You Decide To Quit Smoking,* which is available at http://www.cancer.gov/cancertopics/factsheet/tobacco/help-quitting on the Internet.

There are many groups that can help smokers quit:

Go online to **Smokefree.gov** (http://www.smokefree.gov), a Web site created by NCI's Tobacco Control Research Branch, and use the Step-by-Step Quit Guide.
Call **NCI's Smoking Quitline** at **1–877–44U–QUIT (1–877–448–7848)** for individualized counseling, printed information, and referrals to other sources.

OTHER INFORMATION SOURCES

What If a Person Wants To Quit?

For additional information on tobacco abuse and addiction, please visit www.smoking.drugabuse.gov.

For more information on how to quit smoking, please visit www.smokefree.gov from the U.S. Department of Health and Human Services, which offers online advice and downloadable information to make cessation easier.

A national toll-free number, 1-800-QUIT-NOW (1-800-784-8669), can help people get the information they need to quit smoking. Callers are routed to their state's smoking cessation quit line or, in states that have not established quit lines, to one maintained by the National Cancer Institute.

REFERENCES

1. Drug addiction. National Institute on Drug Abuse (NIDA). What Are the Extent and Impact of Tobacco Use? 2008. http://www.drugabuse.gov/Researchreports/Nicotine/whatis.html
2. The National Institute on Drug Abuse (NIDA). NIDA for Teens: Know the Scene: Want To Look Your Best? Don't Smoke June 2010. http://teens.drugabuse.gov/blog/want-to-look-your-best-don%E2%80%99t-smoke/.
3. National Cancer Institute (NCI)."Light" Cigarettes and Cancer Risk. 2010. http://www.cancer.gov/cancertopics/factsheet/Tobacco/light-cigarettes
4. The National Institute on Drug Abuse (NIDA). "Smokeless Tobacco". 2009 http://www.nida.nih.gov/tib/smokeless.html
5. The National Institute on Drug Abuse (NIDA). Chewing tobacco 2006. http://teens.drugabuse.gov/mom/pdf/english/nicotine.pdf
6. The National Institute on Drug Abuse (NIDA). Alternative Cigarettes May Deliver More Nicotine Than Conventional Cigarettes. 2003. http://archives.drugabuse.gov/NIDA_notes/NNVol18N2/Alternative.html
7. The National Institute on Drug Abuse (NIDA). NIDA for Teens: New Rules for Cigarette Companies 2010. http://teens.drugabuse.gov/blog/tag/public-health/
8. National Cancer Institute (NCI). How To Handle Withdrawal Symptoms and Triggers When You Decide To Quit Smoking. 2010. http://www.cancer.gov/cancertopics/factsheet/Tobacco/symptoms-triggers-quitting.

CHAPTER 8

Health Consequences of Tobacco Use

Shutterstock © Maciej Oleksy, 2011. Under license from Shutterstock, Inc.

OBJECTIVES

After you have finished this chapter, you should be able to

- define and explain tobacco smoking;
- define and explain nicotine;
- describe the history of nicotine;
- describe the pharmacology of nicotine;
- explain the therapeutic use of nicotine;
- describe the adverse health effects of nicotine use;
- explain tobacco use across age groups;
- list the treatments for tobacco addiction.

"I have made it a rule never to smoke more than one cigar at a time."

-Mark Twain

Shutterstock © nutech21, 2011. Under license from Shutterstock, Inc.

Smoking is the most common method of consuming tobacco, and tobacco is the most common substance smoked.

TOBACCO USE[1]

Tobacco use is the leading preventable cause of disease, disability, and death in the United States. Between 1964 and 2004, cigarette smoking caused an estimated 12 million deaths, including 4.1 million deaths from cancer, 5.5 million deaths from cardiovascular diseases, 1.1 million deaths from respiratory diseases, and 94,000 infant deaths related to mothers smoking during pregnancy.

WHAT IS NICOTINE?[2]

Nicotine, a component of tobacco, is the primary reason that tobacco is addictive, although cigarette smoke contains many other dangerous chemicals, including **tar, carbon monoxide, acetaldehyde, nitrosamines,** and more.

Fact

Tobacco use is the leading preventable cause of disease, disability, and death in the United States.

Nicotine is a colorless, oily chemical found in the nightshade family of plants and is one of the most addictive of all drugs. It functions as an antiherbivore chemical with particular specificity to insects; therefore, nicotine was widely used as an insecticide in the past. Nicotine is also found in several other members of the Solanaceae family, with small amounts being present in species such as the eggplant and tomato.

In low concentrations (an average cigarette yields about 1 mg of absorbed nicotine), the substance acts as a stimulant in mammals and is the main factor responsible for the dependence-forming properties of tobacco smoking. According to the American Heart Association, nicotine addiction has historically been one of the hardest addictions to break, while the pharmacological and behavioral characteristics that determine tobacco addiction are similar to those that determine addiction to drugs such as heroin and cocaine. Nicotine content in cigarettes has slowly increased over the years, and one study showed that there was an average increase of 1.6% per year between the years of 1998 and 2005. This was found for all major market categories of cigarettes.

KEY TERMS

Tar - An oily substance resulting from the burning of tobacco and consisting of thousands of chemicals, some of which are carcinogenic or otherwise harmful.
Carbon monoxide - A highly poisonous gas found in tobacco smoke.
Acetaldehyde - A colorless, volatile, water-soluble liquid that is used chiefly in the manufacture of acetic acid, perfumes, and drugs.
Nitrosamines - Various compounds that are believed to be potent cancer-causing agents.
Nicotine - A colorless, oily chemical found in the nightshade family of plants and is one of the most addictive of all drugs.

Many smokers begin during adolescence or early adulthood. Usually during the early stages, smoking provides pleasurable sensations, serving as a source of positive reinforcement. After an individual has smoked for many years, the avoidance of withdrawal symptoms and negative reinforcement become the key motivations to continue.

Is Nicotine Addictive?[2]

Yes. It is actually the nicotine in tobacco that makes tobacco products like cigarettes addictive. Each cigarette contains about 10 mg of nicotine. Because the smoker inhales only some of the smoke from a cigarette, and not all of each puff is absorbed in the lungs, a smoker gets about 1 to 2 mg of the drug from each cigarette. Although that may not seem like much, it is enough to make someone addicted.

Addiction is characterized by compulsive drug seeking and abuse, even in the face of negative health consequences. It is well documented that most smokers identify tobacco use as harmful and express a desire to reduce or stop using it, and nearly 35 million of them want to quit each year. Unfortunately, more than 85 percent of those who try to quit on their own relapse, most within a week.

Is Nicotine the Only Harmful Part of Tobacco?[2]

No. Nicotine is only one of more than 4,000 chemicals, many of which are poisonous, found in the smoke from tobacco products. Smokeless tobacco products also contain many toxins, as well as high levels of nicotine. Many of these other ingredients are things we would never consider putting in our bodies, like tar, carbon monoxide, acetaldehyde, and nitrosamines. Tar causes lung cancer, emphysema, and bronchial diseases. Carbon monoxide causes heart problems, which is one reason why smokers are at high risk for heart disease.

Nicotine is only one of more than 4,000 chemicals, many of which are poisonous, found in the smoke from tobacco products.

What Are the Common Street Names?[2]

One might hear cigarettes referred to as "smokes," "cigs," or "butts." Smokeless tobacco is often called "chew," "dip," "spit tobacco," "snus," or "snuff." People may refer to hookah smoking as "narghile," "argileh," "shisha," "hubble-bubble," or "goza."

PHARMACOLOGY OF NICOTINE[1]

Nicotine is readily absorbed into the bloodstream when a tobacco product is chewed, inhaled, or smoked. Upon entering the bloodstream, nicotine immediately stimulates the adrenal glands to release the hormone epinephrine (adrenaline). Epinephrine stimulates the central nervous system and increases blood pressure, respiration, and heart rate. Glucose is released into the blood while nicotine suppresses insulin output from the pancreas, which means that smokers have chronically elevated blood sugar levels.

Effects on the Central Nervous System[1]

Like cocaine, heroin, and marijuana, nicotine increases levels of the neurotransmitter dopamine, which affects the brain pathways that control reward and pleasure. For many tobacco users, long-term brain changes induced by continued nicotine exposure result in addiction, a condition of compulsive drug seeking and use, even in the face of negative consequences.

Dependence and Withdrawal[1]

When an addicted user tries to quit, he or she experiences withdrawal symptoms including irritability, attention difficulties, sleep disturbances, increased appetite, and powerful cravings for tobacco. Treatments can help smokers manage these symptoms and improve the likelihood of successfully quitting.

What Other Adverse Effects Does Tobacco Have on Health?[1]

Cigarette smoking accounts for about one-third of all cancers, including 90 percent of lung cancer cases. Smokeless tobacco (such as chewing tobacco and snuff) also increases the risk of cancer, especially oral cancers. In addition to cancer, smoking causes lung diseases such as chronic bronchitis and emphysema, and increases the risk of heart disease, including stroke, heart attack, vascular disease, and aneurysm. Smoking has also been linked to leukemia, cataracts, and pneumonia. On average, adults who smoke die 14 years earlier than nonsmokers.

Although nicotine is addictive and can be toxic if ingested in high doses, it does not cause cancer. Other chemicals are responsible for most of the severe health consequences of tobacco use. Tobacco smoke is a complex mixture of chemicals such as carbon monoxide, tar, formaldehyde, cyanide, and ammonia; many of which are known carcinogens. Carbon monoxide increases the chance of cardiovascular diseases. Tar exposes the user to an increased risk of lung cancer, emphysema, and bronchial disorders.

Effects on the Brain

Research has shown how nicotine acts on the brain to produce a number of effects. Of primary importance to its addictive nature are findings that nicotine activates reward pathways, the brain circuitry that regulates feelings of pleasure. A key brain chemical involved in mediating the desire to consume drugs is the neurotransmitter dopamine, and research has shown that nicotine increases levels of dopamine in the reward pathways. This reaction is similar to that seen with other drugs of abuse and is thought to underlie the pleasurable sensations experienced by many smokers. For many tobacco users, long-term brain changes, induced by continued nicotine exposure result in addiction.[3]

Preliminary research supported by the National Institute on Drug Abuse (NIDA), a component of the National Institutes of Health, has shown that some smokers with damage to a part of the brain called the **insula** may have their addiction to nicotine practically eliminated.[4]

"The researchers found that smokers with insula lesions were 136 times more likely to have their addiction to nicotine erased than smokers with other brain injuries," said NIDA Director Dr. Nora Volkow in a January 2007 news release from NIDA. "Research that identifies a way to alter the function of this area could have major implications for smokers and addiction treatment in general." Thus, damage to the insula could lead smokers to feel that their bodies have "forgotten" the urge to smoke.[4]

"Cigarette smoking is the most common preventable cause of illness and death in the modern world, and it is an addictive behavior," Dr. Volkow said. "While additional research is needed to replicate these findings, the current study suggests that damage to the insula can impact the conscious 'urge' to smoke, making it easier for smokers to quit and remain abstinent."[4]

Cigarette smoking is the most common preventable cause of illness and death in the modern world.

How Does Tobacco Deliver Its Effects?[5]

With each puff of a cigarette, a smoker pulls nicotine and other harmful substances into the lungs, where it is absorbed into the blood. It takes just eight seconds for nicotine to hit the brain. Nicotine happens to be shaped like the natural brain chemical acetylcholine. **Acetylcholine** is one of many chemicals called neurotransmitters that carry messages between brain cells. **Neurons** (brain cells) have specialized proteins called **receptors,** into which specific neurotransmitters can fit, like a key fitting into a lock. Nicotine locks into acetylcholine receptors, rapidly causing changes in the brain and body. For instance, nicotine increases blood pressure, heart rate, and respiration (breathing).

Nicotine also attaches to **cholinergic** receptors on neurons that release a neurotransmitter called dopamine. Dopamine is released normally when you experience something pleasurable like good food, surfing, or the company of people you love. But smoking cigarettes causes neurons to release excess dopamine, which is responsible for the feelings of pleasure experienced by the smoker. However, this effect wears off rapidly, causing smokers to get the urge to light up again for another dose of the drug.

KEY TERMS

Insula - A cerebral cortex structure deep within the lateral fissure between the temporal lobe and the frontal lobe.
Acetylcholine - One of many chemicals called neurotransmitters that carry messages between brain cells.
Neurons - Nerve cells that transmit nerve signals to and from the brain.
Receptor - A protein molecule to which one or more specific kinds of signaling molecules may attach.
Cholinergic - Cholinergic is related to the neurotransmitter acetylcholine, and is typically used in a neurological perspective.

Nicotine may be the primary addictive component in tobacco but it's not the only ingredient that is biologically important. Using advanced neuroimaging technology, scientists have found that smokers have a significant reduction in the levels of an enzyme called monoamine oxidase (**MAO**) in the brain and throughout the body. This enzyme is responsible for the breakdown of dopamine, other neurotransmitters involved in mood regulation, and in a variety of bodily functions. Having lower amounts of MAO in the brain may lead to higher dopamine levels and be another reason that smokers continue to smoke to sustain the pleasurable feelings that high dopamine levels create.

What Happens When Someone Uses Tobacco for Long Periods of Time?[25]

Long-term use of nicotine frequently leads to addiction. Research is just beginning to document all of the changes in the brain that accompany nicotine addiction. The behavioral consequences of these changes are well documented, however.

The way that nicotine is absorbed and metabolized by the body enhances its addictive potential. Each inhalation brings a rapid distribution of nicotine to the brain peaking within ten seconds and then disappearing quickly, along with the associated pleasurable feelings. Over the course of the day, tolerance develops, meaning that higher (or more frequent) doses are required to produce the same initial effects. Some of this tolerance is lost overnight, and smokers often report that the first cigarette of the day is the strongest or the "best."

When a person quits smoking, he or she usually experiences withdrawal symptoms, which often drive the person back to tobacco use. Nicotine withdrawal symptoms include irritability, cognitive and attention deficits, sleep disturbances, increased appetite, and cravings. Craving, an intense urge for nicotine that can persist for six months or longer, is an important but poorly understood component of the nicotine withdrawal syndrome. Some people describe it as a major stumbling block to quitting.

Nicotine withdrawal symptoms include irritability, cognitive and attention deficits, sleep disturbances, increased appetite, and craving.

Withdrawal symptoms usually peak within the first few days and may subside within a few weeks. The withdrawal syndrome is related to the pharmacological effects of nicotine, but many behavioral factors also affect the severity and persistence of withdrawal symptoms. For example, the cues associated with smoking at the end of a meal; the sight or smell of a cigarette; the ritual of obtaining, handling, lighting, and smoking the cigarette; and alcohol use all can be powerful triggers of craving that can last or re-emerge months or even years after smoking has ceased. Although nicotine gum and patches may stop the pharmacological aspects of withdrawal, cravings often persist.

KEY TERMS

MAO - This enzyme, called monoamine oxidase, is responsible for the breakdown of dopamine, other neurotransmitters involved in mood regulation, and in a variety of bodily functions.

WHAT ARE OTHER ADVERSE HEALTH EFFECTS?[5]

Tobacco abuse harms every organ in the body. It has been conclusively linked to leukemia, cataracts, and pneumonia, and accounts for about one-third of all cancer deaths. The overall rates of death from cancer are twice as high among smokers as nonsmokers, with heavy smokers having rates that are four times greater than those of nonsmokers. Perhaps unsurprisingly, foremost among the cancers caused by tobacco use is lung cancer. In fact, cigarette smoking has been linked to about 90 percent of all lung cancer cases, the No. 1 cancer killer of both men and women. Tobacco abuse is also associated with cancers of the mouth, pharynx, larynx, esophagus, stomach, pancreas, cervix, kidney, ureter, and bladder.

Smokers also lose some of their sense of smell and taste, don't have the same stamina for exercise and sports they once did, and may smell of smoke. After smoking for a long time, smokers find that their skin ages faster and their teeth discolor or turn brown.

ENVIRONMENTAL TOBACCO SMOKE[6]

Environmental tobacco smoke (ETS), also known as **secondhand smoke,** is a mixture of the smoke given off by the burning end of tobacco products (**sidestream smoke**) and the (**mainstream smoke**) exhaled by smokers, and contains more than 4,000 chemicals, including more than 60 known carcinogens, nicotine, and carbon monoxide.

Shutterstock © Aleksey Klints, 2011. Under license from Shutterstock, Inc.

It's not just the smokers who are affected. Nonsmokers are exposed to "secondhand smoke," "sidestream smoke" and "mainstream smoke".

GENDER DIFFERENCES IN TOBACCO SMOKING

Large-scale smoking cessation trials show that women are less likely to initiate quitting and may be more likely to relapse if they do quit. Several avenues of research now indicate that men and women differ in their smoking behaviors. For instance, women smoke fewer cigarettes per day, tend to use cigarettes with lower nicotine content, and do not inhale as deeply as men. However, it is unclear whether this is from differences in sensitivity to nicotine or other factors that affect women differently, such as social factors or the sensory aspects of smoking.[7]

KEY TERMS

Environmental tobacco smoke (ETS) - Is also known as secondhand smoke.
Sidestream smoke - The smoke given off by the burning end of tobacco products
Maintream smoke - Smoke that is exhaled by a smoker.

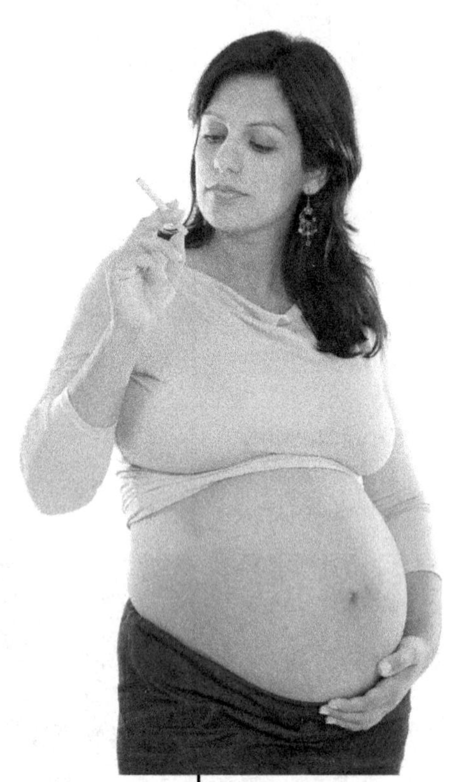

Shutterstock © Gelpi, 2011. Under license from Shutterstock, Inc.

Nicotine concentrates in fetal blood, amniotic fluid, and breast milk, exposing both fetuses and infants to toxic effects.

The number of smokers in the United States declined in the 1970s and 1980s, remained relatively stable throughout the 1990s, and declined further through the early 2000s. Because this decline in smoking was greater among men than women, the prevalence of smoking is only slightly higher for men today than it is for women.[7]

Smoking causes cancers of the lung, esophagus, larynx (voice box), mouth, throat, kidney, bladder, pancreas, stomach, and cervix, as well as acute myeloid leukemia . In 1987, lung cancer surpassed breast cancer to become the leading cause of cancer death in U.S. women. Unlike early breast cancer and many other types of cancer, lung cancer is rarely curable. Most deaths from lung cancer among U.S. women are caused by smoking.[8]

What are the immediate benefits of quitting smoking for women?[8]

The immediate health benefits of quitting smoking are substantial. Within a few hours, the level of carbon monoxide in the blood begins to decline. (Carbon monoxide reduces the blood's ability to carry oxygen.) The former smoker's heart rate and blood pressure, which were abnormally high while smoking, begin to return to normal. Within a few weeks, women who quit smoking have improved circulation, don't produce as much phlegm, and don't cough or wheeze as often. Women can also expect significant improvements in lung function within several months of quitting.

SMOKING AND PREGNANCY[5]

In the United States between 2007 and 2008, 20.6 percent of teens ages fifteen to seventeen smoked cigarettes during their pregnancies. Carbon monoxide and nicotine from tobacco smoke may interfere with fetal oxygen supply, and because nicotine readily crosses the placenta, it can reach concentrations in the fetus that are much higher than maternal levels. Nicotine concentrates in fetal blood, amniotic fluid, and breast milk, exposing both fetuses and infants to toxic effects. These factors can have severe consequences for the fetuses and infants of smoking mothers, including increased risk for stillbirth, infant mortality, sudden infant death syndrome, preterm birth, and respiratory problems. In addition, smoking more than a pack a day during pregnancy nearly doubles the risk that the child will become addicted to tobacco if he or she starts smoking.

Fact

Carbon monoxide and nicotine from tobacco smoke may interfere with fetal oxygen supply and because nicotine readily crosses the placenta, it can reach concentrations in the fetus that are much higher than maternal levels.

HOW IS TOBACCO ADDICTION TREATED?[9]

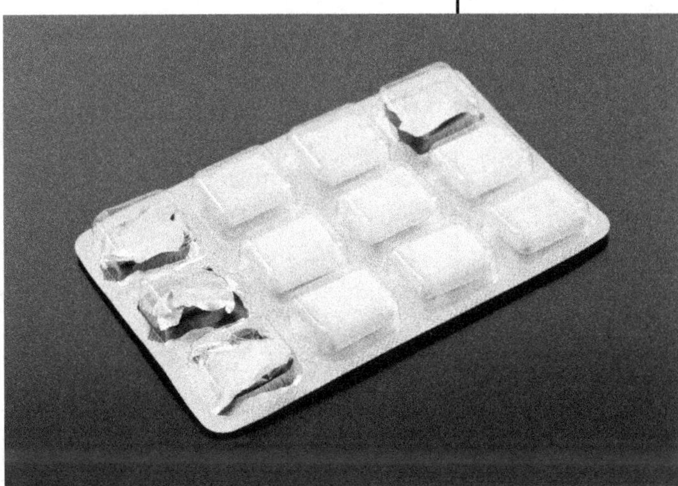

Shutterstock © jcjgphotography, 2011. Under license from Shutterstock, Inc.

Nicotine lozenges contain a dose of nicotine which dissolves slowly in the mouth to release the nicotine.

The good news is that treatments for tobacco addiction do work. Although some smokers can quit without help, many people need help. Behavioral treatment programs help smokers learn about and change their behaviors using self-help materials, counselor-staffed telephone "quitlines," and individual therapy. Over-the-counter medications, such as the nicotine patch, nicotine gum, **nicotine inhaler**, **nicotine lozenges**, and **nicotine spray** replace nicotine and relieve the symptoms of withdrawal. It is important to know that nicotine replacement medicines can be safely used as a medication when taken properly. They have lower overall nicotine levels than tobacco and they have little abuse potential since they do not produce the pleasurable effects of tobacco products. They also don't contain the carcinogens and gases found in tobacco smoke, making them a good treatment approach for quitting.

There are also prescription medications now available for smoking cessation, such as **bupropion** (Zyban) and **varenicline tartrate** (Chantix), that have been shown to help people quit.

Nicotine Replacement Treatments[10]

Nicotine replacement therapies (NRTs), such as **nicotine gum** and the **transdermal nicotine patch,** were the first pharmacological treatments approved by the Food and Drug Administration (FDA) for use in smoking cessation therapy. NRTs are used (in conjunction with behavioral support) to relieve withdrawal symptoms—they produce less severe physiological alterations than tobacco-based

KEY TERMS

Nicotine inhaler - Nicotine-containing inhaler that delivers nicotine in a vapor that is absorbed in the mouth.
Nicotine lozenge - A tablet (usually flavored) that contains a dose of nicotine that dissolves slowly in the mouth to release the nicotine.
Nicotine nasal spray - A nasal spray that contains a small dose of nicotine, which enters the blood by being absorbed through the lining of the nose.
Bupropion - Was the first non-nicotine medication shown to be effective for smoking cessation and was approved by the FDA for that use in1997.
Varenicline tartrate - A prescription medication used to treat smoking addiction.
Nicotine replacement therapies (NRTs) - Were the first pharmacological treatments approved by the Food and Drug Administration (FDA) for use in smoking cessation therapy.
Nicotine gum - A gum that contains a dose of nicotine.
Transdermal nicotine patch - A transdermal patch that releases nicotine into the body through the skin. It is usually used as a method to quit smoking.

systems and generally provide users with lower overall nicotine levels than they receive with tobacco. An added benefit is that these forms of nicotine have little abuse potential. Behavioral treatments, even beyond what is recommended on packaging labels, have been shown to enhance the effectiveness of NRTs and improve long-term outcomes.

The FDA approved of nicotine gum in 1984, marking the availability, by prescription, of the first NRT. Then in 1996, the FDA approved Nicorette gum for over-the-counter (OTC) sales. Whereas nicotine gum provides some smokers with the desired control over dosage and the ability to relieve cravings, others are unable to tolerate the taste and chewing demands. In 1991 and 1992, the FDA approved four transdermal nicotine patches, two of which became OTC products in 1996. In 1996 a nicotine nasal spray, and in 1998 a nicotine inhaler, also became available by prescription, thus meeting the needs of many additional tobacco users. All the NRT products gum, patch, spray, and inhaler appear to be equally effective.

Behavioral Treatments[9]

Behavioral interventions play an integral role in smoking cessation treatment, either in conjunction with medication or alone. A variety of methods can assist smokers with quitting, ranging from self-help materials to individual cognitive-behavioral therapy. These interventions teach individuals to recognize high-risk smoking situations, develop alternative coping strategies, manage stress, improve problem solving skills, and increase social support.

ADDITIONAL INFORMATION

What If a Person Wants To Quit?[5]

If someone who is smoking or using tobacco in another way and wants to quit, he or she should talk to a parent, school guidance counselor, or other trusted adult. A national toll-free number, 1-800-QUIT-NOW (1-800-784-8669), can help people get the information they need to quit smoking. Callers to the number are routed to their state's smoking cessation quitline or, in states that have not established quitlines, to one maintained by the National Cancer Institute. In addition, a new Web site (www.smokefree.gov) from the U.S. Department of Health and Human Services, offers online advice and downloadable information to make cessation easier.

The bottom line: People who quit smoking can have immediate health benefits. Believe it or not, within twenty-four hours of quitting, a person's blood pressure decreases and the chance of having a heart attack goes down. Over the long haul, quitting means less chance of stroke, lung and other cancers, and coronary heart disease, and more chance for a long and healthy life.

REFERENCES

1. NIDA InfoFacts: Cigarettes and Other Tobacco Products. NIDA. 2010. http://www.drugabuse.gov/Infofacts/tobacco.html
2. The National Institute on Drug Abuse (NIDA). NIDA for Teens: What is tobacco addiction? June 2008. http://teens.drugabuse.gov/facts/facts_nicotine1.php. Accessed April 22, 2011
3. Research Report Series: Tobacco Addiction. The National Institute on Drug Abuse (NIDA). http://www.nida.nih.gov/researchreports/nicotine/addictive.html. Accessed April 23, 2011.
4. Damage to specific part of the brain may make smokers 'forget' to smoke [news release]. National Institutes on Drug Abuse; January 25, 2007. http://www.nida.nih.gov/pdf/news/NR0125a.pdf. Accessed April 23, 2011.
5. Tobacco addiction. The National Institute on Drug Abuse (NIDA) for Teens. http://teens.drugabuse.gov/facts/facts_nicotine2.php. Accessed April 23, 2011.
6. The National Cancer Institute (NCI). Secondhand Smoke and Cancer. 2011 http://www.cancer.gov/cancertopics/factsheet/Tobacco/ETS
7. Research Report Series: Tobacco Addiction. NIDA. 2007. http://www.nida.nih.gov/researchreports/nicotine/adolescenceGender.html. Accessed April 23, 2011.
8. The National Cancer Institute (NCI). Women and Smoking. 2010 http://www.cancer.gov/cancertopics/factsheet/Tobacco/women
9. Tobacco Addiction. The National Institute on Drug Abuse NIDA For Teens. Research Report Series: How Is Tobacco Addiction Treated? http://teens.drugabuse.gov/facts/facts_nicotine2.php#treated
10. Tobacco Addiction. The National Institute on Drug Abuse NIDA. Research Report Series: Nicotine Replacement Treatments http://teens.drugabuse.gov/facts/facts_nicotine2.php#treated

CHAPTER 9

Stimulants

Shutterstock © Lyle E. Doberstein, 2011. Under license from Shutterstock, Inc.

OBJECTIVES

After you have finished this chapter, you should be able to

- explain what stimulants are;
- list the types of stimulants;
- describe the pharmacological effects of cocaine;
- describe the physiological effects of cocaine use;
- explain what amphetamines are;
- describe the psychological effects of amphetamines use;
- explain what methamphetamines are;
- describe how methamphetamines affect the brain;
- explain what methylphenidate is;
- list what treatments are available for stimulant abusers.

"Cocaine isn't habit-forming. I should know—I've been using it for years"

-Tallulah Bankhead

WHAT ARE STIMULANTS?[1]

As the name suggests, stimulants increase alertness, attention, and energy, as well as elevate blood pressure and increase heart rate and respiration. **Stimulants** historically were used to treat asthma and other respiratory problems, obesity, **neurological disorders,** and a variety of other ailments. But as their potential for abuse and addiction became apparent, the medical use of stimulants began to wane. Now, stimulants are prescribed for the treatment of only a few health conditions, including **narcolepsy,** attention deficit hyperactivity disorder (ADHD), and depression that has not responded to other treatments.

TYPES OF STIMULANTS

Cocaine[2]

Cocaine is a powerfully addictive stimulant that directly affects the brain. Cocaine was labeled the drug of the 1980s and 1990s because of its extensive popularity and use during that period. However, cocaine is not a new drug. In fact, it is one of the oldest known psychoactive substances. Coca leaves, the source of cocaine, have been chewed and ingested for thousands of years, and the purified chemical, cocaine hydrochloride, has been an abused substance for more than 100 years. In the early 1900s, for example, purified cocaine was the main active ingredient in most of the tonics and elixirs that were developed to treat a wide variety of illnesses.

History of Cocaine[2]

Pure cocaine was originally extracted from the leaf of the erythroxylon coca bush, which grew primarily in Peru and Bolivia. After the 1990s, and following crop reduction efforts in those countries, Colombia became the nation with the largest cultivated coca crop. Today, cocaine is a Schedule II drug, which means that it has high potential for abuse but can be administered by a doctor for legitimate medical uses, such as local anesthesia for some eye, ear, and throat surgeries.

Fact

Pure cocaine was originally extracted from the leaf of the erythroxylon coca bush, which grew primarily in Peru and Bolivia.

Cocaine is generally sold on the street as a fine, white, crystalline powder and is also known as "coke," "C," "**snow,**" "flake," or "blow." Street dealers generally dilute it with inert substances such as cornstarch, talcum powder, or sugar, or with active drugs such as procaine (a chemically related local anesthetic) or amphetamine (another stimulant). Some users combine cocaine with heroin in what is termed a "**speedball.**"

KEY TERMS

Stimulants - Increase alertness, attention, and energy, as well as elevate blood pressure and increase heart rate and respiration.
Neurological disorders - Those disorders that affect the brain, spinal cord, nerves, or muscles.
Narcolepsy - A sleep disorder characterized by sudden and uncontrollable episodes of deep sleep.
Cocaine - A powerfully addictive stimulant that directly affects the brain.
Snow - A street name for Cocaine.
Speedball - A mix of heroin and cocaine.

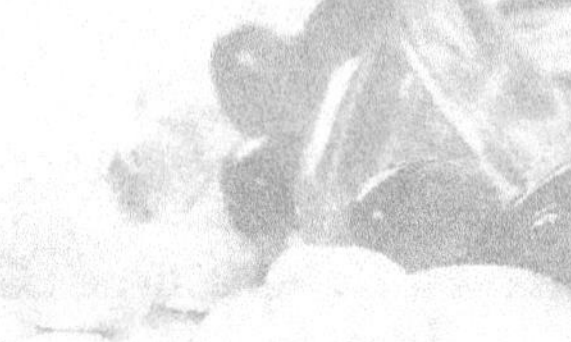

The Two Forms of Cocaine[2]

There are two chemical forms of cocaine that are abused: the water-soluble hydrochloride salt and the water insoluble cocaine base (or freebase). When abused, the hydrochloride salt, or powdered form of cocaine, can be injected or snorted. The base form of cocaine has been processed with ammonia or sodium bicarbonate (baking soda) and water, and then heated to remove the hydrochloride to produce a smokable substance. The term "**crack**," which is the street name given to freebase cocaine, refers to the crackling sound heard when the mixture is smoked.

Cocaine Use in the United States[3]

Cocaine abuse and addiction continue to plague our nation. In 2008, almost 15 percent of Americans had tried cocaine, with 6 percent having tried it by their senior year of high school. Recent discoveries about the inner workings of the brain and the harmful effects of cocaine offer us unprecedented opportunities for addressing this persistent public health problem.

The 2009 Monitoring the Future survey, an annual gauge of teen attitudes and drug use, indicated that while there has been a significant decline in the thirty-day prevalence of powder cocaine use among eighth, tenth, and twelfth graders from its peak use in the late 1990s, there was no significant change in current cocaine use from 2001 to 2008; however, crack use declined significantly during this timeframe among eighth and twelfth graders.

Repeated cocaine use can produce addiction and other adverse health consequences. In 2008, according to the National Survey on Drug Use and Health, nearly 1.6 million Americans met Diagnostic and Statistical Manual of Mental Disorders criteria for dependence on or abuse of cocaine (in any form) in the preceding twelve months. Further, data from the 2005 Drug Abuse Warning Network report showed that cocaine was involved in 448,481 of the total 1,449,154 visits to emergency departments for drug misuse or abuse. This translates to almost one in three drug misuse or abuse emergency department visits (31 percent) that involved cocaine.

Fact

Three routes of administration are commonly used for cocaine: snorting, injecting, and smoking.

How Is Cocaine Abused?[4]

Three routes of administration are commonly used for cocaine: snorting, injecting, and smoking. **Snorting** is the process of inhaling cocaine powder through the nose, where it is absorbed into the bloodstream through the nasal tissues. **Injecting** is the use of a needle to insert the drug directly into the bloodstream. **Smoking**

KEY TERMS

Crack - The street name given to freebase cocaine, refers to the crackling sound heard when the mixture is smoked.
Snorting - The process of inhaling cocaine powder through the nose, where it is absorbed into the bloodstream through the nasal tissues.
Injecting - The use of a needle to insert the drug directly into the bloodstream.
Smoking - Inhaling cocaine vapor or smoke into the lungs, where absorption into the bloodstream is as rapid as it is by injection.

Shutterstock © Anja Peternelji, 2011. Under license from Shutterstock, Inc.

powdered form of cocaine, can be injected or snorted.

involves inhaling cocaine vapor or smoke into the lungs, where absorption into the bloodstream is as rapid as it is by injection. All three methods of cocaine abuse can lead to addiction and other severe health problems, including increasing the risk of contracting HIV/AIDS and other infectious diseases.

The intensity and duration of cocaine's effects, which include increased energy, reduced fatigue, and mental alertness, depend on the route of drug administration. The faster cocaine is absorbed into the bloodstream and delivered to the brain, the more intense the high. Injecting or smoking cocaine produces a quicker, stronger high than snorting. On the other hand, faster absorption usually means shorter duration of action: the high from snorting cocaine may last fifteen to thirty minutes, but the high from smoking may last only five to ten minutes. To sustain the high, a cocaine abuser has to administer the drug again. For this reason, cocaine is sometimes abused in binges taken repeatedly within a relatively short period of time, at increasingly higher doses.

Statistics[5]

The National Institute on Drug Abuse-funded 2010 Monitoring the Future Survey showed that 1.6% of eighth graders, 2.2% of tenth graders, and 2.9% of twelfth graders had abused cocaine in any form and 1.0% of eighth graders, 1.0% of tenth graders, and 1.4% of twelfth graders had abused crack at least once in the year prior to being surveyed.

Pharmacological Effects of Cocaine Use

Effects on the Central Nervous System[4]

Cocaine is a strong central nervous system (CNS) stimulant that increases levels of dopamine, a brain chemical (or neurotransmitter) associated with pleasure and movement, in the brain's reward pathways. Certain brain cells, or neurons, use dopamine to communicate. Normally, dopamine is released by a neuron in response to a pleasurable signal (e.g., the smell of good food) and then recycled back into the cell that released it, thus shutting off the signal between neurons. Cocaine acts by preventing the dopamine from being recycled, causing excessive amounts of the neurotransmitter to build up, amplifying the message to and response of the receiving neuron, and ultimately disrupting normal communication. It is this excess of dopamine that is responsible for cocaine's euphoric effects. With repeated use, cocaine can cause long-term changes in the brain's reward system and in other brain systems as well, which may eventually lead to addiction. With repeated use, tolerance to the cocaine high also often develops. Some users will increase their dose in an attempt to intensify and prolong the euphoria, but this also can increase the risk of adverse psychological or physiological effects.

Physiological Effects of Cocaine Use

Short-Term Effects[6]

The short-term physiological effects of cocaine use include constricted blood vessels; dilated pupils; and increased body temperature, heart rate, and blood pressure. Large amounts of cocaine may intensify the user's high but also can lead to bizarre, erratic, and violent behavior. Some cocaine users report feelings of restlessness, irritability, anxiety, panic, and **paranoia**. Users also may experience tremors, **vertigo**, and muscle twitches.

Long-Term Effects[6]

Cocaine is a powerfully addictive drug. Thus, it is unlikely that an individual would be able to reliably predict or control the extent to which he or she would continue to want or use the drug. And, if addiction takes hold, the risk for relapse is high even following long periods of abstinence. Recent studies have shown that during periods of abstinence, the memory of the cocaine experience or exposure to cues associated with drug use can trigger tremendous craving and relapse to drug use.

Cardiovascular Effects[6]

There also can be severe medical complications associated with cocaine abuse. Some of the most frequent are cardiovascular effects, including disturbances in heart rhythm and heart attacks; neurological effects, including strokes, seizures, headaches, and coma; and gastrointestinal complications, including abdominal pain and nausea. In rare instances, sudden death can occur on the first use of cocaine or unexpectedly thereafter. Cocaine-related deaths are often a result of cardiac arrest or seizures followed by respiratory arrest.

Polydrug Use[4]

Polydrug use of more than one drug is common among substance abusers. When people consume two or more psychoactive drugs together, such as cocaine and alcohol, they compound the danger each drug poses and unknowingly perform a complex chemical experiment within their bodies. Researchers have found that the human liver combines cocaine and alcohol to produce a third substance, **cocaethylene,** which intensifies cocaine's euphoric effects. Cocaethylene is associated with a greater risk of sudden death than cocaine alone.

KEY TERMS

Paranoia - A psychological disorder characterized by delusions of persecution or grandeur.
Vertigo - A feeling of being about to fall.
Cocaethylene - A substance created in the body when cocaine and alcohol are used together.

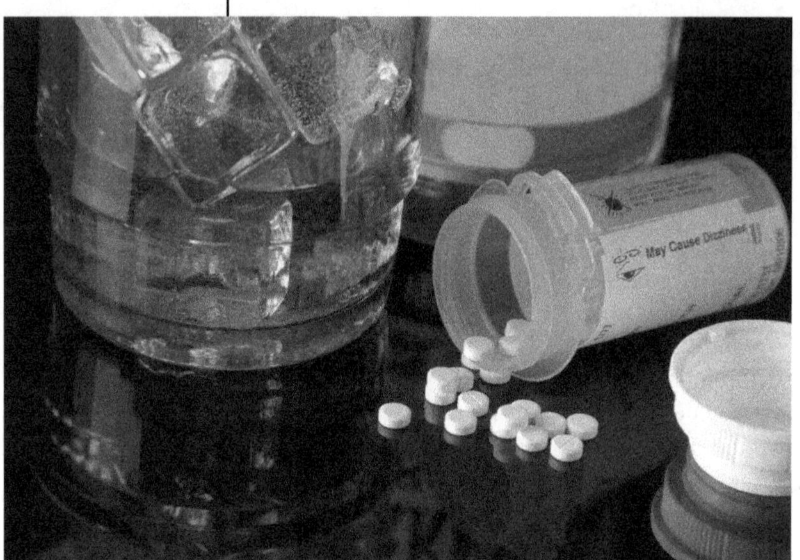

Shutterstock © Donna Cuic, 2011. Under license from Shutterstock, Inc.

When people consume two or more psychoactive drugs together, such as cocaine and alcohol, they compound the danger each drug poses and unknowingly perform a complex chemical experiment within their bodies.

Can a User Develop a Tolerance to Cocaine?[4]

Many cocaine addicts report that they seek but fail to achieve as much pleasure as they did from their first experience, suggesting tolerance to some effects of cocaine. Users also can become more sensitive to cocaine's anesthetic and convulsant effects over time. This increased sensitivity may explain why some deaths occur after apparently low doses of cocaine.

What Are the Effects of Maternal Cocaine Use?[8]

It is difficult to estimate the full extent of the consequences of maternal drug abuse and to determine the specific hazard of a particular drug to the unborn child. This is because multiple factors such as the amount and number of all drugs abused, including nicotine; extent of prenatal care; exposure to violence in the environment; socioeconomic conditions; maternal nutrition; other health conditions; and exposure to sexually transmitted diseases can all interact to impact maternal, fetal, and child outcomes.

Some may recall that **"crack babies"** or babies born to mothers who abused crack cocaine while pregnant, were at one time written off as a lost generation. They were predicted to suffer from severe, irreversible damage, including reduced intelligence and social skills. It was later found that this was a gross exaggeration. However, the fact that most of these children appear normal should not be over interpreted to indicate that there is no cause for concern. Using sophisticated technologies, scientists are now finding that exposure to cocaine during fetal development may lead to subtle, yet significant, later deficits in some children, including deficits in some aspects of cognitive performance, information processing, and attention to tasks abilities that are important for the realization of a child's full potential.

Amphetamines[9]

Amphetamines are a powerful stimulant drug that affect the brain in many ways. They cause increased heart rate and blood pressure, sleeplessness, decreased appetite, decreased tiredness, shaking, cloudy thinking, and violent behavior. This can be dangerous! In the brain, amphetamine increases the amount of the neurotransmitters

KEY TERMS

"Crack babies" - Babies born to mothers who abused crack cocaine while pregnant,
Amphetamines - Are a powerful stimulant drug that affect the brain in many ways.

dopamine and norepinephrine in the **synapse** (space between the neurons).

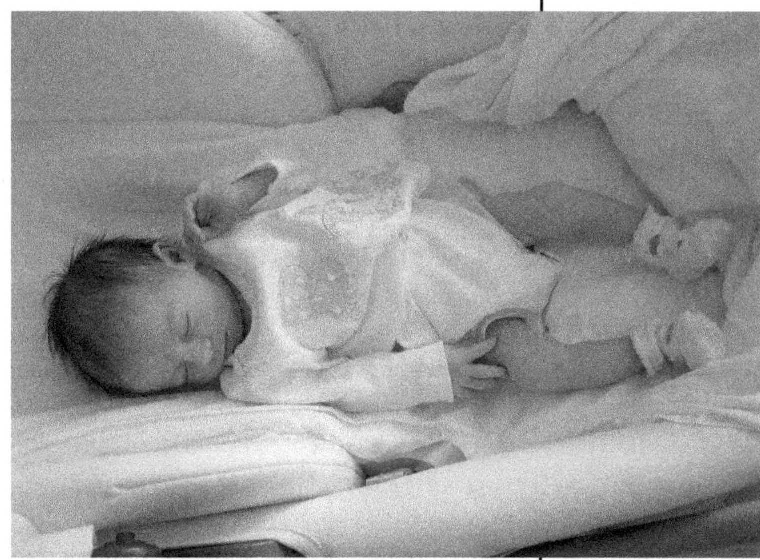

Shutterstock © jovannig, 2011. Under license from Shutterstock, Inc.

Babies born to mothers who abused crack cocaine while pregnant, were at one time written off as a lost generation.

Amphetamine-type substances come in different forms and with different names. **"Speed"** ("meth," "crank,") is a powdered methamphetamine of relatively low purity and is sold in grams or ounces. It can be snorted or injected. "Pills" can be pharmaceutical grade stimulants such as dextroamphetamine, Dexedrine, Adderall, or Ritalin (methylphenidate), or they can be methamphetamine powder that has been pressed into tablets and sold as amphetamines or ecstasy. Pills can be taken orally, crushed for inhalation, or dissolved in water for injection. There is also a damp, sticky powder of higher purity than "Speed" that is known as "Base" in Australia and "Peanut Butter" in parts of the United States. "Ice," also known as "Crystal" or "Tina," is methamphetamine that has been "washed" in a solvent to remove impurities; it has longer-lasting physical effects and purity levels above 80 percent. Ice can be smoked in a glass pipe, "chased" on aluminum foil, mixed with marijuana and smoked through a bong, or injected.[11]

Methamphetamine Use[10]

Methamphetamine is a CNS stimulant drug that is similar in structure to amphetamine. Because of its high potential for abuse, methamphetamine is classified as a Schedule II drug and is available only through a prescription that cannot be refilled. Although methamphetamine can be prescribed by a doctor, its medical uses are limited, and the doses that are prescribed are much lower than those typically abused. Most of the methamphetamine abused in this country comes from foreign or domestic super-labs, although it can also be made in small, illegal laboratories, where its production endangers the people in the labs, neighbors, and the environment.

How Is Methamphetamine Abused?[10]

Methamphetamine is commonly known as "speed," "meth," and **"chalk."** In its smoked form, it is often referred to as **"ice,"** "crystal," "crank," and "glass." It is a

KEY TERMS

Synapse - The space between the neurons.
Speed - Street name for amphetamine.
Methamphetamine - A central nervous system stimulant drug that is similar in structure to amphetamine.
"chalk" - Street name for Methamphetamine.
"ice" - Street name for the smokable form of methamphetamine.

white, odorless, bitter-tasting crystalline powder that easily dissolves in water or alcohol. The drug was developed early in this century from its parent drug, amphetamine, and was used originally in nasal decongestants and bronchial inhalers.

How Do Methamphetamines Affect the Brain?[10]

Methamphetamines increase the release and block the reuptake of the brain chemical (or neurotransmitter) dopamine, leading to high levels of the chemical in the brain, a common mechanism of action for most drugs of abuse. Dopamine is involved in reward, motivation, the experience of pleasure, and motor function. Methamphetamine's ability to release dopamine rapidly in reward regions of the brain produces the intense euphoria, or "rush," that many users feel after snorting, smoking, or injecting the drug.

Repeated methamphetamine abuse also can lead to addiction, a chronic relapsing disease characterized by compulsive drug seeking and use, which is accompanied by chemical and molecular changes in the brain. Some of these changes persist long after methamphetamine abuse is stopped. Reversal of some of the changes, however, may be observed after sustained periods of abstinence (e.g., more than one year).

What Other Adverse Effects Do Methamphetamines Have on Health?[10]

Taking even small amounts of methamphetamines can result in many of the same physical effects as those of other stimulants, such as cocaine or amphetamines, including increased wakefulness, increased physical activity, decreased appetite, increased respiration, rapid heart rate, irregular heartbeat, increased blood pressure, and hyperthermia.

Long-term methamphetamine abuse has many negative health consequences, including extreme weight loss, severe dental problems **("meth mouth"),** anxiety, confusion, insomnia, mood disturbances, and violent behavior. Chronic methamphetamine abusers can also display a number of psychotic features, including paranoia, visual and auditory hallucinations, and delusions (e.g., the sensation of insects crawling under the skin).

Methylphenidate[12]

Methylphenidate is often prescribed to treat individuals diagnosed with attention-deficit hyperactivity disorder (ADHD). ADHD is characterized by a persistent pattern of inattention and/or hyperactivity-impulsivity that is more frequently

KEY TERMS

"meth mouth" - An informal name for advanced tooth decay attributed to heavy methamphetamine use.
Methylphenidate - Is often prescribed to treat individuals diagnosed with attention-deficit hyperactivity disorder (ADHD).

displayed and more severe than is typically observed in individuals at a comparable level of development. This pattern of behavior usually becomes evident in the preschool or early elementary years, and the median age of onset of ADHD symptoms is 7 years. For many individuals, ADHD symptoms improve during adolescence or as age increases, but the disorder can persist into adulthood. In the United States, ADHD is diagnosed in an estimated 8 percent of children ages 4–17 and in 2.9–4.4 percent of adults.

Mild Stimulants

Mild stimulants such as caffeine, chocolate, coffee, soft drinks, tea, and energy drinks were discussed in greater detail in Chapter 4. Other mild stimulants are contained in over-the-counter medications, such as cold and hay fever products; these will be mentioned briefly in this chapter but discussed at greater length in Chapter 14.

WHAT TREATMENTS ARE AVAILABLE FOR STIMULANT ABUSERS?[10]

Currently, the most effective treatments for stimulant abusers are comprehensive cognitive behavioral interventions. For example, the **Matrix Model,** a behavioral treatment approach that combines behavioral therapy, family education, individual counseling, 12-step support, drug testing, and encouragement for nondrug related activities has been shown to be effective. Contingency management interventions, which provide tangible incentives in exchange for engaging in treatment and maintaining abstinence, have also been shown to be effective. Methamphetamine and cocaine recovery support groups also appear to be effective additions to behavioral therapies.

WHAT SHOULD ONE DO IF SOMEONE HE OR SHE KNOWS IS USING COCAINE, CRACK, METHAMPHETAMINE, OR ANOTHER STIMULANT?[7]

When someone has a drug problem, it's not always easy to know what to do. If someone is using a stimulant, he or she should talk to a parent, school guidance counselor, or another trusted adult. In addition, the Substance Abuse and Mental Health Services Administration (SAMHSA) has a toll-free phone number (1-800-662-4357) to help direct a caller to treatment available nearby. SAMHSA's Web-based Substance Abuse Treatment Facility Locator presents information on treatment centers by state.

KEY TERMS

Matrix Model - A behavioral treatment approach that combines behavioral therapy, family education, and individual counseling.

REFERENCES

1. What are stimulants? The National Institute on Drug Abuse (NIDA). 2009. http://drugabuse.gov/ResearchReports/Prescription/prescription4.html. Accessed April 23, 2011.
2. Research Report Series: Cocaine: Abuse and Addiction. NIDA. 2009. http://www.nida.nih.gov/ResearchReports/Cocaine/whatis.html. Accessed April 23, 2011.
3. What is Cocaine? NIDA. 2008. http://www.nida.nih.gov/ResearchReports/Cocaine/Cocaine.html. Accessed April 23, 2011.
4. NIDA InfoFacts: Cocaine. NIDA. 2009. http://www.nida.nih.gov/Infofacts/cocaine.html. Accessed April 23, 2011.
5. Cocaine. NIDA. 2009. http://www.nida.nih.gov/DrugPages/Cocaine.html. Accessed April 23, 2011.
6. Research Report Series: Cocaine: Abuse and Addiction. NIDA. http://www.nida.nih.gov/researchreports/cocaine/effects.html. Accessed April 23, 2011.
7. Volkow ND. Scientific Research on the Scope, Pharmacology, and Health Consequences of Cocaine Abuse and Addiction, Before the Subcommittee on Crime and Drugs, Committee on the Judiciary, United States Senate. February 12, 2008. http://www.drugabuse.gov/Testimony/2-12-08Testimony.html. Accessed April 23, 2011.
8. The National Institute on Drug Abuse (NIDA) What Are the Effects of Maternal Cocaine Use? http://www.drugabuse.gov/ResearchReports/Cocaine/treatment.html#maternal
9. The National Institute on Drug Abuse (NIDA) Module 4: How stimulants affectthenervoussystem.http://www.drugabuse.gov/JSP3/MOD4/Mod4.pdf
10. NIDA InfoFacts: methamphetamine. The National Institute on Drug Abuse (NIDA). 2008. http://www.nida.nih.gov/infofacts/methamphetamine.html. Accessed April 23, 2011.
11. The National Institute on Drug Abuse (NIDA). Stimulants, 2007. http://www.drugabuse.gov/PDF/CEWG/Vol2_606.pdf
12. The National Institute on Drug Abuse (NIDA). NIDA InfoFacts: Stimulant ADHD Medications - Methylphenidate and Amphetamines, 2009. http://www.drugabuse.gov/Infofacts/ADHD.html

CHAPTER 10

Central Nervous System Depressants

OBJECTIVES

After you have finished this chapter, you should be able to

- define and explain central nervous system (CNS) depressants.
- list the three groups of CNS depressants;
- describe how the CNS depressants affect the brain and body;
- list the types of CNS depressants;
- define and explain barbiturates;
- define and explain benzodiazepines;
- define and explain Gamma-hydroxybutyrate (GHB).

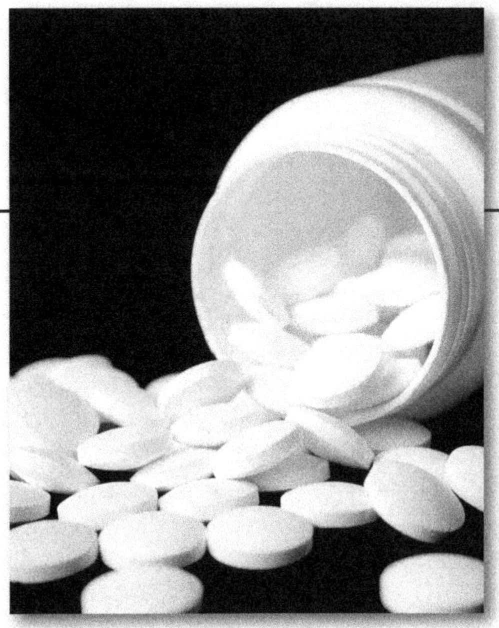

Shutterstock © marylooo, 2011. Under license from Shutterstock, Inc.

"Let us not forget who we are. Drug abuse is a repudiation of everything America is."

-Ronald Reagan

CENTRAL NERVOUS SYSTEM (CNS) DEPRESSANTS[1]

CNS depressants, sometimes referred to as sedatives and tranquilizers, are substances that can slow normal brain function. Because of this property, some CNS depressants are useful in the treatment of anxiety and sleep disorders.

CNS depressants can be divided into three groups, based on their chemistry and pharmacology:

- **Barbiturates.** This group includes mephobarbital (Mebaral) and sodium pentobarbital (Nembutal), which are used as preanesthetics and promote sleep.
- **Benzodiazepines.** This group includes diazepam (Valium), alprazolam (Xanax), and estazolam (ProSom), which can be prescribed to treat anxiety, acute stress reactions, panic attacks, convulsions, and sleep disorders. For the latter, benzodiazepines are usually prescribed only for short-term relief of sleep problems because of the risks of addiction or developing tolerance.
- **Newer sleep medications.** Including zolpidem (Ambien), zaleplon (Sonata), and eszopiclone (Lunesta), newer sleep medications are now more commonly prescribed than benzodiazepines for treating sleep disorders. These medications are nonbenzodiazepines that act at a subset of the benzodiazepine receptors and appear to have a lower risk for abuse and addiction.

Depressants can be used to induce sleep.

Shutterstock © iofoto, 2011. Under license from Shutterstock, Inc.

How Do CNS Depressants Affect the Brain and Body?[2]

CNS depressants usually come in pill or capsule form. Drug abusers might take a CNS depressant not prescribed for them or take a larger dose than prescribed. Sometimes people take them with other drugs or to counteract the effects of other drugs, such as stimulants. Most CNS depressants affect the brain in the same way, they enhance the activity of gamma-aminobutyric acid (GABA). **GABA** is a neurotransmitter, one of the naturally occurring chemicals in the brain that sends messages between cells. GABA works by slowing down brain activity. Although different classes of CNS depressants work in unique ways, they ultimately increase GABA activity, which produces a drowsy or calming effect.

KEY TERMS

CNS depressants - Substances that can slow normal brain function.
GABA (gamma-aminobutyric acid) - A neurotransmitter, one of the naturally occurring chemicals in the brain that sends messages between cells.

Possible Consequences of CNS Depressant Use and Abuse[2]

Although CNS depressants can help people suffering from seizures, anxiety, or sleep disorders, they can be addictive and should be used only as prescribed. During the first few days of taking a CNS depressant, a person usually feels sleepy and uncoordinated. With continuing use, the body becomes accustomed to these effects and they lessen. This is known as tolerance, which means that larger doses are needed to achieve the same initial effects. Continued use can lead to physical dependence and, when stopped, withdrawal. CNS depressants should not be combined with any medication or substance that causes drowsiness, including prescription pain medicines, certain over-the-counter cold and allergy medications, or alcohol. If combined, they can slow both the heart and respiration, which can lead to death.

Abuse of high doses of CNS depressants can lead to physical dependence and, when reduced or stopped, serious withdrawal symptoms. CNS depressants work by slowing the brain's activity, so when someone stops taking a CNS depressant, activity in the brain can rebound and race out of control to the point that seizures can occur. Someone who is either thinking about discontinuing use, or who has stopped and is suffering withdrawal, should seek medical treatment.

TYPES OF CNS DEPRESSANTS

Tranquilizers (Benzodiazepines)[3]

Tranquilizers are psychotherapeutic drugs that are legally sold only by prescription, like amphetamines. They are central nervous depressants and, for the most part, are comprised of benzodiazepines (minor tranquilizers), although some nonbenzodiazepines have been introduced. Valium and Xanax are the two tranquilizers most commonly used by students.

Trends in Use[3]

During the late 1970s and all of the 1980s, tranquilizers fell steadily from popularity, with 12th graders' use declining by three fourths over the 15 year interval between 1977 and 1992. Their use then increased, as happened with many other drugs during the 1990s. Annual prevalence more than doubled among 12th graders, rising steadily through 2002, before leveling. Use also rose steadily among 10th graders, but began to decline some in 2002. Use peaked much earlier among 8th graders, in 1996, and then declined slightly for two years. Tranquilizer use has remained relatively stable since then among 8th graders, at considerably lower levels than the upper two grades. From 2002 to 2005 there was some decline among 10th graders,

KEY TERMS

Tranquilizers - Are psychotherapeutic drugs that are legally sold only by prescription, like amphetamines. They are central nervous system depressants.

followed by a leveling, while among 12th graders there was a very gradual decline from 2002 through 2007, before leveling. This staggered pattern of change suggests that a cohort effect is at work. At present the prevalence of use of these prescription-type drugs remains near recent peak levels.

Sedatives (Barbiturates)[3]

Like tranquilizers, **sedatives** are prescription controlled psychotherapeutic drugs that act as central nervous system depressants. They are used to assist sleep and relieve anxiety.

Trends in Use[3]

As with tranquilizers, the use of sedatives (barbiturates) fell steadily among 12th graders from the mid-1970s through the early 1990s. From 1975 to 1992, use fell by three fourths, from 10.7% annual prevalence to 2.8%. As with many other drugs, a gradual, long-term resurgence in sedative use occurred after 1992, and use continued to rise steadily through 2005, well beyond the point where the use of many illegal drugs began falling. Use has declined some since 2005, but in 2009 the annual prevalence rate is down only about one fourth from its recent peak. The sedative methaqualone has never been as popular as barbiturates, and use rates have generally been declining since 1975, reaching an annual prevalence of just 0.5% in 2006, about where it has remained.

Perceived Risk[3]

Trying sedatives (barbiturates) was never seen by most students as very dangerous. Perceived risk cannot explain the trends in use that occurred from 1975 through 1986, when perceived risk was actually declining along with use. But then perceived risk shifted up some through 1991 while use was still falling. It dropped back some through 1995, as use was increasing, and then remained relatively stable for a few years. Perceived risk has generally been at quite low levels, which may help to explain why this class of psychotherapeutic drugs (and likely others) has stayed at relatively high levels in this decade. However, it began to rise after 2000, foretelling the decline in use that began after 2005. When the term "sedatives" was changed to "sedatives/barbiturates" in 2004, the trend line shifted down slightly, but perceived risk has continued to climb since then. As perceived risk has risen, use has declined somewhat.

Gamma-hydroxybutyrate (GHB)

Gamma-hydroxybutyrate (GHB) is a central nervous system (CNS) depressant that was approved by the Food and Drug Administration (FDA) in 2002 for use

KEY TERMS

Sedatives - Are prescription controlled psychotherapeutic drugs that act as central nervous system depressants.

Gamma-hydroxybutyrate (GHB) - Is a central nervous system (CNS) depressant that was approved by the Food and Drug Administration (FDA) in 2002 for use in the treatment of narcolepsy (a sleep disorder).

in the treatment of narcolepsy (a sleep disorder). This approval came with severe restrictions, including its use only for the treatment of narcolepsy, and the requirement for a patient registry monitored by the FDA. GHB is also a metabolite of the inhibitory neurotransmitter gamma-aminobutyric acid (GABA). It exists naturally in the brain, but at much lower concentrations than those found when GHB is abused.[5]

The use of GHB continues to spread across the country. It has been involved in poisonings, overdoses, date rapes, and even fatalities in Boston, Colorado, Detroit, Miami, New York, Phoenix, Seattle, and Texas. Availability is also reported in Atlanta, Baltimore, and Minneapolis/St. Paul. It is associated with the club scene, raves, gay circuit parties, and fitness centers and gyms. It is frequently consumed with alcohol, and sometimes with marijuana, LSD, or ecstasy. In New Orleans, it is mixed with amphetamine in an alcoholic drink called "max." Only in San Francisco did ethnographers report a decline in 1998. Its names include "grievous bodily harm," "cherry meth," "easy lay," "gamma," "Georgia home boy," "G," "liquid E," "liquid ecstasy," "liquid X," "great hormones at bedtime," "everclear," "g-riffic," and "salty water." In addition, gamma butyrolactone (GBL) is contained in commercial products (Blue Nitro, RenewTrient, and ReVivarin) legally sold as health supplements; it metabolizes into GHB and produces clinical symptoms identical to GHB. Labeling may cause a critical lag time in seeking help for GBL toxicity.

Another club drug, ketamine ("Special K" or "vitamin K"), is popular in cities such as Atlanta, Boston, Miami, Minneapolis/St. Paul, San Diego, and Seattle. It is usually snorted, but injection is reported among young users in some areas, including Boston and Minneapolis/St. Paul. In the latter city, being under the influence of ketamine is known as being "in the hole" or "in the K hole." The drug has been involved in DUI cases and poison control calls in Miami and in one death in San Diego.

Clonazepam - (Klonopin or Rivotril) has been termed "street drug of the 90s" in Boston. Juveniles in Texas commonly use it in combination with beer. It is sold in Atlanta to enhance the effects of methadone, and it is commonly diverted in Phoenix. Alprazolam (Xanax, or "sticks") is increasingly replacing diazepam on the street in New York; it is also a common street drug in Boston. Diazepam is appearing in Atlanta crack houses. An emerging trend in Seattle involves concomitantly injecting heroin and a depressant, typically diazepam -a longtime practice in Chicago. Flunitrazepam (Rohypnol) reports continue to decline in Miami, but still appear in Minnesota and in Texas treatment and survey data. Use of this "date-rape" drug was suspected in a syphilis outbreak among white, middle-class adolescent girls in Atlanta. Trazodone (Desyrel) has been involved in numerous poisonings and one death in Detroit.[4]

Shutterstock © Vlue, 2011. Under license from Shutterstock, Inc.

Insomnia is an inability to sleep.

Rohypnol

Rohypnol (flunitrazepam) use began gaining popularity in the United States in the early 1990s. It is a benzodiazepine (chemically similar to sedative-hypnotic drugs such as Valium or Xanax), but it is not approved for medical use in this country, and its importation is banned.[5]

Chloral Hydrate[6]

Chloral hydrate, a sedative, is used in the short-term treatment of insomnia (to help individuals fall asleep and stay asleep for a proper rest) and to relieve anxiety and induce sleep before surgery. It is also used after surgery for pain and to treat alcohol withdrawal.

Chloral hydrate comes as a capsule and liquid to take by mouth and as a suppository to insert rectally. Chloral hydrate can be habit-forming.

Chloral hydrate may cause these side effects:

- drowsiness
- upset stomach
- vomiting
- diarrhea

General Concerns about Benzodiazepines[7]

There may be an increased risk of congenital malformations associated with the use of benzodiazepine drugs. There may also be non-teratogenic risks associated with the use of benzodiazepines during pregnancy. **Neonatal flaccidity** refers to respiratory and feeding difficulties, and hypothermia in children born to mothers who have been receiving benzodiazepines late in pregnancy. In addition, children born to mothers receiving benzodiazepines late in pregnancy may be at some risk of experiencing withdrawal symptoms during the postnatal period.

If a person is abusing or misusing prescription drugs, or has a friend who is, he or she should talk to a parent, school guidance counselor, or other trusted adult. There are

KEY TERMS

Rohypnol (flunitrazepam) - A benzodiazepine (chemically similar to sedative-hypnotic drugs such as Valium or Xanax), but it is not approved for medical use in this country, and its importation is banned.
Chloral hydrate - A sedative, is used in the short-term treatment of insomnia.
Neonatal flaccidity - Respiratory and feeding difficulties in children born to mothers who have been receiving benzodiazepines late in pregnancy.

also anonymous resources, such as the National Suicide Prevention Lifeline (1–800–273–TALK) and the Treatment Referral Helpline (1–800–662–HELP). The National Suicide Prevention Lifeline is a crisis hotline that can help with a lot of issues, not just suicide. For example, anyone who feels sad, hopeless, or suicidal; family and friends who are concerned about a loved one; or anyone interested in mental health treatment referrals can call this Lifeline. Callers are connected with a professional nearby who will talk with them about what they're feeling or about concerns for family and friends. In addition, the Treatment Referral Helpline (1–800–662–HELP)—offered by the Substance Abuse and Mental Health Services Administration's Center for Substance Abuse Treatment—refers callers to treatment facilities, support groups, and other local organizations that can provide help for their specific needs. Treatment centers can also located bystate by going to www.findtreatment.samhsa.gov.

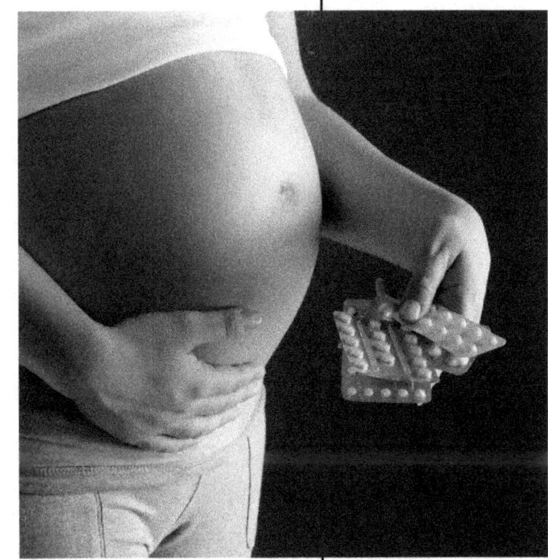

Shutterstock © newphotoservice, 2011. Under license from Shutterstock, Inc.

Neonatal flaccidity, respiratory and feeding difficulties, and hypothermia in children born to mothers who have been receiving benzodiazepines late in pregnancy.

REFERENCES

1. CNS depressants National Institute on Drug Abuse (NIDA). 2009. http://www.drugabuse.gov/researchreports/prescription/prescription3.html. Accessed April 19, 2011.
2. Facts on CNS Depressants. NIDA. October 2009. http://teens.drugabuse.gov/peerx/pdf/PEERx_Toolkit_Depressants.pdf. Accessed April 19, 2011.
3. National Institute on Drug Abuse (NIDA). Overview of Key Findings, 2009. 2009. http://www.drugabuse.gov/PDF/overview2009.pdf
4. National Institute on Drug Abuse (NIDA). http://www.drugabuse.gov/about/organization/ICAW/Epidemiology/epidemiologyfindings999.html
5. National Institute on Drug Abuse NIDA InfoFacts: Club Drugs (GHB, 2010. Ketamine, and Rohypnol) http://www.drugabuse.gov/infofacts/clubdrugs.html
6. National Institute on Health (NIH), Chloral Hydrate 2009.http://www.nlm.nih.gov/medlineplus/druginfo/meds/a682201.html#side-effects
7. National Institute on Health (NIH), General Concerns about Benzodiazepines, 2010. http://dailymed.nlm.nih.gov/dailymed/drugInfo.cfm?id=23848

CHAPTER 11

Marijuana

Shutterstock © jocic, 2011. Under license from Shutterstock, Inc.

OBJECTIVES

After you have finished this chapter, you should be able to

- define what marijuana is;
- explain how marijuana is abused;
- describe how you can tell if someone has been using marijuana;
- describe what happens after a person smokes marijuana;
- describe the effects of marijuana;
- explain how marijuana affects the brain;
- explain the effects of marijuana on the heart and lungs;
- explain how marijuana affects driving;
- explain why it is not recommended to use marijuana during pregnancy.

Marijuana is the most frequently used illegal drug in the United States

"I now have absolute proof that smoking even one marijuana cigarette is equal in brain damage to being on Bikini Island during an H-bomb blast."

-Ronald Reagan

Shutterstock © Kuzma, 2011. Under license from Shutterstock, Inc.

By the time they graduate from high school, about 42 percent of teens will have tried marijuana. Although current use among U.S. teens has dropped dramatically in the past decade (to a prevalence of about 14 percent in 2009), this decline has stalled during the past several years. These data are from the Monitoring the Future study, which has been tracking drug use among teens since 1975. Still, the World Health Organization ranks the United States first among 17 European and North American countries for prevalence of marijuana use. And more users start every day. In 2008, an estimated 2.2 million Americans used marijuana for the first time; greater than half were under age 18.[1]

WHAT IS MARIJUANA?[2,3]

Fact

By the time they graduate from high school, about 42 percent of teens will have tried marijuana.

Marijuana is a dry, shredded green and brown mix of flowers, stems, seeds, and leaves derived from the hemp plant *Cannabis sativa.* **Cannabis** is a term that refers to marijuana and other drugs made from the same plant. Strong forms of cannabis include **sinsemilla** (sin-seh-me-yah), **hashish** ("hash" for short), and **hash oil**. All forms of cannabis are mind-altering (psychoactive) drugs; they all contain **THC (delta-9-tetrahydrocannabinol),** the main active chemical in marijuana. They also contain more than 400 other chemicals.

Marijuana's effect on the user depends on the strength or potency of the THC it contains. THC potency has increased since the 1970s and continues to increase. The strength of the drug is measured by the average amount of THC in test samples confiscated by law enforcement agencies. For the year 2006, most ordinary marijuana contained, on average, 7 percent THC.

KEY TERMS

Cannabis - A term that refers to marijuana and other drugs made from the Cannabis sativa plant.
Sinsemilla - A seedless variety of high-potency marijuana, originally grown in California and prepared from the unpollinated female cannabis plant.
Hashish - Purified resinous extract of the hemp plant; used as a hallucinogen.
Hash oil - A sticky, honey-colored residue extracted from marijuana that has a high level of THC.
THC (delta-9-tetrahydrocannabinol) - The main active chemical in marijuana.

Marijuana Abuse in the United States[4]

In 2009, more than 28 million Americans (11.3%) ages twelve or older reported abusing marijuana within the past year, according to the National Survey on Drug Use and Health (NSDUH).

The NIDA-funded 2010 Monitoring the Future Study showed that 13.7% of 8th graders, 27.5% of 10th graders, and 34.8% of 12th graders had abused marijuana at least once in the year prior to being surveyed.

Marijuana Use and Perceived Risk of Use among Adolescents[5]

- Based on SAMHSA's annual National Surveys on Drug Use and Health from 2002 to 2007, past month marijuana use among adolescents (i.e., youths aged twelve to seventeen) generally decreased from 2002 (8.2%) to 2005 (6.8%), and then remained constant between 2005 and 2007.
- The percentage of adolescents who perceived great risk from smoking marijuana once a month increased between 2002 (32.4 percent) and 2003 (34.9 percent), and then remained relatively stable between 2003 and 2007.
- Adolescents who perceived great risk from smoking marijuana once a month were much less likely to have used marijuana in the past month than those who perceived moderate to no risk (1.4 vs. 9.5 percent).

What Are the Current Slang Terms for Marijuana?[6]

There are many different names for marijuana. Slang terms for drugs change quickly, and they vary from one part of the country to another. They may even differ across sections of a large city.

Terms from years ago, such as "pot," "herb," "grass," "weed," "Mary Jane," and "reefer," are still used. Other slang terms for marijuana include "Aunt Mary," "skunk," "boom," "gangster," "kif," and "ganja."

There are also street names for different strains or "brands" of marijuana, such as "**Texas tea,**" "Maui wowie," and "chronic." There are many different terms for various kinds of marijuana.

How Many People Smoke Marijuana?[6]

A recent government survey tells us that marijuana is the most frequently used illegal drug in the United States. Nearly 98 million Americans over the age of twelve

KEY TERMS

Texas tea - A street name for a different strain or "brand" of marijuana.

Fact

Marijuana is the most frequently used illegal drug in the United States.

have tried marijuana at least once. Additionally, more than 14 million Americans over the age of twelve had used the drug in the month before the survey.

The Monitoring the Future Survey, which is conducted yearly, includes students from eighth, tenth, and twelfth grades. In 2006, the survey showed that 15.7 percent of eighth graders had tried marijuana at least once, and among tenth graders, 14.2 percent were "current" users (that is, had used within the past month). Among twelfth graders, 42.3 percent had tried marijuana at least once, and about 18 percent were current users.

Other researchers have found that use of marijuana and other drugs usually peaks in the late teens and early twenties, then declines in later years.

Marijuana is usually smoked as a cigarette (joint) or in a pipe.

Shutterstock © Amihays, 2011. Under license from Shutterstock, Inc.

HOW IS MARIJUANA ABUSED?[2]

Marijuana is usually smoked as a cigarette (**joint**) or in a pipe. It is also smoked in **blunts,** which are cigars that have been emptied of tobacco and refilled with a mixture of marijuana and tobacco. This mode of delivery combines marijuana's active ingredients with nicotine and other harmful chemicals. Marijuana also can be mixed in food or brewed as a tea. As a more concentrated, resinous form, it is called hashish; and as a sticky black liquid, hash oil. Marijuana smoke has a pungent and distinctive, usually sweet-and-sour odor.

What are the signs that Someone Has Been Using Marijuana?[7]

If someone is high on marijuana, he or she might

- seem dizzy and have trouble walking;
- seem silly and giggly for no reason;
- have very red, bloodshot eyes; and
- have a hard time remembering things that just happened.

When the early effects fade, the user can become very sleepy.

Marijuana users also may exhibit changes in behavior, although these signs can be hard to notice in teenagers. Behavioral changes can include withdrawal, depression, fatigue, carelessness with grooming, hostility, and deteriorating relationships with

KEY TERMS

Joint - Marijuana leaves rolled into a cigarette for smoking.
Blunts - Cigars that have been emptied of tobacco and refilled with a mixture of marijuana and tobacco.

family members and friends. In addition, changes in academic performance, increased absenteeism or truancy, lost interest in sports or other favorite activities, and changes in eating or sleeping habits could be related to drug use. However, these signs may also indicate problems other than use of drugs.

Other signs that someone is using marijuana include

- signs of drugs and drug paraphernalia, including pipes and rolling papers;
- odor on clothes and in the bedroom;
- use of incense and other deodorizers;
- use of eye drops; and
- clothing, posters, jewelry, and other items that promote drug use.

Why Do Young People Use Marijuana?[28]

Children and young teens start using marijuana for many reasons. Curiosity and the desire to fit into a social group are common reasons. Certainly, youngsters who have already begun to smoke cigarettes and/or use alcohol are at high risk for marijuana use.

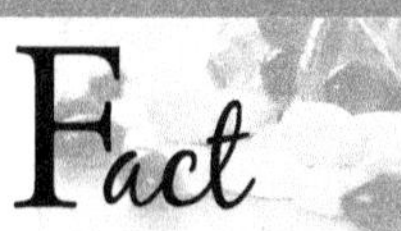

For children and young teens curiosity and the desire to fit into a social group are common reasons to start using marijuana.

Also, research from NIDA suggests that the use of alcohol and drugs by other family members plays a strong role in whether children start using drugs. Parents, grandparents, and older brothers and sisters in the home are models for children to follow. Some young people who take drugs do not get along with their parents. Some have a network of friends who use drugs and urge them to do the same (peer pressure). All aspects of a child's environment—home, school, neighborhood—help to determine whether the child will try drugs.

Children who become heavily involved with marijuana can become dependent, making it difficult for them to quit. Others mention psychological coping as a reason for their use to deal with feelings such as anxiety, anger, depression, and boredom. But marijuana use is not an effective method for coping with life's problems, and staying high can be a way of simply not dealing with the problems and challenges of growing up.

Researchers have found that children and teens (both male and female) who are physically and sexually abused are at greater risk than other young people of using marijuana and other drugs and of beginning drug use at an early age.

Does Using Marijuana Lead to Other Drugs?[28]

Though few young people use cocaine, the risk of doing so is much greater for youths who have tried marijuana than for those who have never tried it. Although research has not fully explained this association, growing evidence suggests a combination of biological, social, and psychological factors is involved.

Researchers are examining the possibility that long-term marijuana use may create changes in the brain that make a person more at risk of becoming addicted to other drugs, such as alcohol or cocaine. Although many young people who use marijuana do not go on to use other drugs, further research is needed to determine who will be at greatest risk.

Fact

Within a few minutes of inhaling marijuana smoke, blood vessels in the eye expand, so the user's eyes look red.

What Happens After a Person Smokes Marijuana?[9]

Within a few minutes of inhaling marijuana smoke, the user will likely feel, along with intoxication, a dry mouth, rapid heartbeat, some loss of coordination and balance, and a slower than normal reaction time. Blood vessels in the eye expand, so the user's eyes look red.

For some people, marijuana raises blood pressure slightly and can double the normal heart rate. This effect can be greater when other drugs are mixed with marijuana, but users do not always know when drugs are added. As the immediate effects fade, usually after two to three hours, the user may become sleepy.

WHAT ARE THE EFFECTS OF MARIJUANA?[8]

The effects of marijuana on each person depend on the:

- type of cannabis and how much THC it contains;
- way the drug is taken (e.g., smoking or eating);
- experience and expectations of the user;
- setting where the drug is used; and
- use of other drugs and/or alcohol.

Some people feel nothing at all when they first try marijuana. Others may feel high (intoxicated and/or **euphoric**).

It is common for marijuana users to become engrossed with ordinary sights, sounds, or tastes, and trivial events may seem extremely interesting or funny. Time seems to pass very slowly, so minutes feel like hours. Sometimes the drug causes users to feel thirsty and very hungry, an effect called "the munchies."

Fact

THC in marijuana is readily absorbed by fatty tissues in various organs.

How Long Does Marijuana Stay in the User's Body?[9]

THC in marijuana is readily absorbed by fatty tissues in various organs. Generally, traces (metabolites) of THC can be detected by standard urine testing methods several days after a smoking session. In heavy, chronic users, however, traces can sometimes be detected for weeks after they have stopped using marijuana.

KEY TERMS

Euphoric - Exaggerated feeling of well-being or elation.

Can a User Have a Bad Reaction?[9]

Yes. Some users, especially those who are new to the drug or in a strange setting, may suffer acute anxiety and have paranoid thoughts. This is more likely to happen with high doses of THC. These scary feelings will fade as the drug's effects wear off. In rare cases, a user who has taken a very high dose of the drug can have severe **psychotic** symptoms and need emergency medical treatment.

Other kinds of bad reactions can occur when marijuana is mixed with other drugs, such as PCP or cocaine.

How is Marijuana Harmful?[9]

Marijuana can be harmful in a number of ways, through immediate effects and through damage to health over time.

Marijuana hinders the user's short-term memory (memory for recent events), and he or she may have trouble handling complex tasks. With the use of more potent varieties of marijuana, even simple tasks can be difficult.

Because of the drug's effects on perceptions and reaction time, users could be involved in auto crashes. Drug users also may become involved in risky sexual behaviors, which could lead to the spread of HIV, the virus that causes AIDS.

Under the influence of marijuana, students may find it hard to study and learn. Young athletes could find their performance is off; timing, movements, and coordination are all affected by THC.

How Does Marijuana Affect the Brain?[2]

Scientists have learned a great deal about how THC acts in the brain to produce its many effects. When someone smokes marijuana, THC rapidly passes from the lungs into the bloodstream, which carries the chemical to the brain and other organs throughout the body.

THC acts on specific sites in the brain called **cannabinoid receptors,** kicking off a series of cellular reactions that ultimately lead to the "high" that users experience when they smoke marijuana. Some brain areas have many cannabinoid receptors; others have few or none. The highest density of cannabinoid receptors are found in parts of the brain that influence pleasure, memory, thinking, concentrating, sensory and time perception, and coordinated movement.

The highest density of cannabinoid receptors are found in parts of the brain that influence pleasure, memory, thinking, concentrating, sensory and time perception, and coordinated movement.

KEY TERMS

Psychotic - Any severe mental disorder in which contact with reality is lost or highly distorted.
Cannabinoid receptors - A class of cell membrane receptors.

Not surprisingly, marijuana intoxication can cause distorted perceptions, impaired coordination, difficulty with thinking and problem solving, and problems with learning and memory. Research has shown that, in chronic users, marijuana's adverse effect on learning and memory can last for days or weeks after the acute effects of the drug wear off. As a result, someone who smokes marijuana every day may be functioning at a suboptimal intellectual level all of the time.

Research into the effects of long-term cannabis use on the structure of the brain has yielded inconsistent results. It may be that the effects are too subtle for reliable detection by current techniques. A similar challenge arises in studies of the effects of chronic marijuana use on brain function. Brain imaging studies in chronic users tend to show some consistent alterations, but their connection to impaired cognitive functioning is far from clear. This uncertainty may stem from confounding factors such as other drug use, residual drug effects, or withdrawal symptoms in long-term chronic users.

Addictive Potential[2]

Long-term marijuana abuse can lead to addiction; that is, compulsive drug seeking and abuse despite the known harmful effects on functioning in the context of family, school, work, and recreational activities. Estimates from research suggest that about 9 percent of users become addicted to marijuana; this number increases among those who start young (to about 17 percent) and among daily users (25 to 50 percent).

Long-term marijuana abusers trying to quit report withdrawal symptoms including irritability, sleeplessness, decreased appetite, anxiety, and drug craving, all of which can make it difficult to remain abstinent. These symptoms begin within about one day following abstinence, peak at two to three days, and subside within one or two weeks following drug cessation.

Marijuana and Mental Health[2]

A number of studies have shown an association between chronic marijuana use and increased rates of anxiety, depression, and **schizophrenia.** Some of these studies have shown age at first use to be an important risk factor, where early use is a marker of increased vulnerability to later problems. However, at this time, it is not clear whether marijuana use causes mental problems, exacerbates them, or reflects an attempt to self-medicate symptoms already in existence.

KEY TERMS

Schizophrenia - A mental disorder characterized by abnormalities in the perception or expression of reality.

Chronic marijuana use, especially in a very young person, also may be a marker of risk for mental illnesses including addiction stemming from genetic or environmental vulnerabilities, such as early exposure to stress or violence. Currently, the strongest evidence links marijuana use and schizophrenia and/or related disorders. High doses of marijuana can produce an acute psychotic reaction; in addition, use of the drug may trigger the onset or relapse of schizophrenia in vulnerable individuals.

What Other Adverse Effect Does Marijuana Have on Health?[2]

Effects on the Heart

Marijuana increases heart rate by 20-100 percent shortly after smoking; this effect can last up to 3 hours. In one study, it was estimated that marijuana users have a greater increase in the risk of heart attack in the first hour after smoking the drug. This may be due to increased heart rate as well as the effects of marijuana on heart rhythms, causing **palpitations** and **arrhythmias.** This risk may be greater in aging populations or in those with cardiac vulnerabilities.

Effects on the Lungs

Numerous studies have shown marijuana smoke to contain **carcinogens** and to be an irritant to the lungs. In fact, marijuana smoke contains 50-70 percent more carcinogenic hydrocarbons than tobacco smoke. Marijuana users usually inhale more deeply and hold their breath longer than tobacco smokers do, which further increase the lungs' exposure to carcinogenic smoke. Marijuana smokers show dysregulated growth of **epithelial cells** in their lung tissue, which could lead to cancer; however, a recent case-controlled study found no positive associations between marijuana use and lung, upper respiratory, or upper digestive tract cancers. Thus, the link between marijuana smoking and these cancers remains unsubstantiated at this time.

Nonetheless, marijuana smokers can have many of the same respiratory problems as tobacco smokers, such as daily cough and phlegm production, more frequent acute chest illness, and a heightened risk of lung infections. A study of 450 individuals found that people who smoke marijuana frequently but do not smoke tobacco have more health problems and miss more days of work than nonsmokers. Many of the extra sick days among the marijuana smokers in the study were for respiratory illnesses.

KEY TERMS

Palpitations - A palpitation is an abnormality of heartbeat that causes a conscious awareness of its beating, whether it is too slow, too fast, irregular.
Arrhythmias - An irregular heartbeat.
Carcinogens - Any substance that produces cancer.
Epithelial cells - Cells that line the insides of the lungs.

Marijuana affects many skills required for safe driving: alertness, concentration, coordination, and reaction time.

How does marijuana affect driving?[9]

Marijuana affects many skills required for safe driving: alertness, concentration, coordination, and reaction time. Marijuana use can make it difficult to judge distances and react to signals and sounds on the road.

There are data showing that marijuana can play a role in motor vehicle crashes. Studies show that approximately 4–14 percent of drivers who sustained injury or died in traffic accidents tested positive for THC (tetrahydrocannabinol, the main psychoactive substance in marijuana). In many of these cases, alcohol was detected as well. When users combine marijuana with alcohol, as they often do, the hazards of driving can be more severe than with either drug alone. In a study conducted by the National Highway Traffic Safety Administration (NHTSA), a moderate dose of marijuana alone was shown to impair driving performance; however, the effects of even a low dose of marijuana combined with alcohol were markedly greater than those of either drug alone.

In one study conducted in Memphis, Tennessee, researchers found that, of 150 reckless drivers who were tested for drugs at the arrest scene, 33 percent tested positive for marijuana and 12 percent tested positive for both marijuana and cocaine. Data also show that while smoking marijuana, people display the same lack of coordination on standard "drunk driver" tests as do people who have had too much to drink.

What about Pregnancy? Will Smoking Marijuana Hurt the Baby?[10]

Doctors advise pregnant women not to use any drugs because they might harm the growing fetus. Although one animal study has linked marijuana use to loss of the fetus very early in pregnancy, two studies in humans found no association between marijuana use and early pregnancy loss. More research is necessary to fully understand the effects of marijuana use on pregnancy outcomes.

Some scientific studies have shown that babies born to women who used marijuana during their pregnancy displayed altered responses to visual stimulation, increased tremors, and a high-pitched cry, which may indicate problems with nervous system development. During preschool and early school years, marijuana-exposed children have been reported to have more behavioral problems and difficulties with sustained attention and memory than nonexposed children.

Researchers are not certain whether any effects of maternal marijuana use during pregnancy persist as the child grows up; however, because some parts of the brain continue to develop into adolescence, it is also possible that certain kinds of problems will become more evident as the child matures.

What Happens if a Nursing Mother Uses Marijuana?[10]

When a nursing mother uses marijuana, some of the THC is passed to the baby through breast milk. This is a matter for concern, because the THC in the mother's milk is much more concentrated than that in the mother's blood. One study has shown that the use of marijuana by a mother during the first month of breastfeeding can impair the infant's motor development (control of muscle movement). This work has not been replicated, although similar anecdotal reports exist. Further research is needed to determine whether THC transmitted in breast milk has harmful effects on development.

When a nursing mother uses marijuana, some of the THC is passed to the baby through breast milk.

Do Marijuana Users Lose Their Motivation?[11]

Some frequent, long-term marijuana users show signs of a lack of motivation (sometimes termed **"amotivational syndrome"**). Their problems include not caring about what happens in their lives, no desire to work regularly, fatigue, and a lack of concern about how they look. As a result of these symptoms, some users tend to perform poorly in school or at work. Scientists are still studying these problems.

Can a Person Become Addicted to Marijuana?[4,12]

Long-term marijuana use can lead to addiction; that is, people use the drug compulsively even though it interferes with family, school, work, and recreational activities. According to NSDUH, in 2009 of the estimated 7.1 million Americans classified with dependence on or abuse of illicit drugs, 4.3 million were dependent on or abused marijuana. In 2008, 17 percent of people entering drug abuse treatment programs reported marijuana as their primary drug of abuse (63 percent of those aged twelve to fourteen; and 69 percent of those fifteen to seventeen), representing more than 320,000 treatment admissions. Along with craving, withdrawal symptoms such as irritability, sleeping problems, and anxiety can make it difficult for long-term marijuana smokers to quit. Research has shown that approximately 9 percent of people who used marijuana may become dependent. The risk of addiction goes up to about one in six among those who start using as adolescents, and 25-50 percent of daily users.

Long-term marijuana use can lead to addiction; that is, people use the drug compulsively even though it interferes with family, school, work, and recreational activities.

Some heavy users of marijuana show signs of withdrawal when they do not use the drug. They develop symptoms such as restlessness, loss of appetite, trouble sleeping, weight loss, and shaky hands.

KEY TERMS

Amotivational syndrome - A syndrome characterized by lack of motivation, apathy, lethargy, etc., and which may be linked to use of marijuana or other drugs.

Shutterstock © Juan Camilo Bernal, 2011. Under license from Shutterstock, Inc.

The potential medicinal properties of marijuana have been the subject of substantive research and heated debate.

According to one study, marijuana use by teens who have prior serious antisocial problems can quickly lead to dependence on the drug. That study also showed that, for troubled teens using tobacco, alcohol, and marijuana, progression from their first use of marijuana to regular use was about as rapid as their progression to regular tobacco use and more rapid than the progression to regular use of alcohol.

What is "tolerance" for marijuana?[13]

"Tolerance" means that the user needs increasingly larger doses of the drug to get the same desired results that he or she previously got from smaller amounts. Some frequent, heavy users of marijuana may develop tolerance for it.

Is Marijuana Medicine?[2,12]

The potential medicinal properties of marijuana have been the subject of substantive research and heated debate. Scientists have confirmed that the cannabis plant contains active ingredients with therapeutic potential for relieving pain, controlling nausea, stimulating appetite, and decreasing ocular pressure. **Cannabinoid**-based medications include synthetic compounds, such as dronabinol (Marinol) and nabilone (Cesamet),which are approved by the U.S. Food and Drug Administration, and a new, chemically pure mixture of plant-derived THC and **cannabidiol** called Sativex, formulated as a mouth spray and approved in Canada and parts of Europe for the relief of cancer-associated pain and spasticity and neuropathic pain in multiple sclerosis.

Marijuana itself is an unlikely medication candidate for several reasons:

1. it is an unpurified plant containing numerous chemicals with unknown health effects,
2. it is typically consumed by smoking, further contributing to potential adverse effects, and
3. its cognitive impairing effects may limit its utility.

KEY TERMS

Cannabinoid - The chemical compounds that are the active principles in marijuana.

Cannabidiol - A non-psychoactive cannabinoid present in cannabis that inhibits convulsions, anxiety, vomiting and inflammation.

The promise lies instead in medications developed from marijuana's active components, the goal of which is to design tailored medications for specific conditions or symptoms with improved risk/benefit profiles.

Scientists continue to investigate the medicinal properties of THC and other cannabinoids to better evaluate and harness their ability to help patients suffering from a broad range of conditions, while avoiding the adverse effects of smoked marijuana.

Effects on Daily Life[2]

Research clearly demonstrates that marijuana has the potential to cause problems in daily life or make a person's existing problems worse. In one study, heavy marijuana abusers reported that the drug impaired several important measures of life achievement, including physical and mental health, cognitive abilities, social life, and career status. Several studies associate workers' marijuana smoking with increased absences, tardiness, accidents, workers' compensation claims, and job turnover.

Fact

Several studies associate workers' marijuana smoking with increased absences, tardiness, accidents, workers' compensation claims, and job turnover.

WHAT IS "SPICE"?[14]

"Spice" is used to describe a diverse family of herbal mixtures marketed under many names, including **K2** (fake marijuana), Yucatan Fire, Skunk, Moon Rocks, and others. These products contain dried, shredded plant material and presumably, chemical additives that are responsible for their psychoactive (mind-altering) effects. While Spice products are labeled "not for human consumption," they are marketed to people who are interested in herbal alternatives to marijuana. Spice users report experiences similar to those produced by marijuana, and regular users may experience withdrawal and addiction symptoms.

Spice mixtures are sold in many countries in head shops, gas stations, and via the Internet, although their sale and use are illegal throughout most European countries. Easy access has likely contributed to Spice's popularity.

How Is Spice Abused?[14]

Some Spice products are sold as "incense" but resemble potpourri rather than popular, more familiar incense products (common forms include short cones or long, thin sticks). Like marijuana, Spice is abused mainly by smoking. Sometimes Spice is mixed with marijuana or is prepared as an herbal infusion for drinking.

KEY TERMS

"Spice" - A diverse family of herbal mixtures marketed under many names, including K2, fake marijuana, Yucatan Fire, Skunk, Moon Rocks, and others.

K2 - A synthetic cannabinoid that affects the body like marijuana or pot, but is much more potent in its effects.

What Are the Health Effects of Spice Abuse?[14]

Presently, there are no studies on the effects of Spice on human health or behavior. A variety of mood and perceptual effects have been described, and patients who have been taken to Poison Control Centers in Texas report symptoms that include rapid heart rate, vomiting, agitation, confusion, and hallucinations.

Public Health Concerns[14]

Marketing labels often make unverified claims that Spice products contain up to 3 g of a natural psychoactive material taken from a variety of plants. Because the chemical composition of the various products sold as Spice is unknown, it is likely that some varieties also contain substances with dramatically different effects than those expected by the user. There is also concern about the presence of harmful heavy metal residues in Spice mixtures. However, without further analyses, it is difficult to determine whether these concerns are justified.

Legal Status[14]

The U.S. Drug Enforcement Administration (DEA) recently banned five synthetic cannabinoids in December 2010 by placing them in Schedule I status under the Controlled Substances Act. Schedule I status means that the substance is considered to have a high potential for abuse and no known medical benefits; and as such, it is illegal to possess or sell products that contain the substance. This ban went into effect December 2010, and will continue for one year while the DEA continues to gather information about the chemicals.

A number of states have also instituted bans on Spice and Spice-like products and/or synthetic cannabinoid-containing products, and many others are considering legislation forbidding the sale or possession of Spice.

HOW WIDESPREAD IS MARIJUANA ABUSE?[2]

National Survey on Drug Use and Health (NSDUH)

According to the National Survey on Drug Use and Health, in 2009, 16.7 million Americans ages twelve or older used marijuana at least once in the month prior to being surveyed, an increase over the rates reported in all years between 2002 and 2008. There was also a significant increase among youth ages twelve to seventeen, with current use up from 6.7 percent in 2008 to 7.3 percent in 2009, although this rate was lower than what was reported in 2002 (8.2 percent). Past-month use also increased among those eighteen to twenty-five, from 16.5 percent in 2008 to 18.1 percent in 2009.

How Can Someone Be Prevented from Getting Involved with Marijuana?[15]

There is no magic bullet for preventing drug use. But parents and friends can be influential by talking to their children or friends about the dangers of using marijuana and other drugs, and by remaining actively engaged in their lives. Even after teens enter high school, parents can stay involved in schoolwork, recreation, and social activities with their children's friends. Research shows that appropriate parental monitoring can reduce future drug use, even among those adolescents who may be prone to marijuana use, such as those who are rebellious, cannot control their emotions, and experience internal distress. For those who want to address the issue of drug abuse in their area, it is important that they get involved in drug abuse prevention programs in their community or child's school.

REFERENCES

1. Marijuana abuse: from the director [Research Report Series]. National Institute on Drug Abuse (NIDA). September 2010. http://www.nida.nih.gov/researchreports/marijuana/default.html. Accessed April 19, 2011.
2. NIDA InfoFacts: Marijuana. NIDA. December 2010. http://www.nida.nih.gov/infofacts/marijuana.html. Accessed April 19, 2011.
3. Marijuana: Facts Parents Need To Know. NIDA. http://www.nida.nih.gov/MarijBroch/parentpg3-4N.html. Accessed April 19, 2011.
4. Marijuana—February, 2011 [Topics in Brief]. NIDA. February 2011. http://www.nida.nih.gov/pdf/tib/marijuana.pdf. Accessed April 29, 2011.
5. Marijuana use and perceived risk of use among adolescents: 2002 to 2007. Office of Applied Studies. Updated January 7, 2009. http://www.oas.samhsa.gov/2k9/MJrisks/MJrisks.cfm. Accessed April 19, 2011.
6. Marijuana: facts parents need to know. NIDA. http://www.nida.nih.gov/marijbroch/parentpg5-6n.html. Accessed April 19, 2011.
7. Marijuana: facts parents need to know. NIDA. http://www.nida.nih.gov/marijbroch/parentpg7-8N.html. Accessed April 19, 2011.
8. Marijuana: facts parents need to know. NIDA. http://www.nida.nih.gov/marijbroch/parentpg9-10N.html. Accessed April 19, 2011.
9. Marijuana: facts parents need to know. NIDA. http://www.nida.nih.gov/marijbroch/parentpg11-12N.html. Accessed April 19, 2011.
10. Marijuana: facts parents need to know. NIDA. http://www.nida.nih.gov/marijbroch/parentpg13-14N.html#Pregnancy. Accessed April 19, 2011.
11. Marijuana: facts parents need to know. NIDA. http://www.nida.nih.gov/marijbroch/parentpg17-18N.html. Accessed April 19, 2011.
12. Marijuana. NIDA. http://www.nida.nih.gov/tib/marijuana.html. Accessed April 19, 2011.
13. Marijuana: facts parents need to know. NIDA. http://www.nida.nih.gov/MarijBroch/parentpg17-18N.html#Tolerance. Accessed April 19, 2011.

14. NIDA InfoFacts: Spice. NIDA. http://drugabuse.gov/infofacts/Spice.html. Accessed April 19, 2011.
15. Marijuana: facts parents need to know. NIDA. http://www.nida.nih.gov/marijbroch/parentpg19-20N.html#Prevent. Accessed April 19, 2011

CHAPTER 12

Narcotics (Opioids)

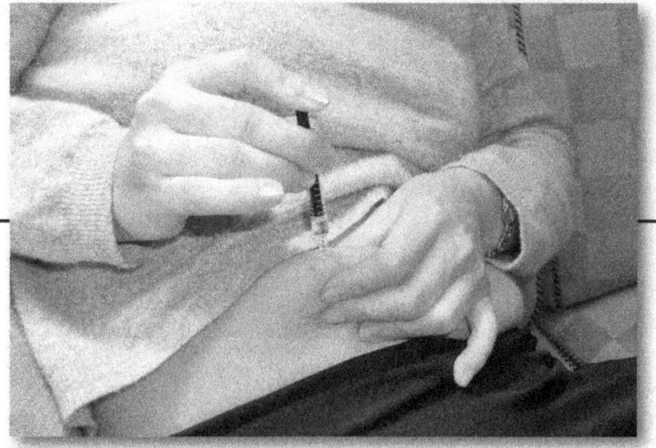

Shutterstock © Ingvald Kaldhussater, 2011. Under license from Shutterstock, Inc.

OBJECTIVES

After you have finished this chapter, you should be able to

- define opioids,
- describe how opioids affect the brain and body,
- describe the possible consequences of opioid use and abuse,
- define morphine,
- define heroin,
- explain how is heroin abused,
- explain how heroin affects the brain,
- list the medication used for opioid addiction,
- define codeine,

"If it keeps you awake, its art; if it puts you to sleep, it's a drug."

-Unknown

Shutterstock © rsirosistvan, 2011. Under license from Shutterstock, Inc.

The first known cultivation of opium poppies was in Mesopotamia.

NARCOTICS (OPIOIDS)[1]

Opioids are narcotics commonly prescribed because of their effective analgesic, or pain-relieving, properties. Medications that fall within this class-referred to as prescription narcotics-include morphine (e.g., Kadian, Avinza), codeine, oxycodone (e.g., OxyContin, Percodan, Percocet), and related drugs. Morphine, for example, is often used before and after surgical procedures to alleviate severe pain. Codeine, on the other hand, is often prescribed for mild pain. In addition to their pain-relieving properties, some of these drugs-codeine and diphenoxylate (Lomotil) for example-can be used to relieve coughs and diarrhea.

How opioids affect the brain and body[1]

Opioids act on the brain and body by attaching to specific proteins called opioid receptors, which are found in the brain, spinal cord, and the gastrointestinal tract. When these drugs attach to certain opioid receptors, they can block the perception of pain. Opioids can produce drowsiness, nausea, constipation, and, depending upon the amount of drug taken, depress respiration. Opioid drugs also can induce euphoria by affecting the brain regions that mediate what we perceive as pleasure. This feeling is often intensified for those who abuse opioids when administered by routes other than those recommended. For example, oxycodone often is snorted or injected to enhance its euphoric effects, while at the same time increasing the risk for serious medical consequences, such as opioid overdose.

Fact

Opioids can produce drowsiness, nausea, constipation, and, depending upon the amount of drug taken, depress respiration.

Possible consequences of opioid use and abuse[1]

Taken as directed, opioids can be used to manage pain effectively. When properly managed, short-term medical use of opioid analgesic drugs is safe and rarely causes addiction-defined as the compulsive and uncontrollable use of drugs despite adverse consequences-or dependence, which occurs when the body adapts to the presence of a drug, and often results in withdrawal symptoms when that drug is reduced or

KEY TERMS

Opioids - Are narcotics commonly prescribed because of their effective analgesic, or pain-relieving, properties.

stopped. Withdrawal symptoms include restlessness, muscle and bone pain, insomnia, diarrhea, vomiting, cold flashes with goose bumps, and involuntary leg movements. Long-term use of opioids can lead to physical dependence and addiction. Taking a large single dose of an opioid could cause severe respiratory depression that can lead to death.

Opioid drug use with other medications[1]

Only under a physician's supervision can opioids be used safely with other drugs. Typically, they should not be used with other substances that depress the central nervous system, such as alcohol, antihistamines, barbiturates, benzodiazepines, or general anesthetics, because these combinations increase the risk of life-threatening respiratory depression.

MORPHINE

Morphine is used to relieve moderate to severe pain. Morphine long-acting tablets and capsules are only used by patients who are expected to need medication to relieve moderate to severe pain around-the-clock for longer than a few days. Morphine is in a class of medications called opiate (narcotic) analgesics. It works by changing the way the body senses pain.[3]

Morphine and other opioids suppress the immune system, the body's innate defense against infections. Because of this effect, the pain-relief benefits of opioids should be weighed against the added risk of infection they pose to patients, particularly those being treated for severe burns or certain cancers. Opioid abusers, many of whom are already infection-prone due to unclean needles, repeated injections, and poor nutrition and living conditions, are rendered even more vulnerable by these drugs.
Morphine affects the body's immune cells in many ways, both directly and indirectly. Morphine suppresses the activity of three different types of white blood cells:

- T lymphocytes;
- B lymphocytes;
- Natural killer (NK) cells.[2]

HEROIN[6]

Heroin is an opiate drug that is synthesized from morphine, a naturally occurring substance extracted from the seed pod of the Asian opium poppy plant. Heroin

KEY TERMS

Morphine - Morphine is used to relieve moderate to severe pain. Morphine is in a class of medications called opiate (narcotic) analgesics.
Heroin - An opiate drug that is synthesized from morphine.

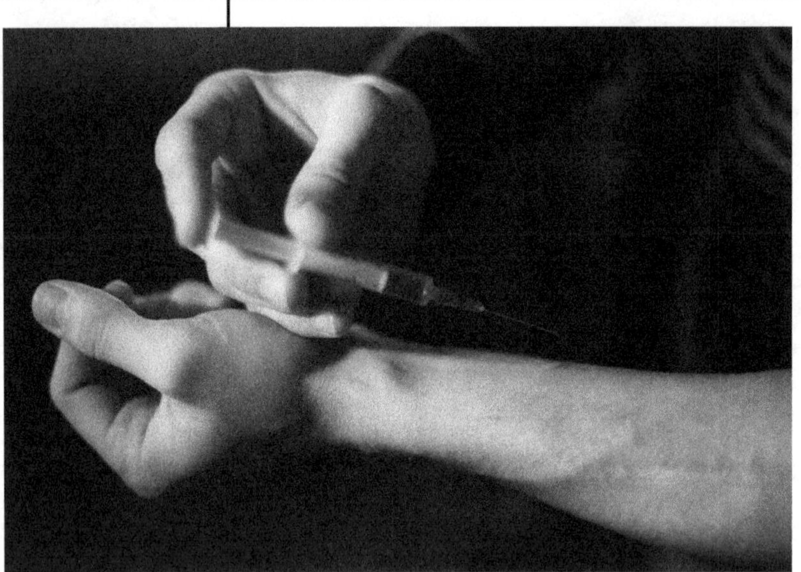
Shutterstock © Ingrid W, 2011. Under license from Shutterstock, Inc.

Heroin can be injected, snorted/sniffed, or smoked.

usually appears as a white or brown powder or as a black sticky substance, known as "black tar heroin."

Heroin Abuse[6]

Heroin can be injected, snorted or sniffed, or smoked. Injecting is the use of a needle to administer the drug directly into the bloodstream. Snorting is the process of inhaling heroin powder through the nose, where it is absorbed into the bloodstream through the nasal tissues. Smoking involves inhaling heroin smoke into the lungs. All three methods of administering heroin can lead to addiction and other severe health problems.

Heroin's Affect on the Brain[6]

Fact

Heroin enters the brain, where it is converted to morphine and binds to opioid receptors.

Heroin enters the brain, where it is converted to morphine and binds to opioid receptors. These receptors are located in many areas of the brain (and in the body), especially those involved in the perception of pain and reward. Opioid receptors are also located in the brain stem where they are important for automatic processes critical for life, such as breathing (respiration), blood pressure, and arousal. Heroin overdoses frequently involve a suppression of respiration.

After an intravenous injection of heroin, users report feeling a surge of euphoria ("rush") accompanied by dry mouth, a warm flushing of the skin, heaviness of the extremities, and clouded mental functioning. Following this initial euphoria, the user goes "on the nod," an alternately wakeful and drowsy state. Users who do not inject the drug may not experience the initial rush, but other effects are the same.

Tolerance[6]

With regular heroin use, **tolerance** develops, in which the user's physiological (and psychological) response to the drug decreases, and more heroin is needed to achieve the same intensity of effect. Heroin users are at high risk for addiction; it is estimated that about 23 percent of individuals who use heroin become dependent.

KEY TERMS

Tolerance - In which the user's physiological (and psychological) response to the drug decreases, and more heroin is needed to achieve the same intensity of effect.

Withdrawal[6]

Chronic use of heroin leads to **physical dependence**, a state in which the body has adapted to the presence of the drug. If a dependent user reduces or stops use of the drug abruptly, he or she may experience severe symptoms of withdrawal. These symptoms can begin as early as a few hours after the last drug administration and can include restlessness, muscle and bone pain, insomnia, diarrhea and vomiting, cold flashes with goose bumps, and kicking movements.

Pregnancy[6]

Heroin abuse during pregnancy, together with related factors like poor nutrition and inadequate prenatal care, has been associated with adverse consequences including low birth weight, an important risk factor for later developmental delay. If the mother is regularly abusing the drug, the infant may be born physically dependent on heroin and could suffer from serious medical complications that require hospitalization.

Treatment Options[6]

A range of treatments exist for heroin addiction, including medications and behavioral therapies. Science indicates that when medication treatment is combined with other supportive services, patients are often able to stop using heroin (or other opiates) and return to stable and productive lives.

Treatment usually begins with medically assisted **detoxification** to help patients withdraw from the drug safely. Medications such as clonidine and buprenorphine can be used to help minimize symptoms of withdrawal. However, detoxification alone is not treatment and has not been shown to be effective in preventing relapse. It is merely the first step. For pregnant heroin abusers, methadone maintenance combined with prenatal care and a comprehensive drug treatment program can improve many of the detrimental maternal and neonatal outcomes associated with untreated heroin abuse.

TREATMENT FOR OPIOID ADDICTION[4]

Individuals who abuse or are addicted to prescription opioid medications can be treated. Initially, they may need to undergo medically supervised detoxification to help reduce withdrawal symptoms; however, that is just the first step. Options for effectively treating addiction to prescription opioids are drawn from research

KEY TERMS

Physical dependence - A state in which the body has adapted to the presence of the drug.
Detoxification - A treatment for addiction to drugs or alcohol intended to remove the physiological effects of the addictive substances

on treating heroin addiction. Behavioral treatments, usually combined with medications, have also been proven effective. Currently used medications include the following:

- ***Methadone.*** A synthetic opioid that eliminates withdrawal symptoms and relieves craving, methoadone has been used successfully for more than thirty years to treat people addicted to heroin as well as opiates.
- ***Buprenorphine.*** Another synthetic opioid, buprenorphine is a more recently approved medication for treating addiction to heroin and other opiates. It can be prescribed in a physician's office.
- ***Naltrexone.*** Naltrexone is a long-acting opioid receptor blocker that can be employed to help prevent relapse. It is not widely used, however, because of poor compliance, except by highly motivated individuals (e.g., physicians at risk of losing their medical license). It should be noted that this medication can only be used for someone who has already been detoxified, because it can produce severe withdrawal symptoms in a person continuing to abuse opioids.
- ***Naloxone.*** A short-acting opioid receptor blocker that counteracts the effects of opioids, naloxone can be used to treat overdoses and sleep disorders.

Shutterstock © Istocksnapp, 2011. Under license from Shutterstock, Inc.

Opium dens were prevalent in many parts of the world in the 19th century.

CODEINE

Codeine is used to relieve mild to moderate pain. It is also used, usually in combination with other medications, to reduce coughing. Combination products that contain codeine and promethazine should not be used in children younger than 16 years of age. Codeine will help relieve symptoms but will not treat the cause of symptoms or speed recovery. Codeine belongs to a class of medications called opiate (narcotic) **analgesics** and to a class of medications called **antitussives.** When codeine is used to treat pain, it works by changing the way the body senses pain. When codeine is used to reduce coughing, it works by decreasing the activity in the part of the brain that causes coughing.[5]

KEY TERMS

Codeine - Codeine is used to relieve mild to moderate pain. Codeine belongs to a class of medications called opiate (narcotic).

Analgesics - Are drugs that relieve pain without causing loss of consciousness.

Antitussives - Are drugs that are capable of relieving or suppressing coughing.

Examples of commercial names for codeine:

- Empirin with Codeine
- Fiorinal with Codeine
- Robitussin A-C
- Tylenol with Codeine

Examples of street names for codeine:

- Captain Cody
- Schoolboy
- Doors & fours
- Loads
- Pancakes and syrup[7]

REFERENCES

1. The National Institute on Drug Abuse (NIDA). What are opioids? http://www.drugabuse.gov/Researchreports/Prescription/prescription2.html
2. The National Institute on Drug Abuse (NIDA). Morphine-Induced Immunosuppression, From Brain to Spleen, Vol. 21, No. 6 (June 2008). http://www.drugabuse.gov/NIDA_notes/NNvol21N6/morphine.html
3. National Institute on Health (NIH), Morphine, 2011. http://www.nlm.nih.gov/medlineplus/druginfo/meds/a682133.html
4. Prescription and over-the-counter medications. NIDA InfoFacts. June 2009. http://www.nida.nih.gov/PDF/Infofacts/PainMed09.pdf. Accessed April 23, 2011.
5. National Institute on Health (NIH), Codeine, 2011. http://www.nlm.nih.gov/medlineplus/druginfo/meds/a682065.html
6. NIDA InfoFacts: Heroin. The National Institute on Drug Abuse (NIDA). 2009. http://www.nida.nih.gov/infofacts/heroin.html. Accessed April 23, 2011.
7. The National Institute on Drug Abuse (NIDA). Selected Prescription Drugs With Potential for Abuse. 2002. http://www.drugabuse.gov/PDF/PrescriptionDrugs.pdf

CHAPTER 13

Hallucinogens (Psychedelics)

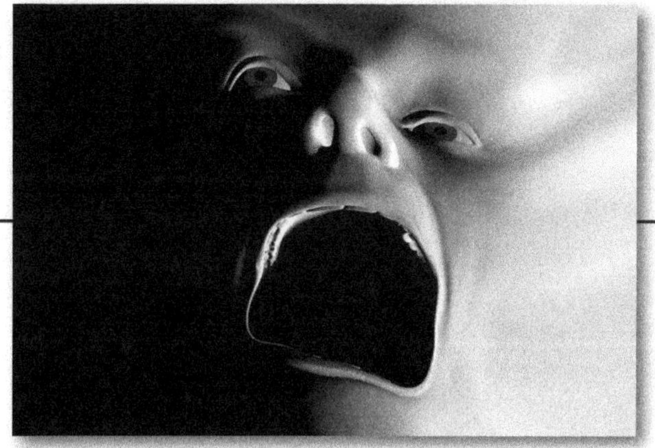

Shutterstock © Chris Harvey, 2011. Under license from Shutterstock, Inc.

OBJECTIVES

After you have finished this chapter, you should be able to

- define what hallucinogens are,
- explain why people take hallucinogens,
- list some of the more common hallucinogens,
- describe the effects of hallucinogens,
- explain how hallucinogens affect the brain,
- define MDMA
- explain how MDMA is abused,
- explain how MDMA affects the brain,
- define what polydrug use is,

"LSD melts your mind, not in your hand."

-Unknown

Shutterstock © Mandy Godbehear, 2011. Under license from Shutterstock, Inc.

Hallucinogens are frequently used at all-night techno dance parties.

WHAT ARE HALLUCINOGENS?[1]

Hallucinogens are drugs that cause hallucinations, profound distortions in a person's perception of reality. Under the influence of hallucinogens, people see images, hear sounds, and feel sensations that seem real but do not exist. Some hallucinogens also produce rapid, intense emotional swings.

Hallucinogens cause their effects by disrupting the interaction of nerve cells and the neurotransmitter serotonin. Distributed throughout the brain and spinal cord, the serotonin system is involved in the control of behavioral, perceptual, and regulatory systems, including mood, hunger, body temperature, sexual behavior, muscle control, and sensory perception. LSD (an abbreviation of the German words for "lysergic acid diethylamide") is the drug most commonly identified with the term "hallucinogen" and the most widely used in this class of drugs. It is considered the typical hallucinogen, and the characteristics of its action and effects apply to the other hallucinogens, including mescaline, psilocybin, and ibogaine.

Why Do People Take Hallucinogens?[1]

Hallucinogenic drugs have played a role in human life for thousands of years. Cultures from the tropics to the arctic have used plants to induce states of detachment from reality and to precipitate "visions" thought to provide mystical insight. These plants contain chemical compounds, such as mescaline, psilocybin, and ibogaine, that are structurally similar to serotonin, and they produce their effects by disrupting normal functioning of the serotonin system. Historically, hallucinogenic plants were used largely for social and religious ritual, and their availability was limited by the climate and soil conditions they require. After the development of LSD, a synthetic compound that can be manufactured anywhere, abuse of hallucinogens became more widespread, and from the 1960s it increased dramatically. All LSD manufactured in the United States is intended for illegal use, since LSD has no accepted medical use in the United States.

KEY TERMS

Hallucinogens - Drugs that cause hallucinations, profound distortions in a person's perceptions of reality.

How Do Hallucinogens Affect the Brain?[2]

LSD, peyote, psilocybin, and PCP(Phenylcyclohexyl piperidine) are drugs that cause hallucinations by initially disrupting the interaction of nerve cells and the neurotransmitter serotonin. Comparatively, PCP acts mainly through a type of glutamate receptor in the brain that is important for the perception of pain, responses to the environment, and learning and memory.

LSD[3]

LSD is a clear or white, odorless, water-soluble material synthesized from lysergic acid, a compound derived from a rye fungus. LSD is the most potent known mood and perception altering drug: oral doses as small as 30 mcg can produce effects that last six to twelve hours. LSD is initially produced in crystalline form. The pure crystal can be crushed to powder and mixed with binding agents to produce tablets known as microdots or thin squares of gelatin called "window panes"; more commonly, it is dissolved, diluted, and applied to paper or other materials. The most common form of LSD is called "blotter acid" sheets of paper soaked in LSD and perforated into one-quarter-inch squares, individual dosage units. Variations in manufacturing and the presence of contaminants can produce LSD in colors ranging from clear or white, in its purest form, to tan or even black. Even uncontaminated LSD begins to degrade and discolor soon after it is manufactured, and drug distributors often apply LSD to colored paper, making it difficult for a buyer to determine the drug's purity or age.

The most common form of LSD is called "blotter acid" sheets of paper soaked in LSD and perforated into ¼-inch square, individual dosage units.

LSD's effects[3]

The precise mechanism by which LSD alters perceptions is still unclear. Some laboratory studies suggest that LSD, like hallucinogenic plants, may act on certain groups of serotonin receptors and that its effects are most prominent in two brain regions: the cerebral cortex, an area involved in mood, cognition, and perception, and the locus ceruleus, which receives sensory signals from all areas of the body and has been described as the brain's "novelty detector" for important external stimuli. LSD's effects typically begin within thirty to ninety minutes of ingestion and may last as long as twelve hours. Users refer to LSD and other hallucinogenic experiences as "trips" and to the acute adverse experiences as "bad trips." Although most LSD trips include both pleasant and unpleasant aspects, the drug's effects are unpredictable and may vary with the amount ingested and the user's personality, mood, expectations, and surroundings. Users of LSD may experience some physiological effects, such as increased blood pressure and heart rate, dizziness, loss of appetite,

LSD's effects typically begin within 30 to 90 minutes of ingestion and may last as long as 12 hours.

KEY TERMS

LSD - Is a clear or white, odorless, water soluble material synthesized from lysergic acid, a compound derived from a rye fungus.

dry mouth, sweating, nausea, numbness, and tremors; but the drug's major effects are emotional and sensory. The user's emotions may shift rapidly through a range from fear to euphoria, with transitions so rapid that the user may seem to experience several emotions simultaneously. LSD also has dramatic effects on the senses. Colors, smells, sounds, and other sensations seem highly intensified. In some cases, sensory perceptions may blend in a phenomenon known as synesthesia, in which a person seems to hear or feel colors and see sounds.

LSD users quickly develop a high degree of tolerance for the drug's effects; after repeated use, they need increasingly larger doses to produce similar effects. LSD use also produces tolerance for other hallucinogenic drugs such as psilocybin and mescaline, but not to drugs such as marijuana, amphetamines, or PCP, which do not act directly on the serotonin receptors affected by LSD. Tolerance for LSD is short-lived; it is lost if the user stops taking the drug for several days.

There is no evidence that LSD produces physical withdrawal symptoms when chronic use is stopped. Two long-term effects that have been associated with use of LSD are persistent psychosis and hallucinogen persisting perception disorder (HPPD), more commonly referred to as "flashbacks." The causes of these effects, which in some users occur after a single experience with the drug, are not known.

Psychosis[3]

The effects of LSD can be described as drug induced **psychosis distortion** or disorganization of a person's capacity to recognize reality, think rationally, or communicate with others. Some LSD users experience devastating psychological effects that persist after the trip has ended, producing a long-lasting psychotic-like state.

LSD-induced persistent psychosis may include dramatic mood swings from mania to profound depression, vivid visual disturbances, and hallucinations. These effects may last for years and can affect people who have no history or other symptoms of psychological disorder.

Hallucinogen Persisting Perception Disorder[3]

Episodes of HPPD that are experienced by former LSD users are spontaneous, repeated, and sometimes continuous recurrences of some of the sensory distortions originally produced by LSD. The experience may include hallucinations, but it most commonly consists of visual disturbances, such as seeing false motion on the edges of the field of vision, bright or colored flashes, and halos or trails attached to moving

KEY TERMS

Psychosis distortion - Disorganization of a person's capacity to recognize reality, think rationally, or communicate with others.

objects. This condition is typically persistent and in some cases remains unchanged for years after an individual has stopped using the drug.

Because **HPPD** symptoms may be mistaken for those of other neurological disorders such as stroke or brain tumors, sufferers may consult a variety of clinicians before the disorder is accurately diagnosed. There is no established treatment for HPPD, although some antidepressant drugs may reduce the symptoms. Psychotherapy may help patients adjust to the confusion associated with visual distraction and minimize the fear, expressed by some, that they are suffering brain damage or psychiatric disorder.

PCP[4]

Shutterstock © Coulerfield, 2011. Under license from Shutterstock, Inc.

PCP is sprinkled on marijuana and then smoked and the onset of effects is rapid.

Phenylcyclohexyl piperidine, commonly initialized as **PCP**, developed in the 1950s as an intravenous surgical anesthetic, is classified as a dissociative anesthetic. Its sedative and anesthetic effects are trance-like, and patients experience a feeling of being "out of body" and detached from their environment when they take it. PCP was used in veterinary medicine but was never approved for human use because of problems that arose during clinical studies, including delirium and extreme agitation upon emergence from anesthesia. During the 1960s, PCP in pill form became widely abused, but the surge in illicit use receded rapidly as users became dissatisfied with the long delay between taking the drug and feeling its effects, and with the unpredictable and often violent behavior associated with its use.

Powdered PCP known as "ozone," "rocket fuel," "love boat," "hog," "**embalming fluid**," or "superweed," appeared in the 1970s. In powdered form, the drug is sprinkled on marijuana, tobacco, or parsley, and then smoked, and the onset of effects is rapid. Users sometimes ingest PCP by snorting the powder or by swallowing it in tablet form. Normally a white crystalline powder, PCP is sometimes colored with water soluble or alcohol-soluble dyes. PCP, which is not a true hallucinogen, can affect many neurotransmitter systems. When snorted or smoked, PCP rapidly passes to the brain to disrupt the functioning of sites known as NMDA receptor complexes, which are receptors for the neurotransmitter glutamate. Glutamate receptors play a major role in the perception of pain, in cognition including learning and memory, and in emotion. In the brain, PCP also alters the actions of dopamine,

KEY TERMS

HPPD - Hallucinogen Persisting Perception Disorder.
PCP - Phenylcyclohexyl piperidine, commonly initialized as PCP, developed in the 1950s as an intravenous surgical anesthetic, is classified as a dissociative anesthetic.
"Embalming fluid" - A street name for PCP.

a neurotransmitter responsible for the euphoria and "rush" associated with many abused drugs.

At low PCP doses (5 mg or less), physical effects of PCP include shallow, rapid breathing, increased blood pressure and heart rate, and elevated temperature. Doses of 10 mg or more cause dangerous changes in respiration, often accompanied by nausea, blurred vision, dizziness, and decreased awareness of pain. Muscle contractions may cause uncoordinated movements and bizarre postures. When severe, the muscle contractions can result in bone fracture or in kidney damage or failure as a consequence of muscle cells breaking down. Very high doses of PCP can cause convulsions, coma, hyperthermia, and death.

PCP's effects are unpredictable. Typically, they are felt within minutes of ingestion and last for several hours. Some users report that they experience the drug's effects for days. One drug-taking episode may produce feelings of detachment from reality, including distortions of space, time, and body image; another may produce hallucinations, panic, and fear. Some users report feelings of invulnerability and exaggerated strength. PCP users may become severely disoriented, violent, or suicidal.

Repeated use of PCP can result in addiction, and repeated or prolonged use of PCP can cause withdrawal syndrome when drug use is stopped. Symptoms such as memory loss and depression may persist for as long as a year after a chronic user stops taking PCP.

KETAMINE[3]

Ketamine ("K," "**Special K**," "cat Valium") is a dissociative anesthetic developed in 1963 to replace PCP and is used in human anesthesia and veterinary medicine. Much of the ketamine sold on the street has been diverted from veterinarians' offices. Although it is manufactured as an injectable liquid, in illicit use, ketamine is generally evaporated to form a powder that is snorted or compressed into pills.

Ketamine's chemical structure and mechanism of action are similar to those of PCP, and its effects are similar, but ketamine is much less potent than PCP and has effects of much shorter duration. Users report sensations ranging from a pleasant feeling of floating to being separated from their bodies. Some ketamine experiences involve a terrifying feeling of almost complete sensory detachment that is likened to a near-death experience. These experiences, similar to a bad trip on LSD, are called the "**K-hole**."

KEY TERMS

Ketamine - Is a dissociative anesthetic developed in 1963 to replace PCP and currently used in human anesthesia and veterinary medicine.
"Special K" - A street name for Ketamine.
"K-hole" - Similar to a "bad trip" on LSD.

Ketamine is odorless and tasteless, so it can be added to beverages without being detected, and it induces amnesia. Because of these properties, the drug is sometimes given to unsuspecting victims and used in the commission of sexual assaults referred to as "drug rape."

DXM[4]

Dextromethorphan ("**DXM**" or "robo") is a cough-suppressing ingredient in a variety of over-the-counter cold and cough medications. Like PCP and ketamine, DXM acts as an NMDA receptor antagonist. The most common source of abused DXM is extra-strength cough syrup, which typically contains 3 mg of the drug per mL of syrup. At the doses recommended for treating coughs (one-sixth to one-third of an ounce of medication, containing 15 mg to 30 mg DXM), the drug is safe and effective. At much higher doses (4 oz or more), DXM produces dissociative effects similar to those of PCP and ketamine.

Fact

The most common source of abused DXM is extra-strength cough syrup.

The effects vary with dose, and DXM users describe a set of distinct dose-dependent plateaus ranging from a mild stimulant effect with distorted visual perceptions at low doses (approximately 2-oz) to a sense of complete dissociation from one's body at doses of 10 ounces or more. The effects typically last for 6 hours. Over-the-counter medications that contain dextromethorphan often contain antihistamine and decongestant ingredients as well, and high doses of these mixtures can seriously increase risks of dextromethorphan abuse.

PSILOCYBIN[2]

Psilocybin (4-phosphoryloxy-N, N-dimethyltryptamine) is obtained from certain types of mushrooms that are indigenous to tropical and subtropical regions of South America, Mexico, and the United States. These mushrooms typically contain less than 0.5 percent psilocybin plus trace amounts of psilocin, another hallucinogenic substance.

Mushrooms containing psilocybin are available fresh or dried and are typically taken orally. Psilocybin (4-phosphoryloxy-N, N-dimethyltryptamine) and its biologically active form, psilocin (4-hydroxy-N, N-dimethyltryptamine), cannot be inactivated by cooking or freezing preparations. Thus, they may also be brewed as a tea or added to other foods to mask their bitter flavor. The effects of psilocybin, which appear within 20 minutes of ingestion, last approximately 6 hours.

KEY TERMS

DXM - Dextromethorphan is a cough-suppressing ingredient in a variety of over-the-counter cold and cough medications.
Psilocybin - Is obtained from certain types of mushrooms that are indigenous to tropical and subtropical regions of South America, Mexico, and the United States.

Fact

Psilocybin can produce muscle relaxation or weakness, uncoordinated movements, excessive pupil dilation, nausea, vomiting, and drowsiness.

Psilocybin can produce muscle relaxation or weakness, uncoordinated movements, excessive pupil dilation, nausea, vomiting, and drowsiness. Individuals who abuse psilocybin mushrooms also risk poisoning if one of many existing varieties of poisonous mushrooms is incorrectly identified as a psilocybin mushroom.

The active compounds in psilocybin (**"magic" mushrooms**) have LSD-like properties and produce alterations of autonomic function, motor reflexes, behavior, and perception. The psychological consequences of psilocybin use include hallucinations, an altered perception of time, and an inability to discern fantasy from reality. Panic reactions and psychosis also may occur, particularly if a user ingests a large dose.

Shutterstock © Charlie Edward, 2011. Under license from Shutterstock, Inc.

Peyote is a small, spineless cactus. It is native to southwestern Texas and through Mexico.

PEYOTE[2]

Peyote is a small, spineless cactus in which the principal active ingredient is mescaline. This plant has been used by natives in northern Mexico and the southwestern United States as a part of religious ceremonies. Mescaline can also be produced through chemical synthesis.

The top of the peyote cactus, also referred to as the crown, consists of disc-shaped buttons that are cut from the roots and dried. These buttons are generally chewed or soaked in water to produce an intoxicating liquid. The hallucinogenic dose of mescaline is about 0.3 to 0.5 grams, and its effects last about 12 hours. Because the extract is so bitter, some individuals prefer to prepare a tea by boiling the cacti for several hours. Its effects can be similar to those of LSD, including increased body temperature and heart rate, uncoordinated movements, profound sweating, and flushing.

MDMA[5]

MDMA (3, 4-methylenedioxymethamphetamine) is a synthetic, psychoactive drug that is chemically similar to the stimulant methamphetamine and the hallucinogen

KEY TERMS

"magic" mushrooms - A street name for psilocybin.
Peyote - A small, spineless cactus in which the principal active ingredient is mescaline.
MDMA - Is a synthetic, psychoactive drug that is chemically similar to the stimulant methamphetamine and the hallucinogen mescaline.

mescaline. MDMA produces feelings of increased energy, euphoria, emotional warmth, and distortions in time, perception, and tactile experiences.

How Is MDMA Abused?[25]

MDMA is taken orally, usually as a capsule or tablet. It was initially popular among Caucasian adolescents and young adults in the nightclub scene or at weekend-long dance parties known as raves. However, the profile of the typical MDMA user has changed, with the drug now affecting a broader range of ethnic groups. MDMA is also popular among urban gay males.

How Does MDMA Affect the Brain?[25]

MDMA exerts its primary effects in the brain on neurons that use the chemical (or neurotransmitter) serotonin to communicate with other neurons. The serotonin system plays an important role in regulating mood, aggression, sexual activity, sleep, and sensitivity to pain. MDMA binds to the serotonin transporter, which is responsible for removing serotonin from the synapse (or space between adjacent neurons) to terminate the signal between neurons; thus MDMA increases and prolongs the serotonin signal. MDMA also enters the serotonergic neurons via the transporter (because MDMA resembles serotonin in chemical structure) where it causes excessive release of serotonin from the neurons. MDMA has similar effects on another neurotransmitter norepinephrine, which can cause increases in heart rate and blood pressure. MDMA also releases dopamine, but to a much lesser extent.

MDMA can produce confusion, depression, sleep problems, drug craving, and severe anxiety. These problems can occur soon after taking the drug or, sometimes, even days or weeks after taking MDMA. In addition, chronic users of MDMA perform more poorly than nonusers on certain types of cognitive or memory tasks, although some of these effects may be due to the use of other drugs in combination with MDMA.

What Other Adverse Effects Does MDMA Have on Health?[25]

MDMA can also be dangerous to overall health and, on rare occasions, lethal. MDMA can have many of the same physical effects as other stimulants, such as cocaine and amphetamines. These include increases in heart rate and blood pressure which present risks of particular concern for people with circulatory problems or heart disease and other symptoms such as muscle tension, involuntary teeth clenching, nausea, blurred vision, faintness, and chills or sweating.

In high doses, MDMA can interfere with the body's ability to regulate temperature. On rare but unpredictable occasions, this can lead to a sharp increase in body temperature (hyperthermia), which can result in liver, kidney, cardiovascular system failure, or death. MDMA can interfere with its own metabolism (breakdown within the body); therefore, potentially harmful levels can be reached by repeated MDMA administration within short periods of time. Other drugs that are chemically similar to MDMA, such as MDA (methylenedioxyamphetamine, the parent drug of MDMA) and PMA (paramethoxyamphetamine, associated with fatalities in the United States and Australia), are sometimes sold as ecstasy. These drugs can be neurotoxic or create additional health risks to the user. Furthermore, ecstasy tablets may contain other substances, such as ephedrine (a stimulant); dextromethorphan; ketamine; caffeine; cocaine; and methamphetamine. Although the combination of MDMA with one or more of these drugs may be inherently dangerous, users who also combine these with additional substances such as marijuana and alcohol may be putting themselves at even higher risk for adverse health effects.

What Treatment Options Exist?[5]

There are no specific treatments for MDMA abuse and addiction. The most effective treatments for drug abuse and addiction in general are cognitive-behavioral interventions that are designed to help modify the patient's thinking, expectancies, and behaviors related to their drug use and to increase skills in coping with life stressors. Drug abuse recovery support groups may also be effective in combination with behavioral interventions to support long-term, drug-free recovery. There are currently no pharmacological treatments for addiction to MDMA.

POLYDRUG[6]

Polydrug use is the use of more than one drug and is common among substance abusers. When people consume two or more psychoactive drugs together, such as cocaine and alcohol, they compound the danger each drug poses and unknowingly perform a complex chemical experiment within their bodies. For example, the human liver combines cocaine and alcohol to produce a third substance, cocaethylene, which intensifies cocaine's euphoric effects. Cocaethylene is associated with a greater risk of sudden death than cocaine alone.

KEY TERMS

Polydrug use - Is the use of more than one drug and is common among substance abusers.

REFERENCES

1. The National Institute on Drug Abuse (NIDA). Hallucinogens and Dissociative Drugs. March 2001. http://www.drugabuse.gov/PDF/RRHalluc.pdf. Accessed April 23, 2011.
2. NIDA InfoFacts: Hallucinogens - LSD, Peyote, Psilocybin, and PCP. NIDA. http://www.nida.nih.gov/infofacts/hallucinogens.html. Accessed April 23, 2011.
3. Research Report Series - Hallucinogens and Dissociative Drugs. NIDA. http://www.nida.nih.gov/researchreports/hallucinogens/halluc3.html. Accessed April 23, 2011.
4. Research Report Series - Hallucinogens and Dissociative Drugs. The National Institute on Drug Abuse (NIDA). 2009. http://www.drugabuse.gov/ResearchReports/hallucinogens/halluc4.html. Accessed April 23, 2011.
5. NIDA InfoFacts: National Institute on Drug Abuse (NIDA). 2010. MDMA (Ecstasy). http://www.nida.nih.gov/infofacts/ecstasy.html.
6. NIDA InfoFacts, cocaine: National Institute on Drug Abuse (NIDA). 2010. http://www.drugabuse.gov/infofacts/cocaine.html

CHAPTER 14

Prescription, Over-the-Counter, and Herbal Drugs

Shutterstock © Natalia Bratslavsky, 2011. Under license from Shutterstock, Inc.

OBJECTIVES

After you have finished this chapter, you should be able to

- define and explain prescription drug abuse,
- list the most commonly abused prescription drugs,
- explain how prescription drugs are abused,
- define and explain over-the-counter (OTC) medications,
- list the most common OTC medications,
- define aspirin,
- define tylenol,
- explain laxative abuse,
- define and explain Reye's syndrome,
- define and explain Herbal medicine,
- list the most popular herbal remedies and dietary supplements.

"I had some eyeglasses. I was walking down the street when suddenly the prescription ran out."

-Stephen Wright

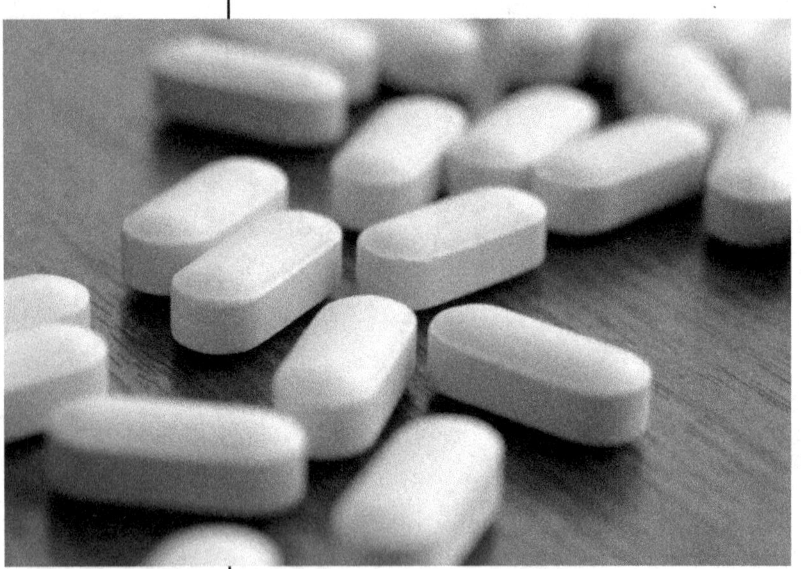

Shutterstock © Liv friis-larsen, 2011. Under license from Shutterstock, Inc.

Abusing prescription drugs can have negative short-and long-term health consequences.

PRESCRIPTION DRUG ABUSE[1]

Prescription drug abuse is the intentional use of a medication without a prescription; in a way other than as prescribed; or for the experience or feeling it causes. It is not a new problem, but one that deserves renewed attention. For although prescription drugs can be powerful allies, they also pose serious health risks related to their abuse.

In 2009, approximately 7.0 million persons were current users of psychotherapeutic drugs taken nonmedically. This class of drugs is broadly described as those targeting the central nervous system, including drugs used to treat psychiatric disorders.

Among adolescents, prescription and over-the-counter medications account for most of the frequently abused drugs by high school seniors (excluding tobacco and alcohol).

Prescription Drug Abuse[2]

Prescription drug abuse is when someone takes a medication that was prescribed for someone else or takes their own prescription in a manner or dosage other than what was prescribed. Abuse can include taking a friend's or relative's prescription to get high, to help with studying, or even to treat pain.

Abusing prescription drugs can have negative short- and long-term health consequences. Stimulant abuse can cause paranoia, dangerously high body temperatures, and an irregular heartbeat, especially if taken in high doses or by routes other than in pill form. The abuse of opioids can cause drowsiness, nausea, and constipation, and depending on the amount taken, slow breathing. Abusing depressants can cause slurred speech, shallow breathing, fatigue, disorientation, lack of coordination, and seizures (upon withdrawal from chronic abuse). Abuse of any of these substances may result in physical dependence or addiction.

KEY TERMS

Prescription drug abuse - When someone takes a medication that was prescribed for someone else or takes their own prescription in a manner or dosage other than what was prescribed.

Many people think that abusing prescription drugs is safer than abusing illicit drugs like heroin because the manufacturing of prescription drugs is regulated or because they are prescribed by physicians. But that doesn't mean these drugs are safe for someone other than the person with the prescription to use. Many prescription drugs can have powerful effects in the brain and body and people sometimes take them in ways that can be just as dangerous (e.g., crushing pills and snorting or injecting the contents) as illicit drug abuse. In fact, opioid painkillers act on the same sites in the brain as heroin, which is one reason why they can be so dangerous when abused. Also, abusing prescription drugs is illegal and that includes sharing prescriptions with friends.

Doctors consider the potential benefits and risks to each patient before prescribing medications. Doctors ask about patients' medical history, including what other health problems they have, what other medications they take, and whether they have a history of problems with addiction or other mental illnesses. Based on this and other information (e.g., age and weight), physicians can prescribe drugs while minimizing the risks. But when abused, some prescription drugs can be dangerous and can lead to severe health consequences, including addiction, just like illicit drugs can.

Most Commonly Abused Prescription Drugs[3]

Opioids (such as the pain relievers OxyContin and Vicodin), central nervous system depressants (e.g., Xanax, Valium), and stimulants (e.g., Concerta, Adderall) are the most commonly abused prescription drugs.

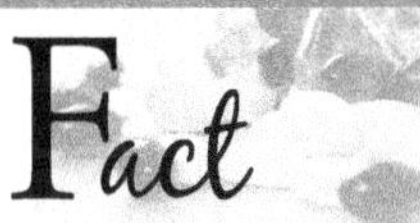

Opioids (such as the pain relievers OxyContin and Vicodin), central nervous system depressants (e.g., Xanax, Valium), and stimulants (e.g., Concerta, Adderall) are the most commonly abused prescription drugs.

How Are Prescription Drugs Abused?[3]

Some people take other people's drugs for their intended purposes (e.g., to relieve pain, to stay awake, to fall asleep). Others take them to get high, often at larger doses than prescribed or by a different route of administration. Most prescription drugs come in pill or capsule form. Sometimes, drug users break or crush the pill or capsule, then swallow the drug, sniff it, or "cook" it by turning it to liquid and then injecting it.

Side Effects[3]

Prescription drugs are designed to treat a particular illness or condition, but they often have other effects on the body, some of which can be dangerous. These are referred to as side effects. For example, Vicodin stops pain, but it also causes constipation and drowsiness and slows breathing. Stimulants such as Adderall increase attention but also raise blood pressure and heart rate. These side effects can be made worse when prescription drugs are not taken as prescribed or are abused in combination with other substances including alcohol, other prescription drugs, and even OTC drugs, such as cold medicine. For instance, some people mix alcohol and benzodiazepines (e.g., Valium), both of which can slow breathing. This combination could stop breathing all together, requiring emergency care, or worse, it could be fatal.

Addiction[3]

Studies show that when people take a medication as it is prescribed for a medical condition such as pain or attention deficit hyperactivity disorder, they usually do not become addicted because the medication is prescribed in dosages and forms that are considered safe. The drug is compensating for a problem, which makes the person feel better, not high. But medications that affect the brain can change the way it functions, especially when they are taken repeatedly. They can alter the reward system, making it harder to feel good without the drug and leading to some of the intense cravings people develop, which make it hard to stop using. This is no different from what can happen when someone takes illicit drugs.

Withdrawal[3]

Taking drugs repeatedly over a period of time causes changes in the body as well as the brain, resulting in physical dependence. That is, the body adapts to the drug's presence, and when its use is abruptly stopped, the person can experience withdrawal symptoms. This can happen even in someone who is prescribed medications and takes them appropriately, which is why a physician should be consulted when stopping prescription medications as well as when starting them. The withdrawal symptoms depend on the drug itself for opioids; they can include nausea, chills, vomiting, muscle pain, and diarrhea. These symptoms often can be controlled or diminished with proper medical supervision.

OTC MEDICATIONS[4]

Cough and cold medications are some of the most commonly abused over-the-counter (OTC) medications.

Cough and cold medications are some of the most commonly abused OTC medications. Many contain an ingredient called **dextromethorphan (DXM)**. However, to get the "high" or "dissociative" state that abusers crave, large quantities are needed. At high doses, DXM causes effects similar to that of the drugs ketamine or PCP by affecting similar sites in the brain. Ketamine and PCP are considered **dissociative drugs,** which make people feel disconnected from their normal selves. They affect memory, feelings, and thoughts. DXM is similar, and its abuse can affect control over movement; cause numbness, nausea, and vomiting; and can increase heart rate and blood pressure.

KEY TERMS

"Dissociative" drugs - Drugs that make people feel disconnected from their normal selves.

Dextromethorphan (DXM) - An oral cough suppressant available in the US without a prescription but which is sometimes abused as a recreational drug.

When taken as directed, OTC medications are safe and effective, but high doses can cause problems. And, some OTC medications can produce dangerous health effects when taken with alcohol. It is important to understand these risks, read bottle labels, and take OTC medications only as directed.

Aspirin[5]

Aspirin is used to relieve the symptoms of rheumatoid arthritis (arthritis caused by swelling of the lining of the joints), osteoarthritis (arthritis caused by breakdown of the lining of the joints), systemic lupus erythematosus (condition in which the immune system attacks the joints and organs and causes pain and swelling) and certain other rheumatologic conditions (conditions in which the immune system attacks parts of the body). Nonprescription aspirin is used to reduce fever and to relieve mild to moderate pain from headaches, menstrual periods, arthritis, colds, toothaches, and muscle aches. Nonprescription aspirin is also used to prevent heart attacks in people who have had a heart attack in the past or who have angina (chest pain that occurs when the heart does not get enough oxygen). Nonprescription aspirin is also used to reduce the risk of death in people who are experiencing or who have recently experienced a heart attack. Nonprescription aspirin is also used to prevent ischemic strokes (strokes that occur when a blood clot blocks the flow of blood to the brain) or mini-strokes (strokes that occur when the flow of blood to the brain is blocked for a short time) in people who have had this type of stroke or mini-stroke in the past. Aspirin will not prevent hemorrhagic strokes (strokes caused by bleeding in the brain). Aspirin is in a group of medications called salicylates. It works by stopping the production of certain natural substances that cause fever, pain, swelling, and blood clots. Aspirin is also available in combination with other medications such as antacids, pain relievers, and cough and cold medications.

Prescription aspirin comes as an extended-release tablet (tablet that releases medication slowly over a period of time). Nonprescription aspirin comes as a regular tablet, an enteric-coated, delayed-release tablet (tablet that first begins to release medication some time after it is taken), a chewable tablet, powder, and a gum to take by mouth and a suppository to use rectally. Prescription aspirin is usually taken two or more times a day. Nonprescription aspirin is usually taken once a day to lower the risk of a heart attack or stroke, or taken every 4 to 6 hours as needed to treat fever or pain.

Aspirin is also sometimes used to treat rheumatic fever (a serious condition that may develop after a strep throat infection and may cause swelling of the heart valves) and Kawasaki disease (an illness that may cause heart problems in children). Aspirin is also sometimes used to lower the risk of blood clots in patients who have artificial

KEY TERMS

Aspirin - Is used to relieve the symptoms of rheumatoid arthritis, to reduce fever and to relieve mild to moderate pain from headaches, menstrual periods, arthritis, colds, toothaches, and muscle aches.

heart valves or certain other heart conditions and to prevent certain complications of pregnancy.

Acetaminophen (Tylenol)[6]

Acetaminophen (Tylenol) is used to relieve mild to moderate pain from headaches, muscle aches, menstrual periods, colds and sore throats, toothaches, backaches, and reactions to vaccinations (shots), and to reduce fever. Acetaminophen may also be used to relieve the pain of osteoarthritis (arthritis caused by the breakdown of the lining of the joints). Acetaminophen is in a class of medications called analgesics (pain relievers) and antipyretics (fever reducers). It works by changing the way the body senses pain and by cooling the body.

Acetaminophen comes as a tablet, chewable tablet, capsule, suspension or solution (liquid), drops (concentrated liquid), powder, extended-release (long-acting) tablet, and orally disintegrating tablet (tablet that dissolves quickly in the mouth). Acetaminophen also comes as a suppository to use rectally. Acetaminophen is available without a prescription, but a doctor may prescribe acetaminophen to treat certain conditions. Taking more than the recommended amount may cause damage to the liver.

Acetaminophen comes in combination with other medications to treat cough and cold symptoms. A doctor or pharmacist should be asked for advice on which product is best for specific symptoms. Nonprescription cough and cold product labels should be carefully checked before using two or more products at the same time. These products may contain the same active ingredient(s) and taking them together could cause an overdose. This is especially important if giving cough and cold medications to a child.

Acetaminophen may also be used in combination with aspirin and caffeine to relieve the pain associated with migraine headache.

Acetaminophen may cause side effects. Some side effects can be serious and include:

- Rash
- Hives
- Itching
- Swelling of the face, throat, tongue, lips, eyes, hands, feet, ankles, or lower legs
- Hoarseness
- Difficulty breathing or swallowing

KEY TERMS

Acetaminophen (Tylenol) - Is used to relieve mild to moderate pain from headaches, muscle aches, menstrual periods, colds and sore throats, toothaches, backaches, and reactions to vaccinations (shots), and to reduce fever.

REYE SYNDROME[7]

Reye syndrome is a rare illness that can affect the blood, liver and brain of someone who recently had a viral infection. It always follows another illness. Although it mostly affects children and teens, anyone can get it. It can develop quickly and without warning. It is most common during flu season. Symptoms include:

- Nausea and vomiting
- Listlessness
- Personality change - such as irritability, combativeness or confusion
- Delirium
- Convulsions
- Loss of consciousness

If these symptoms occur soon after a viral illness, seek medical attention immediately. Reye syndrome can lead to a coma and brain death, so quick diagnosis and treatment are critical. Treatment focuses on preventing brain damage. There is no cure. The cause of Reye syndrome is unknown.

Shutterstock © StockLite, 2011. Under license from Shutterstock, Inc.

Cough and cold medications are some of the most commonly abused over-the-counter (OTC) medications.

ABUSE OF LAXATIVES[9]

The common belief that people must have a daily bowel movement has led to self-medicating with over-the-counter (OTC) laxative products. Although people may feel relief when they use laxatives, typically they must increase the dose over time because the body grows reliant on laxatives in order to have a bowel movement. As a result, laxatives may become habit-forming.

HERBAL MEDICINE[10]

An **herb** is a plant or plant part used for its scent, flavor or therapeutic properties. Herbal medicine products are dietary supplements that people take to improve their health. Many herbs have been used for a long time for claimed health benefits. They are sold as tablets, capsules, powders, teas, extracts and fresh or dried plants. However, some can cause health problems, some are not effective and some may interact with other drugs you are taking.

KEY TERMS

Reye syndrome - Is a rare illness that can affect the blood, liver and brain of someone who recently had a viral infection.
Herb - A plant or plant part used for its scent, flavor or therapeutic properties.

Shutterstock © rebvi, 2011. Under license from Shutterstock, Inc.

Herbal medicine products are dietary supplements that people take to improve their health.

To use an herbal product as safely as possible:

- Consult your doctor first
- Do not take a bigger dose than the label recommends
- Take it under the guidance of a trained medical professional
- Be especially cautious if you are pregnant or nursing

POPULAR HERBAL REMEDIES AND DIETARY SUPPLEMENTS

Garlic[11]

Garlic's most common uses as a dietary supplement are for high cholesterol, heart disease, and high blood pressure. Garlic is also used to prevent certain types of cancer, including stomach and colon cancers.

Garlic cloves can be eaten raw or cooked. They may also be dried or powdered and used in tablets and capsules. Raw garlic cloves can be used to make oils and liquid extracts.

Garlic appears to be safe for most adults but there are some side effects:

- breath and body odor
- heartburn
- upset stomach
- allergic reactions

Ginkgo[12]

Common name is Ginkgo Biloba. Ginkgo leaf extract has been used to treat a variety of ailments and conditions, including asthma, bronchitis, fatigue, and tinnitus (ringing or roaring sounds in the ears).

Today, people use ginkgo leaf extracts hoping to improve memory; to treat or help prevent Alzheimer's disease and other types of dementia; to decrease intermittent claudication (leg pain caused by narrowing arteries); and to treat sexual dysfunction, multiple sclerosis, tinnitus, and other health conditions. Extracts are usually taken from the ginkgo leaf and are used to make tablets, capsules, or teas. Occasionally, ginkgo extracts are used in skin products.

Side effects of ginkgo may include headache, nausea, gastrointestinal upset, diarrhea, dizziness, or allergic skin reactions.

St. John's Wort[13]

St. John's wort has been used for centuries to treat mental disorders and nerve pain. St. John's wort has also been used as a sedative and a treatment for malaria, as well as a balm for wounds, burns, and insect bites. Today, St. John's wort is used by some for depression, anxiety, and/or sleep disorders.

The flowering tops of St. John's wort are used to prepare teas, tablets, and capsules containing concentrated extracts. Liquid extracts and topical preparations are also used.

The side effects for St. John's wort may cause increased sensitivity to sunlight. Other side effects can include anxiety, dry mouth, dizziness, gastrointestinal symptoms, fatigue, headache, or sexual dysfunction.

Green Tea[14]

Green tea and green tea extracts have been used to prevent and treat a variety of cancers, including breast, stomach, and skin cancers. Green tea and green tea extracts have also been used for improving mental alertness, aiding in weight loss, lowering cholesterol levels, and protecting skin from sun damage. Green tea is usually brewed and drunk as a beverage. Green tea extracts can be taken in capsules and are sometimes used in skin products.

Green tea is safe for most adults when used in moderate amounts. There have been some case reports of liver problems in people taking concentrated green tea extracts. This problem does not seem to be connected with green tea infusions or beverages. Green tea and green tea extracts contain caffeine.

HELPING SOMEONE SUSPECTED OF ABUSING PRESCRIPTION AND OTC DRUGS[4]

When someone has a drug problem, it's not always easy to know what to do. Someone whose drug use (illicit or prescription) is concerning should be encouraged to talk to a parent, school guidance counselor, or other trusted adult. There are also anonymous resources, such as the National Suicide Prevention Lifeline (1-800-273-TALK) and the Treatment Referral Helpline (1-800-662-HELP).

The National Suicide Prevention Lifeline (1-800-273-TALK) is a crisis hotline that can help with many problems, not just suicide. This includes problems caused by drug use. Family members and friends who are concerned about a loved one or anyone interested in mental health treatment referrals can call this Lifeline. Callers are connected with a professional nearby who will talk with them about what they're feeling or about concerns for family and friends.

In addition, the Treatment Referral Helpline (1-800-662-HELP) offered by the Substance Abuse and Mental Health Services Administration's Center for Substance Abuse Treatment refers callers to treatment facilities, support groups, and other local organizations that can provide help for their specific needs. Treatment centers can also be located by state by going to www.findtreatment.samhsa.gov.

REFERENCES

1. National Institute on Drug Abuse (NIDA). Prescription Drug Abuse 2011. http://www.nida.nih.gov/tib/prescription.html.
2. Facts on prescription and over-the-counter drugs. NIDA. September 2009. http://teens.drugabuse.gov/peerx/pdf/PEERx_Toolkit_FactSheets_RxDrugs.pdf. Accessed April 23, 2011.
3. Prescription drug abuse. National Institute on Drug Abuse (NIDA). NIDA for Teens. 2010. http://teens.drugabuse.gov/facts/facts_rx1.php. Accessed April 23, 2011.
4. Prescription drug abuse. NIDA for Teens. 2009. http://teens.drugabuse.gov/facts/facts_rx2.php. Accessed April 23, 2011.
5. National Institute on Health (NIH), Aspirin, 2011. http://www.nlm.nih.gov/medlineplus/druginfo/meds/a682878.html#why
6. National Institute on Health (NIH), Acetaminophen, 2011. http://www.nlm.nih.gov/medlineplus/druginfo/meds/a681004.html#why
7. National Institute on Health (NIH), Reye syndrome, 2011. http://www.nlm.nih.gov/medlineplus/reyesyndrome.html
8. National Institute on Drug Abuse (NIDA). Prescription Drug Abuse, 2009. http://teens.drugabuse.gov/facts/facts_rx2.php
9. National Institute on Health (NIH), Constipation, 2011. http://digestive.niddk.nih.gov/ddiseases/pubs/constipation/Constipation.pdf
10. National Institute on Health (NIH), Herbal Medicine, 2011. http://www.nlm.nih.gov/medlineplus/herbalmedicine.html
11. National Institute on Health (NIH), Garlic, 2011. http://www.nlm.nih.gov/medlineplus/herbalmedicine.html
12. National Institute on Health (NIH), Ginkgo, 2011. http://nccam.nih.gov/health/ginkgo/ataglance.htm#intro
13. National Institute on Health (NIH), St. John's Wort, 2011. http://nccam.nih.gov/health/stjohnswort/ataglance.htm
14. National Institute on Health (NIH), Green Tea, 2011. http://nccam.nih.gov/health/greentea/index.htm#uses.

CHAPTER 15

Performance-Enhancing Drugs

Shutterstock © Carsten Medom Madsen, 2011. Under license from Shutterstock, Inc.

OBJECTIVES

After you have finished this chapter, you should be able to:

- define Performance-enhancing drugs,
- define and explain anabolic steroids,
- list the most common anabolic-androgenic steroids,
- describe how steroids are used,
- describe the effects of steroids use,
- describe cycling, stacking and pyramiding,
- list the most common dietary supplements,

"Steroids are for guys who want to cheat opponents."

-Lawrence Taylor

Ever wondered how those bulky weight lifters got so big?

Shutterstock © Valua Vitaly, 2011. Under license from Shutterstock, Inc.

PERFORMANCE ENHANCING DRUGS

Performance-enhancing drugs are drugs that are injected or taken orally by athletes to increase strength and endurance.[1]

During the 1930s, scientists discovered that anabolic steroids could facilitate the growth of skeletal muscle in laboratory animals, which led to abuse of the compounds first by bodybuilders and weightlifters and then by athletes in other sports. Steroid abuse has become so widespread in athletics that it can affect the outcome of sports contests.

Illicit steroids are often sold at gyms, competitions, and through mail order operations after being smuggled into this country. Most illegal steroids in the United States are smuggled from countries that do not require a prescription for the purchase of steroids. Steroids are also illegally diverted from U.S. pharmacies or synthesized in clandestine laboratories.[3]

ANABOLIC STEROIDS

Ever wondered how those bulky weight lifters got so big? Although some may have gotten their muscles through a strict regimen of weightlifting and diet, others may have gotten that way through the illegal use of anabolic-androgenic steroids. **"Anabolic"** refers to a steroid's ability to help build muscle and **"androgenic"** refers to its role in promoting the development of male sexual characteristics. Other types of steroids, like cortisol, estrogen, and progesterone, do not build muscle, are not anabolic, and therefore do not have the same harmful effects.

Anabolic-androgenic steroids are usually synthetic substances similar to the male sex hormone testosterone. They do have legitimate medical uses. Sometimes doctors prescribe them to help people with certain kinds of anemia and men who don't produce enough testosterone on their own. But doctors never prescribe anabolic steroids to young, healthy people to help them build muscle. Without a prescription from a doctor, anabolic steroids are illegal.[2]

KEY TERMS

Performance-enhancing drugs - Are drugs that are injected or taken orally by athletes to increase strength and endurance.
"Anabolic" - Refers to a steroid's ability to help build muscle.
"Androgenic" - Refers to its role in promoting the development of male sexual characteristics.

There are many different anabolic-androgenic steroids. Here's a list of some of the most common ones taken today:

Oral Steroids

- Anadrol (oxymetholone)
- Dianabol (methandrostenolone)
- Oxandrin (oxandrolone)
- Winstrol (stanozolol)

Injectable Steroids

- Deca-Durabolin (nandrolone decanoate)
- Depo-Testosterone (testosterone cypionate)
- Durabolin (nandrolone phenpropionate)
- Equipoise (boldenone undecylenate)3

Common Street Names[2]

Slang words for steroids are hard to find. Most people just say steroids. On the street, steroids may be called "roids" or "juice."

How Are They Used?[2]

Some steroid users pop pills. Others use hypodermic needles to inject steroids directly into muscles. When users take drugs without regard for their legality or their adverse health effects they are called **"abusers."** Steroid abusers have been known to take doses ten to 100 times higher than the amount prescribed by a doctor for medical reasons.

The Effects[2]

A major health consequence from abusing anabolic steroids can include prematurely stunted growth through early skeletal maturation and accelerated puberty changes. This means that teens risk remaining short for the remainder of their lives if they take anabolic steroids before they stop growing. Other effects include jaundice (yellowish coloring of skin, tissues, and body fluids), fluid retention, high blood pressure, increases in **LDL** (bad cholesterol), decreases in **HDL** (good cholesterol), severe acne, trembling, and in very rare cases, liver and kidney tumors. In addition, there are some gender-specific side effects:

- Males can exhibit shrinking of the testicles, reduced sperm count, infertility, baldness, breast development, and an increased risk for prostate cancer.

KEY TERMS

"Abusers" - When users take drugs without regard for their legality or their adverse health effects.
LDL - Low-density lipoprotein (bad cholesterol).
HDL - High-Density Lipoproteins (good cholesterol).

- Females can exhibit growth of facial hair, male-pattern baldness, changes in or cessation of the menstrual cycle, enlargement of the clitoris, and a permanently deepened voice.

Steroid abuse also can have an effect on behavior. Many users report feeling good about themselves while on anabolic steroids, but researchers report that extreme mood swings also can occur, including manic-like symptoms leading to violence. This is because anabolic steroids act in a part of the brain called the limbic system, which influences mood and also is involved in learning and memory.

Steroids also can cause other changes in mood, such as feelings of depression or irritability. Depression, which can be life-threatening, often is seen when the drugs are stopped and may contribute to the continued use of anabolic steroids.

Are Anabolic Steroids Addictive?[2]

It is possible that some steroid abusers may become addicted to the drugs, as evidenced by their continued use in spite of physical problems and negative effects on social relationships. Also, they spend large amounts of time and money obtaining the drugs and, when they stop using them, they experience withdrawal symptoms such as depression, mood swings, fatigue, restlessness, loss of appetite, insomnia, reduced sex drive, and the desire to take more steroids.

Can Steroid Abuse Be Fatal?[2]

Fact

Steroids are not friendly to the heart. In rare cases steroid abuse can create a situation where the body may be susceptible to heart attacks and strokes, which can be fatal.

In some rare cases yes. When steroids enter the body, they go to different organs and muscles. Steroids are not friendly to the heart. In rare cases steroid abuse can create a situation where the body may be susceptible to heart attacks and strokes, which can be fatal. Here's how: Steroid use can lead to a condition called atherosclerosis, which causes fat deposits inside arteries to disrupt blood flow. When blood flow to the heart is blocked, a heart attack can occur. If blood flow to the brain is blocked, a stroke can result.

Cycling, stacking and pyramiding[3]

Steroids are often abused in patterns called **"cycling,"** which involve taking multiple doses of steroids over a specific period of time, stopping for a period, and starting again. Users also frequently combine several different types of steroids in a process known as **"stacking."** Steroid abusers typically "stack" the drugs, meaning that they take two or more different anabolic steroids, mixing oral and/or injectable types,

KEY TERMS

"Cycling" - Involves taking multiple doses of steroids over a specific period of time, stopping for a period, and starting again.
"Stacking" - Combining several different types of steroids.

and sometimes even including compounds that are designed for veterinary use. Abusers think that the different steroids interact to produce an effect on muscle size that is greater than the effects of each drug individually, a theory that has not been tested scientifically. Another mode of steroid abuse is referred to as **"pyramiding."** This is a process in which users slowly escalate steroid abuse (increasing the number of steroids or the dose and frequency of one or more steroids used at one time), reaching a peak amount at mid-cycle and gradually tapering the dose toward the end of the cycle. Often, steroid abusers pyramid their doses in cycles of 6 to 12 weeks. At the beginning of a cycle, the person starts with low doses of the drugs being stacked and then slowly increases the doses. In the second half of the cycle, the doses are slowly decreased to zero. This is sometimes followed by a second cycle in which the person continues to train but without drugs. Abusers believe that pyramiding allows the body time to adjust to the high doses.

Shutterstock © Richard Paul Kane, 2011. Under license from Shutterstock, Inc.

At least half of the individuals arrested for major crimes including homicide, theft, assault, and domestic violence were under the influence of illicit drugs around the time of their arrest.

CREATINE[4]

Creatine is a naturally occurring compound in the body made from amino acids that supplies energy to muscles. Creatine is also found in meat and fish. The use of creatine supplements by athletes became popular in the 1990s as a way to reportedly enhance athletic performance and build lean muscle mass. Today, creatine remains one of the more widely used supplements by athletes, particularly among adolescents.

DIETARY SUPPLEMENTS[5]

The majority of adults in the United States take one or more dietary supplements either every day or occasionally. Today's **dietary supplements** include vitamins, minerals, herbals and botanicals, amino acids, enzymes, and many other products. Dietary supplements come in a variety of forms: traditional tablets, capsules, and powders, as well as drinks and energy bars. Popular supplements include vitamins D and E; minerals like calcium and iron; herbs such as echinacea and garlic; and specialty products like glucosamine, probiotics, and fish oils.

KEY TERMS

"Pyramiding" - A process in which users slowly escalate steroid abuse.
Creatine - A naturally occurring compound in the body made from amino acids that supplies energy to muscles.
Dietary supplements - Include vitamins, minerals, herbals and botanicals, amino acids, enzymes, and many other products.

Shutterstock © Laurin Rinder, 2011. Under license from Shutterstock, Inc.

Most prevention efforts in the United States today focus on athletes involved with the Olympics and professional sports.

The Dietary Supplement Label[5]

All products labeled as a dietary supplement carry a Supplement Facts panel that lists the contents, amount of active ingredients per serving, and other added ingredients (like fillers, binders, and flavorings). The manufacturer suggests the serving size, but you or your health care provider might decide that a different amount is more appropriate for you.

Effectiveness[5]

If you don't eat a nutritious variety of foods, some supplements might help you get adequate amounts of essential nutrients. However, supplements can't take the place of the variety of foods that are important to a healthy diet.

Safety and Risk[5]

Many supplements contain active ingredients that can have strong effects in the body. Always be alert to the possibility of unexpected side effects, especially when taking a new product.

Supplements are most likely to cause side effects or harm when people take them instead of prescribed medicines or when people take many supplements in combination. Some supplements can increase the risk of bleeding or, if a person takes them before or after surgery, they can affect the person's response to anesthesia. Dietary supplements can also interact with certain prescription drugs in ways that might cause problems. Caution should be taken ingesting dietary supplements during pregnancy or nursing. Also, care should be taken when giving them (beyond a basic multivitamin/mineral product) to a child. Most dietary supplements have not been well tested for safety in pregnant women, nursing mothers, or children.

WHAT CAN BE DONE TO PREVENT STEROID ABUSE?[6]

Most prevention efforts in the United States today focus on athletes involved with the Olympics and professional sports; few school districts test for abuse of illicit drugs. It has been estimated that close to nine percent of secondary schools conduct some sort of drug testing program, presumably focused on athletes, and that less than four percent of the nation's high schools test their athletes for steroids. Studies are currently underway to determine whether such testing reduces drug abuse.
Research on steroid educational programs has shown that simply teaching students about steroids' adverse effects does not convince adolescents that they can be adversely affected. Nor does such instruction discourage young people from taking

steroids in the future. Presenting both the risks and benefits of anabolic steroid use is more effective in convincing adolescents about steroids' negative effects, apparently because the students find a balanced approach more credible, according to researchers.

WHAT TREATMENTS ARE EFFECTIVE FOR ANABOLIC STEROID ABUSE?[6]

Few studies of treatments for anabolic steroid abuse have been conducted. Current knowledge is based largely on the experiences of a small number of physicians who have worked with patients undergoing steroid withdrawal. The physicians have found that supportive therapy is sufficient in some cases. Patients are educated about what they may experience during withdrawal and are evaluated for suicidal thoughts. If symptoms are severe or prolonged, medications or hospitalization may be needed.

Some medications that have been used for treating steroid withdrawal restore the hormonal system after its disruption by steroid abuse. Other medications target specific withdrawal symptoms; for example, antidepressants to treat depression and analgesics for headaches and muscle and joint pains.

PREVENTING STEROID ABUSE[3]

A more sophisticated approach has shown promise for preventing steroid abuse among players on high school sports teams. The Adolescents Training and Learning to Avoid Steroids (ATLAS) program is showing high school football players that they do not need steroids to build powerful muscles and improve athletic performance. By educating student athletes about the harmful effects of anabolic steroids and providing nutrition and weight-training alternatives to steroid use, the ATLAS program has increased football players' healthy behaviors and reduced their intentions to abuse steroids. In the program, coaches and team leaders teach the harmful effects of anabolic steroids and other illicit drugs on immediate sports performance, and discuss how to refuse offers of drugs.

The Athletes Targeting Healthy Exercise and Nutrition Alternatives (ATHENA) program was patterned after the ATLAS program, but designed for adolescent girls on sports teams. Results of the ATHENA program showed significant decreases in risky behaviors. In addition, ATHENA team members were less likely to be sexually active, more likely to wear seatbelts, less likely to ride in a car with a driver who had been drinking, and they experienced fewer injuries during the sports season.

The primary reason why girls use steroids is to lose fat and gain lean muscle.

***Adolescent Girls Abuse Steroids, Too*[7]**

What do anabolic steroids have in common with amphetamines, tobacco, diet pills, laxatives, and anorectics? They all are drugs used by adolescent girls seeking to stay thin. The use of these drugs, which often goes hand in hand with eating disorders, is particularly prominent among adolescent girls engaged in athletic activities ranging from track and field, soccer, basketball, and volleyball to school dance and drill teams.

The primary reason that these girls use steroids is to lose fat and gain lean muscle.

REFERENCES

1. The National Institute on Drug Abuse (NIDA). Performance-enhancing drugs are drugs that are injected or taken orally. Module 6 Drugs in the News, 2007 http://www.drugabuse.gov/JSP4/MOD6/Mod6.pdf
2. The National Institute on Drug Abuse (NIDA). NIDA for Teens: Anabolic Steroids, 2009. http://teens.drugabuse.gov/facts/facts_ster1.php. Accessed April 23, 2011.
3. Research Report Series: Anabolic Steroids Abuse. The National Institute on Drug Abuse (NIDA). Research Report Series: Anabolic Steroids Abuse. 2007.www.drugabuse.gov/PDF/RRSteroids.pdf
4. National Institute on Health (NIH), Creatine, 2011. http://nccam.nih.gov/health/creatine/
5. National Institute on Health (NIH), Dietary supplements, 2011. ods.od.nih.gov/pubs/DS_WhatYouNeedToKnow.pdf
6. Research Report Series - Are anabolic steroids addictive? The National Institute on Drug Abuse (NIDA). 2009. http://www.nida.nih.gov/ResearchReports/Steroids/anabolicsteroids5.html. Accessed April 23, 2011.
7. The National Institute on Drug Abuse (NIDA). Nida Notes. Anabolic Steroids Abuse, 2009. www.drugabuse.gov/PDF/NNCollections/NNSteroids.pdf

CHAPTER 16

Drug Abuse Prevention

Shutterstock © tacie Stauff Smith Photography, 2011. Under license from Shutterstock, Inc.

OBJECTIVES

After you have finished this chapter, you should be able to:

- define and explain drug abuse prevention;
- list the early signs of risk that may predict later drug abuse;
- define and explain universal, selective, and indicated programs;
- define and explain family, school, and community programs;
- list the three-tier prevention programs;
- describe the BACCHUS network;
- describe the D.A.R.E. program;
- list the Universal Programs,
- describe the HIV prevention program.

"Offer hugs, not drugs."

-Adina Lebowitz

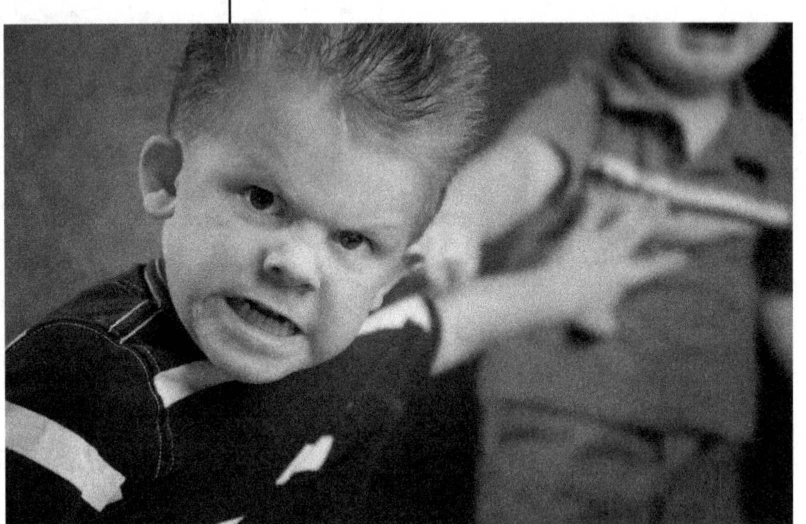

Shutterstock © Cresta Johnson, 2011. Under license from Shutterstock, Inc.

DRUG ABUSE PREVENTION[1]

Each year, drug abuse and addiction cost taxpayers billions in preventable health care, law enforcement, crime, and other costs. The key word in this assessment is "preventable." The best approach to reducing the tremendous toll substance abuse exacts from individuals, families, and communities is to prevent the damage before it occurs.

Signs of risk can be seen as early as infancy or early childhood, such as aggressive behavior, lack of self-control, or difficult temperament.

Early Signs of Risk that May Predict Later Drug Abuse[2]

Some signs of risk can be seen as early as infancy or early childhood, such as aggressive behavior, lack of self-control, or difficult temperament. As the child gets older, interactions with family, at school, and within the community can affect that child's risk for later drug abuse.

Children's earliest interactions occur in the family; sometimes family situations heighten a child's risk for later drug abuse; for example, when there is:

- a lack of attachment and nurturing by parents or caregivers
- ineffective parenting
- a caregiver who abuses drugs

Interactions outside the family can involve risks for both children and adolescents, such as:

- poor classroom behavior or social skills
- academic failure
- association with drug-abusing peers

Families can provide protection from later drug abuse when there is:

- a strong bond between children and parents
- parental involvement in the child's life
- clear limits and consistent enforcement of discipline

Drug availability, drug trafficking, and toleration of drug abuse are other risks factors that can influence young people to start abusing drugs. Gender, ethnicity, and geographic location also can play a role in how and when children begin abusing drugs.

Children's first big transition is when they leave the security of the family and enter school. Later, when they advance from elementary school to middle school, they often experience new academic and social situations, such as learning to get along with a wider group of peers. It is at this stage of early adolescence that children are likely to encounter drugs for the first time.

When they enter high school, adolescents face additional social, emotional, and educational challenges. At the same time, they may be exposed to greater availability of drugs, drug abusers, and social activities involving drugs. These challenges can increase the risk that they will abuse alcohol, tobacco, and other substances.

When young adults leave home for college or work and are on their own for the first time, their risk for abusing alcohol, tobacco, and other drugs is very high. Consequently, young adult interventions are needed as well.

Some children are already abusing drugs at age twelve or thirteen, which likely means that some begin even earlier. Early abuse often includes such substances as tobacco, alcohol, inhalants, marijuana, and prescription drugs such as sleeping pills and anti-anxiety medicines. If drug abuse persists into later adolescence, abusers typically become more heavily involved with marijuana and then advance to other drugs, while continuing their abuse of tobacco and alcohol.

How are risk and protective factors addressed in prevention programs?[3]

Prevention programs are usually designed to reach target populations in their primary setting. However, in recent years it has become more common to find programs for any given target group in a variety of settings, such as holding a family-based program in a school or a church. In addition to setting, prevention programs also can be described by the audience for which they are designed:

- **Universal programs.** Designed for the general population, such as all students in a school.
- **Selective programs.** Target groups at risk or subsets of the general population, such as poor school achievers or children of drug abusers.
- **Indicated programs.** Designed for people already experimenting with drugs.

PREVENTION PROGRAMS[2]

The family prevention programs can strengthen protective factors among young children by teaching parents better family communication skills, appropriate discipline styles, firm and consistent rule enforcement, and other family management approaches. Research confirms the benefits of parents providing consistent rules and discipline, talking to children about drugs, monitoring their activities, getting to know their friends, understanding their problems and concerns, and being involved in their learning. The importance of the parent-child relationship continues through adolescence and beyond.

The school prevention programs focus on children's social and academic skills, including enhancing peer relationships, self-control, coping, and drug-refusal

Shutterstock © Andre Blais, 2011. Under license from Shutterstock, Inc.

In family prevention the importance of the parent-child relationship continues through adolescence and beyond.

skills. If possible, school-based prevention programs should be integrated into the school's academic program, because school failure is strongly associated with drug abuse. Integrated programs strengthen students' bonding to school and reduce their likelihood of dropping out. Other types of interventions include school-wide programs that affect the school environment as a whole.

The community prevention programs work at the community level with civic, religious, law enforcement, and other government organizations to enhance anti-drug norms and pro-social behaviors. Many programs coordinate prevention efforts across settings to communicate consistent messages through school, work, and religious institutions, as well as the media. Research has shown that programs that reach youth through multiple settings can strongly impact community norms. Community-based programs also typically include development of policies or enforcement of regulations, mass media efforts, and community-wide awareness programs.

Fact

Research has shown that programs that reach youth through multiple settings can strongly impact community norms.

Three-tier Drug Prevention Programs

The three-tier prevention programs are created for different levels of users. **Primary drug prevention programs** are aimed at the non-user, or those who have not started using drugs. This program is designed for at-risk groups of youth and families. **Secondary drug prevention programs** are aimed at the new users, those who have just started using drugs like alcohol and tobacco before they can move on to more dangerous substances. **Tertiary drug prevention programs** are aimed at people who are already drug dependent and need treatment.

Prevention Principles[4]

The following sixteen principles from the National Institute on Drug Abuse were developed to help prevention practitioners use the results of prevention research to

KEY TERMS

Primary drug prevention programs - Programs aimed at people who have not started using drugs, the non-user.
Secondary drug prevention programs - Programs aimed at people who have just started using drugs like alcohol and tobacco, the new users.
Tertiary drug prevention programs - Programs aimed at people who are already drug dependent and need treatment.

address drug use among children and adolescents in communities across the country. Some programs can be geared for more than one audience.

Principle 1 - Prevention programs should enhance protective factors and reverse or reduce risk factors (Hawkins et al. 2002).

- The risk of becoming a drug abuser involves the relationship among the number and type of risk factors (e.g., deviant attitudes and behaviors) and protective factors (e.g., parental support) (Wills et al. 1996).
- The potential impact of specific risk and protective factors changes with age. For example, risk factors within the family have greater impact on a younger child, while association with drug-abusing peers may be a more significant risk factor for an adolescent (Gerstein and Green 1993; Dishion et al. 1999).
- Early intervention with risk factors (e.g., aggressive behavior, poor self-control) often has a greater impact than later intervention by changing a child's life path (trajectory) away from problems and toward positive behaviors (Ialongo et al. 2001).
- While risk and protective factors can affect people of all groups, these factors can have a different effect depending on a person's age, gender, ethnicity, culture, and environment (Beauvais et al. 1996; Moon et al. 1999).

Principle 2 - Prevention programs should address all forms of drug abuse, alone or in combination, including the underage use of legal drugs (e.g., tobacco, alcohol); the use of illegal drugs (e.g., marijuana, heroin); and the inappropriate use of legally obtained substances (e.g., inhalants), prescription medications, or over-the-counter drugs (Johnston et al. 2002).

Principle 3 - Prevention programs should address the type of drug abuse problem in the local community, target modifiable risk factors, and strengthen identified protective factors (Hawkins et al. 2002).

Principle 4 - Prevention programs should be tailored to address risks specific to population or audience characteristics, such as age, gender, and ethnicity, to improve program effectiveness (Oetting et al. 1997).

Principle 5 - Family-based prevention programs should enhance family bonding and relationships and include parenting skills; practice in developing, discussing, and enforcing family policies on substance abuse; and training in drug education and information (Ashery et al. 1998).

Family bonding is the bedrock of the relationship between parents and children. Bonding can be strengthened through skills training on parent supportiveness of children, parent-child communication, and parental involvement (Kosterman et al. 1997).

Parental monitoring and supervision are critical for drug abuse prevention. These skills can be enhanced with training on rule-setting; techniques for monitoring activities; praise for appropriate behavior; and moderate, consistent discipline that enforces defined family rules (Kosterman et al. 2001).

- Drug education and information for parents or caregivers reinforces what children are learning about the harmful effects of drugs and opens opportunities for family discussions about the abuse of legal and illegal substances (Bauman et al. 2001).
- Brief, family-focused interventions for the general population can positively change specific parenting behavior that can reduce later risks of drug abuse (Spoth et al. 2002b).

Principle 6 - Prevention programs can be designed to intervene as early as preschool to address risk factors for drug abuse, such as aggressive behavior, poor social skills, and academic difficulties (Webster-Stratton 1998; Webster-Stratton et al. 2001).

Principle 7 - Prevention programs for elementary school children should target improving academic and social-emotional learning to address risk factors for drug abuse, such as early aggression, academic failure, and school dropout. Education should focus on the following skills (Conduct Problems Prevention Research Group 2002; Ialongo et al. 2001):

- self-control
- emotional awareness
- communication
- social problem-solving
- academic support, especially in reading

Principle 8 - Prevention programs for middle or junior high and high school students should increase academic and social competence with the following skills (Botvin et al. 1995; Scheier et al. 1999):

- study habits and academic support
- communication
- peer relationships
- self-efficacy and assertiveness
- drug resistance skills
- reinforcement of anti-drug attitudes
- strengthening of personal commitments against drug abuse

Principle 9 - Prevention programs aimed at general populations at key transition points, such as the transition to middle school, can produce beneficial effects even among high-risk families and children. Such interventions do not single out risk populations and, therefore, reduce labeling and promote bonding to school and community (Botvin et al. 1995; Dishion et al. 2002).

Principle 10 - Community prevention programs that combine two or more effective programs, such as family-based and school-based programs, can be more effective than a single program alone (Battistich et al. 1997).

Principle 11 - Community prevention programs reaching populations in multiple settings--for example, schools, clubs, faith-based organizations, and the media--are most effective when they present consistent, community-wide messages across settings (Chou et al. 1998).

Principle 12 - When communities adapt programs to match their needs, community norms, or differing cultural requirements, they should retain core elements of the original research-based intervention (Spoth et al. 2002b), which include the following:

- structure (how the program is organized and constructed)
- content (the information, skills, and strategies of the program)
- delivery (how the program is adapted, implemented, and evaluated)

Principle 13 - Prevention programs should be long-term with repeated interventions (i.e., booster programs) to reinforce the original prevention goals. Research shows that the benefits from middle school prevention programs diminish without follow-up programs in high school (Scheier et al. 1999).

Principle 14 - Prevention programs should include teacher training on good classroom management practices, such as rewarding appropriate student behavior. Such techniques help to foster students' positive behavior, achievement, academic motivation, and school bonding (Ialongo et al. 2001).

Principle 15 - Prevention programs are most effective when they employ interactive techniques, such as peer discussion groups and parent role-playing, that allow for active involvement in learning about drug abuse and reinforcing skills (Botvin et al. 1995).

Principle 16 - Research-based prevention programs can be cost-effective. Similar to earlier research, recent research shows that for each dollar invested in prevention, a savings of up to $10 in treatment for alcohol or other substance abuse can be seen (Aos et al. 2001; Hawkins et al. 1999; Pentz 1998; Spoth et al. 2002a).

OTHER PREVENTION PROGRAMS

BACCHUS/GAMMA Peer Education Network[5]

BACCHUS/GAMMA Peer Education Network, trains volunteer student leaders to implement a variety of awareness and educational programs and to serve as role

KEY TERMS

BACCHUS - Boosting Alcohol Consciousness Concerning the Health of University Students.
GAMMA - Greeks Advocating for Mature Management of Alcohol.

models for other students to emulate. This type of strategic intervention focuses on the group; it often uses peer-to-peer communication.

At the individual level activities may work to increase student awareness of alcohol-related problems, change individual attitudes and beliefs, and foster each student's determination to avoid high-risk drinking and to intervene to protect other students whose alcohol use has put them in danger. Typical activities may include educational efforts during freshman orientation, alcohol awareness weeks and other special events, and curriculum infusion, where faculty members introduce alcohol-related facts and issues into regular academic courses.

D.A.R.E. Program[6]

Traditional law enforcement could not control Los Angeles' growing drug and alcohol problems. To stem the growth, the police department developed a new program in cooperation with the Los Angeles Unified School District *Drug Abuse Resistance Education (D.A.R.E.).* **D.A.R.E.** is aimed at preventing youngsters from having their first drug experience and has spread quickly throughout the country and around the world. Officers representing 3,500 law enforcement agencies are trained to teach D.A.R.E. and in 1991 reached more than 5 million children.

Specially selected and trained uniformed police officers teach a prevention school curriculum once a week for 17 weeks.

The core lessons are to:

- inform students of alcohol and drug dangers,
- provide them with resistance and decision-making skills to combat peer pressure,
- build self-esteem,
- develop alternatives to drug use.

Initially the program targeted only 5th and 6th graders, but it quickly expanded to other grades. To become a D.A.R.E. instructor, officers complete a mandatory 80-hour training course.

UNIVERSAL PROGRAMS[7]

Project ALERT[7]

Project ALERT is a 2-year, universal program for middle school students, designed to reduce the onset and regular use of drugs among youth. It focuses on preventing the use of alcohol, tobacco, marijuana, and inhalants. Project ALERT Plus, an

KEY TERMS

D.A.R.E. - Drug Abuse Resistance Education.

Project ALERT - A 2-year, universal program for middle school students, designed to reduce the onset and regular use of drugs among youth.

enhanced version, has added a high school component, which is being tested in 45 rural communities.

Life Skills Training (LST)[7]

LST is a universal program for middle school students designed to address a wide range of risk and protective factors by teaching general personal and social skills, along with drug resistance skills and education. An elementary school version was recently developed and the LST booster program for high school students helps to retain the gains of the middle school program.

The Strengthening Families Program (SFP)[7]

SFP, is a universal and selective multi-component, family-focused prevention program, provides support for families with 6- to 11-year-olds. The program, which began as an effort to help drug-abusing parents improve their parenting skills and reduce their children's risk for subsequent problems, has shown success in elementary schools and communities.

Skills, Opportunity, And Recognition (SOAR)[7]

SOAR is a universal school-based intervention program for grades one through six seeks to reduce childhood risks for delinquency and drug abuse by enhancing protective factors. The multi-component intervention combines training for teachers, parents, and children during the elementary grades to promote children's bonding to school, positive school behavior, and academic achievement.

Project STAR[7]

Project STAR is a comprehensive drug abuse prevention community program to be used by schools, parents, community organizations, the media, and health policymakers. The middle school portion focuses on social influence and is included in classroom instruction by trained teachers over a 2-year timetable. The parent program helps parents work with children on homework, learn family communication skills, and get involved in community action.

KEY TERMS

Life Skills Training (LST) - A universal program for middle school students designed to address a wide range of risk and protective factors by teaching general personal and social skills, along with drug resistance skills and education.

The Strengthening Families Program (SFP) - A universal and selective multi-component, family-focused prevention program, provides support for families with 6- to 11-year-olds.

Skills, Opportunity, And Recognition (SOAR) - A universal school-based intervention program for grades one through six seeks to reduce childhood risks for delinquency and drug abuse by enhancing protective factors.

Project STAR - A comprehensive drug abuse prevention community program to be used by schools, parents, community organizations, the media, and health policymakers.

SELECTIVE PROGRAMS[7]

Coping Power[7]

Coping Power is a multi-component child and parent preventive intervention directed at pre-adolescent children at high risk for aggressiveness and later drug abuse and delinquency. The Coping Power Child Component is a program for fifth- and sixth-graders, usually in an after-school setting. Training teaches children how to identify and cope with anxiety and anger; control impulses; and develop social, academic, and problem-solving skills. Parents are also provided training.

Focus on Families (FOF) is a selective program for parents receiving methadone treatment and their children which seeks to reduce parents' use of illegal drugs and teaches family management skills to reduce their children's risk for future drug abuse. The promise of the FOF program—particularly for very high-risk families—is evident in the early reduction in family-related risk factors with an overall trend toward positive program effects on child outcomes.

INDICATED PROGRAMS[7]

Project Towards No Drug Abuse (Project TND)[7]

Project TND is an indicated prevention intervention program that targets high school age youth who attend alternative or traditional high schools. The goal is to prevent the transition from drug use to drug abuse, through considering the developmental issues faced by older teens.

Reconnecting Youth Program (RY)[7]

RY is a school-based indicated prevention program for high school students with poor school achievement and potential for dropping out. The program goals are to increase school performance, reduce drug use, and learn skills to manage mood and emotions.

KEY TERMS

Coping Power - A multi-component child and parent preventive intervention directed at pre-adolescent children at high risk for aggressiveness and later drug abuse and delinquency.

Project Towards No Drug Abuse (Project TND) - A indicated prevention intervention program that targets high school age youth who attend alternative or traditional high schools.

Reconnecting Youth Program (RY) - A school-based indicated prevention program for high school students with poor school achievement and potential for dropping out.

TIERED PROGRAMS[7]

Adolescent Transitions Program (ATP)[7]

ATP is a school-based program that uses a tiered approach to provide prevention services to students in middle and junior high school and their parents. The universal intervention directed to parents of all students in a school establishes a Family Resource Center. The selective intervention level, called the Family Check-Up, offers family assessment and professional support. The indicated level provides direct professional help to the family.

Early Risers "Skills for Success" Risk Prevention Program[7]

Early Risers is a selective, preventive intervention for elementary school children at heightened risk for early onset of serious conduct problems, including legal and illegal drug use. The program's focus is on improving academic ability, self-control, social skills, and parental involvement in the child's activities.

Drug Testing in Schools[8]

Schools that have adopted random student drug testing are hoping to decrease drug abuse among students via two routes. First, schools that conduct testing hope that random testing will serve as a deterrent and give students a reason to resist peer pressure to take drugs. Second, drug testing can identify adolescents who have started using drugs so that interventions can occur early, or identify adolescents who already have drug problems so they can be referred for treatment. Drug abuse not only interferes with a student's ability to learn, but it can also disrupt the teaching environment, affecting other students as well.

In June 2002, the U.S. Supreme Court broadened the authority of public schools to test students for illegal drugs. Voting five to four in *Pottawatomie County v. Earls,* the court ruled to allow random drug tests for all middle and high school students participating in competitive extracurricular activities. The ruling greatly expanded the scope of school drug testing, which previously had been allowed only for student athletes.

In June 2002, the U.S. Supreme Court broadened the authority of public schools to test students for illegal drugs.

Drug Testing[8]

There are several testing methods available that use urine, hair, oral fluids, and sweat (patch). These methods vary in cost, reliability, drugs detected, and detection period. Schools can determine their needs and choose the method that best suits their

KEY TERMS

Adolescent Transitions Program (ATP) - A school-based program that uses a tiered approach to provide prevention services to students in middle and junior high school and their parents.

Early Risers "Skills for Success" Risk Prevention Program - A selective, preventive intervention for elementary school children at heightened risk for early onset of serious conduct problems, including legal and illegal drug use.

Shutterstock © emin kyuliyev, 2011. Under license from Shutterstock, Inc.

There are several testing methods available that use urine, hair, oral fluids, and sweat (patch).

requirements, as long as the testing kits are from a reliable source.

HIV Prevention[9]

Drug users should be advised that stopping all drug use, including drug injection, is the most effective way to reduce their risks for contracting HIV/AIDS and other blood borne diseases, including hepatitis B and hepatitis C. However, not every drug user is ready to stop using drugs, and many of those who stop may relapse.

A variety of HIV/AIDS prevention strategies to protect against becoming infected are available for individuals who may be considering or already injecting drugs. These are described in a hierarchy of HIV/AIDS risk-reduction messages, beginning with the most effective behavioral changes that drug users can make:

- Stop using and injecting drugs.
- Enter and complete drug abuse treatment, including relapse prevention.
- If a person continues to inject drugs, they should take the following steps to reduce personal and public health risks:
    - Never re-use or "share" syringes, water, or drug preparation equipment.
    - Use only sterile syringes obtained from a reliable source (e.g., a pharmacy or a syringe access program).
    - Always use a new, sterile syringe to prepare and inject drugs.
    - If possible, use sterile water to prepare drugs; otherwise use clean water from a reliable source (e.g., fresh tap water)
    - Always use a new or disinfected container ("cooker") and a new filter("cotton") to prepare drugs.
    - Clean the injection site with a new alcohol swab before injecting drugs.
    - Safely dispose of syringes after one use.

The risk and protective factors are the primary targets of effective prevention programs used in family, school, and community settings. The goal of these programs is to build new and strengthen existing protective factors and reverse or reduce risk factors in children and adolescents. If not addressed, negative behaviors can lead to more risks, such as academic failure and social difficulties, which put children at further risk for later drug abuse. An important goal of prevention is to change the balance between risk and protective factors so that protective factors outweigh risk factors.

REFERENCES

1. The National Institute on Drug Abuse (NIDA).Drug Abuse Prevention, 2007. http://drugabuse.gov/tib/prevention.html
2. The National Institute on Drug Abuse (NIDA). Preventing drug abuse among children and adolescents, 2007. http://www.nida.nih.gov/prevention/risk.html. Accessed April 23, 2011.
3. The National Institute on Drug Abuse (NIDA). How are risk and protective factors addressed in prevention programs? http://www.nida.nih.gov/prevention/applying.html
4. The National Institute on Drug Abuse (NIDA). NIDA InfoFacts: Lessons from Prevention Research, 2004. http://www.nida.nih.gov/infofacts/lessons.html
5. NIAAA. How To Reduce High-Risk College Drinking: Use Proven Strategies, Fill Research Gaps, 2005. http://www.collegedrinkingprevention.gov/NIAAACollegeMaterials/Panel02/Appendix_02.aspx.
6. U.S. Department of Health and Human Services (HHS).OFFICE OF. INSPECTOR GENERAL. YOUTH AND ALCOHOL: A SAMPLE OF ENFORCEMENT. AND PREVENTION PROGRAMS, 1991. http://oig.hhs.gov/oei/reports/oei-09-91-00656.pdf
7. The National Institute on Drug Abuse (NIDA). Examples of Research-Based Drug Abuse Prevention Programs. http://www.nida.nih.gov/prevention/examples.html
8. Frequently asked questions about drug testing in schools. NIDA. 2007. http://www.nida.nih.gov/drugpages/testingfaqs.html. Accessed April 23, 2011.
9. Principles of HIV prevention in drug-using populations, NIDA. 2009. http://archives.drugabuse.gov/POHP/FAQ_1.html. Accessed April 23, 2011.

CHAPTER 17

Drug Abuse Treatment

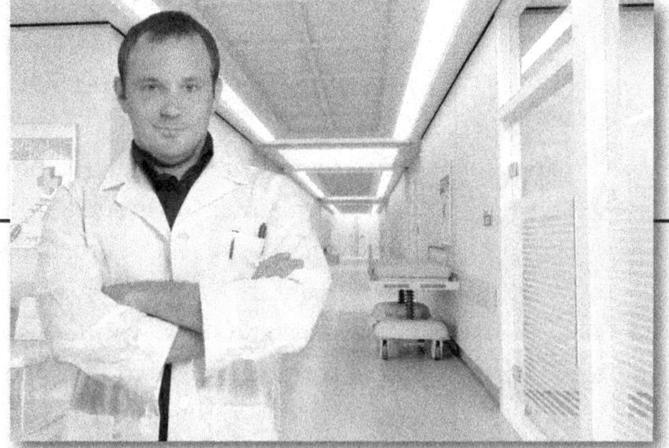
Shutterstock © Franck Boston, 2011. Under license from Shutterstock, Inc.

OBJECTIVES

After you have finished this chapter, you should be able to

- define and explain drug abuse treatment,
- list the types of drug abuse treatment,
- define and explain Alcoholics Anonymous,
- define and explain Al-Anon/Alateen,
- describe the Matrix Model,
- describe the motivational enhancement therapy,
- describe the multisystem therapy,
- describe the multidimensional family therapy for adolescents.

"Reality is a crutch for people who can't cope with drugs."

-Lily Tomlin

DRUG ABUSE TREATMENT[4]

Drug addiction is a complex disorder that can involve virtually every aspect of an individual's functioning: in the family, at work and school, and in the community. Because of addiction's complexity and pervasive consequences, drug addiction treatment typically must involve many components. Some of those components focus directly on the individual's drug use; others, like employment training, focus on restoring the addicted individual to productive membership in the family and society enabling him or her to experience the rewards associated with abstinence.

Treatment for drug abuse and addiction is delivered in many different settings using a variety of behavioral and pharmacological approaches. In the United States, more than 13,000 specialized drug treatment facilities provide counseling, behavioral therapy, medication, case management, and other types of services to persons with substance use disorders.

Along with specialized drug treatment facilities, drug abuse and addiction are treated in physicians' offices and mental health clinics by a variety of providers, including counselors, physicians, psychiatrists, psychologists, nurses, and social workers. Treatment is delivered in outpatient, inpatient, and residential settings. Although specific treatment approaches often are associated with particular treatment settings, a variety of therapeutic interventions or services can be included in any given setting.

Because drug abuse and addiction are major public health problems, a large portion of drug treatment is funded by local, State, and Federal governments. Private and employer-subsidized health plans also may provide coverage for treatment of addiction and its medical consequences. Unfortunately, managed care has resulted in shorter average stays, while a historical lack of or insufficient coverage for substance abuse treatment has curtailed the number of operational programs. The recent passage of parity for insurance coverage of mental health and substance abuse problems will hopefully improve this state of affairs.

TYPES OF TREATMENT

Alcohol Addiction

Alcoholics Anonymous[1]

Alcoholics Anonymous (AA) is a fellowship of men and women who share their experience, strength, and hope with each other that they may solve their common problem and help others to recover from alcoholism. The only requirement for

KEY TERMS

AA - Alcoholics Anonymous.

membership is a desire to stop drinking. There are no dues or fees for AA membership.

Shutterstock © Stephanie Bidouze, 2011. Under license from Shutterstock, Inc.

Alcoholics Anonymous (AA) is an international mutual aid movement declaring its "primary purpose is to stay sober and help other alcoholics achieve sobriety."

Al-Anon/Alateen[1]

For over 50 years, **Al-Anon** (which includes Alateen for younger members) has been offering hope and help to families and friends of alcoholics. It is estimated that each alcoholic affects the lives of at least four other people... alcoholism is truly a family disease. No matter what relationship you have with an alcoholic, whether they are still drinking or not, all who have been affected by someone else's drinking can find solutions that lead to serenity in the Al-Anon/Alateen fellowship.

Matrix Model[2]

The Matrix Model provides a framework for engaging stimulant (e.g., methamphetamine, cocaine) abusers in treatment and helping them achieve abstinence. Abusers learn about issues critical to addiction and relapse, receive direction and support from a trained therapist, become familiar with self-help programs, and are monitored for drug use through urine testing.

The therapist functions simultaneously as teacher and coach, fostering a positive, encouraging relationship with the patient and using that relationship to reinforce positive behavior change. The interaction between the therapist and the patient is authentic and direct but not confrontational or parental. Therapists are trained to conduct treatment sessions in a way that promotes the patient's self-esteem, dignity, and self-worth. A positive relationship between patient and therapist is critical to patient retention.

Treatment materials draw heavily on other tested treatment approaches and, thus, include elements of relapse prevention, family and group therapies, drug education, and self-help participation. Detailed treatment manuals contain worksheets for individual sessions; other components include family education groups, early recovery skills groups, relapse prevention groups, combined sessions, urine tests, twelve-step programs, relapse analysis, and social support groups.

KEY TERMS

Al-Anon - Fellowship of relatives and friends of alcoholics who share their experience.

The Matrix Model - Provides a framework for engaging stimulant abusers in treatment and helping them achieve abstinence.

A number of studies have demonstrated that participants treated using the Matrix Model show statistically significant reductions in drug and alcohol use and risky sexual behaviors associated with HIV transmission, as well as improvements in psychological indicators.

Motivational Enhancement Therapy[2]

Motivational Enhancement Therapy (**MET**) is a patient-centered counseling approach for initiating behavior change by helping individuals resolve ambivalence about engaging in treatment and stopping drug use (e.g., alcohol, marijuana, nicotine). This approach employs strategies to evoke rapid and internally motivated change, rather than guiding people stepwise through the recovery process. This therapy consists of an initial assessment battery session, followed by two to four individual treatment sessions with a therapist. In the first treatment session, the therapist provides feedback to the initial assessment battery, stimulating discussion about personal substance use and eliciting self-motivational statements. Motivational interviewing principles are used to strengthen motivation and build a plan for change. Coping strategies for high-risk situations are suggested and discussed with the patient. In subsequent sessions, the therapist monitors change, reviews cessation strategies being used, and continues to encourage commitment to change or sustained abstinence. Patients sometimes are encouraged to bring a significant other to sessions.

Research on MET suggests that its effects depend on the type of drug used by participants and on the goal of the intervention. This approach has been used successfully with alcoholics to improve both treatment engagement and treatment outcomes (e.g., reductions in problem drinking). MET also has been used successfully with adult marijuana-dependent individuals in combination with cognitive-behavioral therapy, comprising a more comprehensive treatment approach. The results of MET are mixed for participants abusing other drugs (e.g., heroin, cocaine, nicotine) and for adolescents who tend to use multiple drugs. In general, MET seems to be more effective for engaging drug abusers in treatment than for producing changes in drug use.

GENERAL CATEGORIES OF TREATMENT PROGRAMS

Detoxification and Medically Managed Withdrawal[3]

Detoxification is the process by which the body clears itself of drugs and is often accompanied by unpleasant and sometimes even fatal side effects caused by

KEY TERMS

MET - Motivational Enhancement Therapy.

withdrawal. As stated previously, detoxification alone does not address the psychological, social, and behavioral problems associated with addiction and therefore does not typically produce lasting behavioral changes necessary for recovery. The process of detoxification often is managed with medications that are administered by a physician in an inpatient or outpatient setting; therefore, it is referred to as "medically managed withdrawal." Detoxification is generally considered a precursor to or a first stage of treatment because it is designed to manage the acute and potentially dangerous physiological effects of stopping drug use. Medications are available to assist in the withdrawal from opioids, benzodiazepines, alcohol, nicotine, barbiturates, and other sedatives. Detoxification should be followed by a formal assessment and referral to subsequent drug addiction treatment.

Long-Term Residential Treatment[3]

Long-term residential treatment provides care twenty-four hours a day, generally in nonhospital settings. The best-known residential treatment model is the therapeutic community (TC), with planned lengths of stay between six and twelve months. TCs focus on the "resocialization" of the individual and use the program's entire community including other residents, staff members, and social context as active components of treatment. Addiction is viewed in the context of an individual's social and psychological deficits, and treatment focuses on developing personal accountability and responsibility as well as socially productive lives. Treatment is highly structured and can be confrontational at times, with activities designed to help residents examine damaging beliefs, self-concepts, and destructive patterns of behavior and adopt new, more harmonious and constructive ways to interact with others. Many TCs offer comprehensive services, which can include employment training and other support services, on site. Research shows that TCs can be modified to treat individuals with special needs, including adolescents, women, homeless individuals, people with severe mental disorders, and individuals in the criminal justice system.

Short-Term Residential Treatment[3]

Short-term residential treatment provides intensive but relatively brief treatment based on a modified twelve-step approach. These programs were originally designed to treat alcohol problems, but during the cocaine epidemic of the mid 1980s, many began to treat other types of substance use disorders. The original residential treatment model consisted of a three- to six-week hospital-based inpatient treatment phase followed by extended outpatient therapy and participation in a self-help group, such as AA. Following their stays in residential treatment programs, it is important for individuals to remain engaged in outpatient treatment programs and/

KEY TERMS

Long-term residential treatment - Lengths of stay between 6 and 12 months in a non-hospital setting.
Short-term residential treatment - A 3-6-week hospital-based inpatient treatment setting.

or aftercare programs. These programs help reduce the risk of relapse after a patient leaves the residential setting.

Outpatient Treatment Programs[3]

Outpatient treatment varies in the types and intensity of services offered. Such treatment costs less than residential or inpatient treatment and often is more suitable for people with jobs or extensive social supports. It should be noted, however, that low-intensity programs may offer little more than drug education. Other outpatient models, such as intensive day treatment, can be comparable to residential programs in services and effectiveness, depending on the individual patient's characteristics and needs. In many outpatient programs, group counseling can be a major component. Some outpatient programs are also designed to treat patients with medical or other mental health problems in addition to their drug disorders.

Individualized Drug Counseling[3]

Individualized drug counseling not only focuses on reducing or stopping illicit drug or alcohol use, it also addresses related areas of impaired functioning such as employment status, illegal activity, and family/social relations as well as the content and structure of the patient's recovery program. Through its emphasis on short-term behavioral goals, individualized counseling helps the patient develop coping strategies and tools to abstain from drug use and maintain abstinence. The addiction counselor encourages twelve-step participation (at least one or two times per week) and makes referrals for needed supplemental medical, psychiatric, employment, and other services.

Group Counseling[3]

Many therapeutic settings use group therapy to capitalize on the social reinforcement offered by peer discussion and to help promote drug-free lifestyles. Research has shown that when group therapy either is offered in conjunction with individualized drug counseling or is formatted to reflect the principles of cognitive-behavioral therapy or **contingency management,** positive outcomes are achieved.

Drug Abuse Treatment in the Criminal Justice System[3]

Research has shown that combining criminal justice sanctions with drug treatment can be effective in decreasing drug abuse and related crime. Individuals under legal coercion tend to stay in treatment longer and do as well as or better than those not

KEY TERMS

Contingency management - Contingency management is a type of treatment used in the mental health or substance abuse fields.

under legal pressure. Often, drug abusers come into contact with the criminal justice system earlier than other health or social systems, presenting opportunities for intervention and treatment before, during, after, or in lieu of incarceration, which may ultimately interrupt and shorten a career of drug use.

BEHAVIORAL THERAPIES[2]

Behavioral treatments help engage people in drug abuse treatment, provide incentives for them to remain abstinent, modify their attitudes and behaviors related to drug abuse, and increase their life skills to handle stressful circumstances and environmental cues that may trigger intense craving for drugs and prompt another cycle of compulsive abuse. Below are a number of behavioral therapies shown to be effective in addressing substance abuse.

Cognitive-Behavioral Therapy[2]

Cognitive-behavioral therapy was developed as a method to prevent relapse when treating problem drinking and later was adapted for cocaine-addicted individuals. Cognitive-behavioral strategies are based on the theory that learning processes play a critical role in the development of maladaptive behavioral patterns. Individuals learn to identify and correct problematic behaviors by applying a range of different skills that can be used to stop drug abuse and to address a range of other problems that often are concurrent.

Cognitive-behavioral therapy generally consists of a collection of strategies intended to enhance self-control. Specific techniques include exploring the positive and negative consequences of continued use, self-monitoring to recognize drug cravings early on and to identify high-risk situations for use, and developing strategies for coping with and avoiding high-risk situations and the desire to use. A central element of this treatment is anticipating likely problems and helping patients develop effective coping strategies.

Research indicates that the skills individuals learn through cognitive-behavioral approaches remain after the completion of treatment. In several studies, most people receiving a cognitive-behavioral approach maintained the gains they made in treatment throughout the following year.

Current research focuses on how to produce even more powerful effects by combining cognitive-behavioral therapy with medications for drug abuse and with other types of behavioral therapies. Researchers are also evaluating how best to train treatment providers to deliver cognitive-behavioral therapy.

Community Reinforcement Approach Plus Vouchers[2]

Community Reinforcement Approach Plus Vouchers is an intensive twenty-four-week outpatient therapy for treatment of cocaine and alcohol addiction. The treatment goals are twofold:

- to maintain abstinence long enough for patients to learn new life skills to help sustain it and
- to reduce alcohol consumption for patients whose drinking is associated with cocaine use.

Patients attend one or two individual counseling sessions each week, where they focus on improving family relations, learning a variety of skills to minimize drug use, receiving vocational counseling, and developing new recreational activities and social networks. Those who also abuse alcohol receive clinic-monitored **disulfiram therapy**. Patients submit urine samples two or three times each week and receive vouchers for cocaine negative samples. The value of the vouchers increases with consecutive clean samples. Patients may exchange vouchers for personal retail goods that are consistent with a cocaine-free lifestyle.

This approach facilitates patients' engagement in treatment and systematically aids them in gaining substantial periods of cocaine abstinence. The approach has been tested in urban and rural areas and used successfully in outpatient treatment of opioid-addicted adults and with inner-city methadone maintenance patients with high rates of intravenous cocaine abuse.

Contingency Management Interventions and Motivational Incentives[2]

Research has demonstrated the effectiveness of treatment approaches using contingency management principles, which involve giving patients in drug treatment the chance to earn low-cost incentives in exchange for drug-free urine samples. These incentives include prizes given immediately or vouchers exchangeable for food items, movie passes, and other personal goods. Studies conducted in both methadone programs and psychosocial counseling treatment programs demonstrate that incentive-based interventions are highly effective in increasing treatment retention and promoting abstinence from drugs.

Some concerns have been raised that a prize-based contingency management intervention could promote gambling as it contains an element of chance and that pathological gambling and substance use disorders can be **comorbid**. However, studies have shown no differences in gambling over time between those assigned to the contingency management conditions and those in the usual care groups, indicating

KEY TERMS

Disulfiram therapy - Disulfiram is used as a conditioning treatment for alcohol dependence. When taken with alcohol, disulfiram causes many unwanted and unpleasant effects.
Comorbid - The presence of one or more disorders (or diseases) in addition to a primary disease or disorder.

that this prize-based contingency management procedure did not promote gambling behavior.

Behavioral Couples Therapy[2]

Shutterstock © Patricia Marks, 2011. Under license from Shutterstock, Inc.

Behavioral Couples Therapy (**BCT**) is a therapy for drug abusers with partners. BCT uses a **sobriety/abstinence contract** and behavioral principles to reinforce abstinence from drugs and alcohol. It has been studied as an add-on to individual and group therapy and typically involves twelve weekly couple sessions that last approximately sixty minutes each. Many studies support BCT's efficacy with alcoholic men and their spouses; four studies support its efficacy with drug-abusing men and women and their significant others. BCT also has been shown to produce higher treatment attendance, naltrexone adherence, and rates of abstinence than individual treatment, along with fewer drug-related, legal, and family problems at one-year follow-up.

Recent research has focused on making BCT more community-friendly by adapting the therapy for delivery in fewer sessions and in a group format. Research is also being conducted to demonstrate cost effectiveness and to test therapy effectiveness according to therapist training.

Family involvement is a particularly important component for interventions targeting youth.

Behavioral Treatments for Adolescents[2]

Drug-abusing and addicted adolescents have unique treatment needs. Research has shown that treatments designed for and tested in adult populations often need to be modified to be effective in adolescents. Family involvement is a particularly important component for interventions targeting youth. Below are examples of behavioral interventions that employ these principles and have shown efficacy for treating addiction in youth.

Multisystem Therapy[2]

Multisystem Therapy (**MST**) addresses the factors associated with serious antisocial behavior in children and adolescents who abuse alcohol and other drugs. These factors include characteristics of the child or adolescent (e.g., favorable attitudes toward drug use), the family (poor discipline, family conflict, parental drug abuse), the

KEY TERMS

BCT - Behavioral Couples Therapy.
Sobriety/abstinence contract - An agreement to remain sober or abstain from the use of drugs or alcohol.
MST - Multisystem Therapy.

peers (positive attitudes toward drug use), the school (dropout, poor performance), and the neighborhood (criminal subculture). By participating in intensive treatment in natural environments (homes, schools, neighborhood settings), most youths and families complete a full course of treatment. MST significantly reduces adolescent drug use during treatment and for at least six months after treatment. Fewer incarcerations and out-of-home juvenile placements offset the cost of providing this intensive service and maintaining the clinicians' low caseloads.

Multidimensional Family Therapy for Adolescents[2]

Multidimensional Family Therapy (**MDFT**) for adolescents is an outpatient, family-based alcohol and other drug abuse treatment program for teenagers. MDFT views adolescent drug use in terms of a network of influences (individual, family, peer, community) and suggests that reducing unwanted behavior and increasing desirable behavior occur in multiple ways in different settings. Treatment includes individual and family sessions held in the clinic, in the home, or with family members at the family court, school, or other community locations.

During individual sessions, the therapist and adolescent work on important developmental tasks, such as developing decision making, negotiation, and problem solving skills. Teenagers acquire vocational skills and skills in communicating their thoughts and feelings to deal better with life stressors. Parallel sessions are held with family members. Parents examine their particular parenting styles, learning to distinguish influence from control and to have a positive and developmentally appropriate influence on their children.

Brief Strategic Family Therapy[2]

Brief Strategic Family Therapy (**BSFT**) targets family interactions that are thought to maintain or exacerbate adolescent drug abuse and other concurrent problem behaviors. Such problem behaviors include conduct problems at home and at school, oppositional behavior, delinquency, associating with antisocial peers, aggressive and violent behavior, and risky sexual behavior. BSFT is based on a family systems approach to treatment, where family members' behaviors are assumed to be interdependent such that the symptoms of any one member (the drug-abusing adolescent, for example) are indicative, at least in part, of what else is going on in the family system. The role of the BSFT counselor is to identify the patterns of family interaction that are associated with the adolescent's behavior problems and to assist in changing those problem-maintaining family patterns. BSFT is meant to be a flexible approach that can be adapted to a broad range of family situations in various settings (mental health clinics, drug abuse treatment programs, other social service

KEY TERMS

MDFT - Multidimensional Family Therapy
BSFT - Brief Strategic Family Therapy.

settings, families' homes) and in various treatment modalities (as a primary outpatient intervention, in combination with residential or day treatment, and as an aftercare/continuing care service to residential treatment).

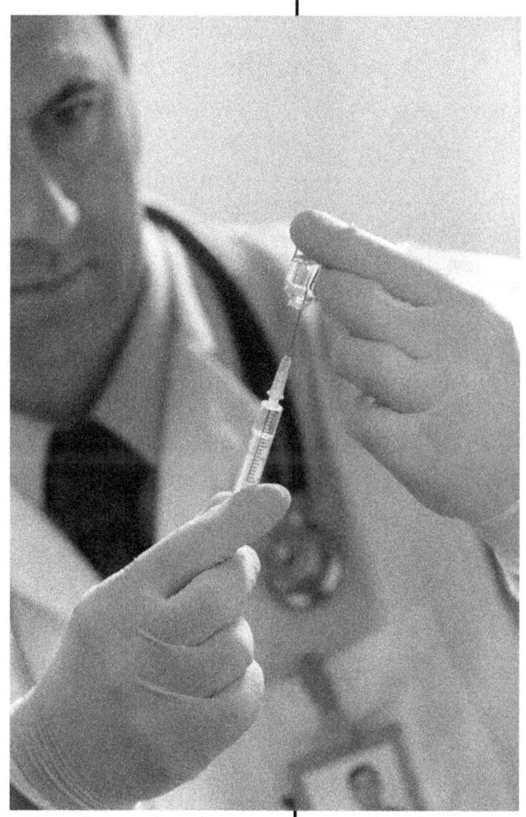
Shutterstock © Wallenrock, 2011. Under license from Shutterstock, Inc.

PHARMACOTHERAPIES

Tobacco Addiction

Nicotine Replacement Treatments

As discussed in Chapter 8, nicotine replacement therapies (NRTs), such as nicotine gum and the transdermal nicotine patch, were the first pharmacological treatments approved by the Food and Drug Administration for use in smoking cessation therapy. NRTs are used (in conjunction with behavioral support) to relieve withdrawal symptoms. They produce less severe physiological alterations than tobacco-based systems and generally provide users with lower overall nicotine levels than they receive with tobacco.[4]

Opioid Addiction

Methadone[5]

Methadone maintenance treatment is usually conducted in specialized settings (e.g., methadone maintenance clinics). These specialized treatment programs offer the long-acting synthetic opioid medication methadone at a dosage sufficient to prevent opioid withdrawal, block the effects of illicit opioid use, and decrease opioid craving.

Methadone maintenance treatment is usually conducted in specialized settings. (e.g., methadone maintenance clinics).

Combined with behavioral treatment: The most effective methadone maintenance programs include individual and/or group counseling, as well as provision of or referral to other needed medical, psychological, and social services. In a study that compared opioid-addicted individuals receiving only methadone to those receiving methadone coupled with counseling, individuals who received only methadone showed some improvement in reducing opioid use; however, the addition of counseling produced significantly more improvement, and the addition of onsite medical/psychiatric, employment, and family services further improved outcomes.

Buprenorphine[5]

Buprenorphine is a partial agonist (it has both agonist and antagonist properties) at opioid receptors and carries a low risk of overdose. It reduces or eliminates withdrawal symptoms associated with opioid dependence but does not produce the euphoria and sedation caused by heroin or other opioids.

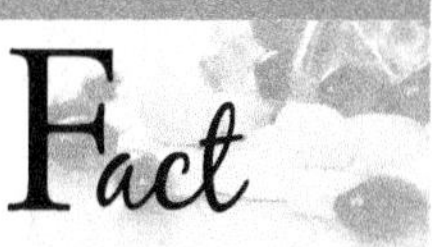

Buprenorphine was the first medication to be approved under the Drug Addiction Treatment Act.

Buprenorphine was the first medication to be approved under the Drug Addiction Treatment Act. Physicians who provide office-based buprenorphine treatment for detoxification and/or maintenance treatment must have special accreditation. These physicians also are required to have the capacity to provide counseling to patients when indicated or, if they do not, to refer patients to those who do. Office-based treatment of opioid addiction is a cost-effective approach that increases the reach of treatment and the options available to patients.

Naltrexone[5]

Naltrexone is a long-acting synthetic opioid antagonist with few side effects. An opioid antagonist blocks opioids from binding to their receptors and thereby prevents an addicted individual from feeling the effects associated with opioid use. Naltrexone as a treatment for opioid addiction is usually prescribed in outpatient medical settings, although initiation of the treatment often begins after medical detoxification in a residential setting. To prevent withdrawal symptoms, individuals must be medically detoxified and opioid-free for several days before taking naltrexone. The medication is taken orally either daily or three times a week for a sustained period. When used this way, naltrexone blocks all the effects, including euphoria, of self-administered opioids. The theory behind this treatment is that the repeated absence of the desired effects and the perceived futility of using the opioid will gradually diminish opioid craving and addiction.

PRINCIPLES OF EFFECTIVE TREATMENT[6]

The following Principles of Drug Addiction Treatment, defined by the National Institute on Drug Abuses, is intended to address addiction to a wide variety of drugs. It is designed to serve as a resource for health care providers, family members, and other stakeholders trying to address the myriad problems faced by patients in need of treatment for drug abuse or addiction.

1. **Addiction is a complex but treatable disease that affects brain function and behavior.** Drugs of abuse alter the brain's structure and function, resulting in changes that persist long after drug use has ceased. This may explain why drug abusers are at risk for relapse even after long periods of abstinence and despite the potentially devastating consequences.
2. **No single treatment is appropriate for everyone.** Matching treatment settings, interventions, and services to an individual's particular problems and needs is critical to his or her ultimate success in returning to productive functioning in the family, workplace, and society.
3. **Treatment needs to be readily available.** Because drug-addicted individuals may be uncertain about entering treatment, taking advantage of available services the moment people are ready for treatment is critical. Potential patients can be lost if treatment is not immediately available or readily accessible. As with other chronic diseases, the earlier treatment is offered in the disease process, the greater the likelihood of positive outcomes.

4. **Effective treatment attends to multiple needs of the individual, not just his or her drug abuse.** To be effective, treatment must address the individual's drug abuse and any associated medical, psychological, social, vocational, and legal problems. It is also important that treatment be appropriate to the individual's age, gender, ethnicity, and culture.
5. **Remaining in treatment for an adequate period of time is critical.** The appropriate duration for an individual depends on the type and degree of his or her problems and needs. Research indicates that most addicted individuals need at least three months in treatment to significantly reduce or stop their drug use and that the best outcomes occur with longer durations of treatment. Recovery from drug addiction is a long-term process and frequently requires multiple episodes of treatment. As with other chronic illnesses, relapses to drug abuse can occur and should signal a need for treatment to be reinstated or adjusted. Because individuals often leave treatment prematurely, programs should include strategies to engage and keep patients in treatment.
6. **Counseling and individual and/or group and other behavioral therapies are the most commonly used forms of drug abuse treatment.** Behavioral therapies vary in their focus and may involve addressing a patient's motivation to change, providing incentives for abstinence, building skills to resist drug use, replacing drug-using activities with constructive and rewarding activities, improving problem solving skills, and facilitating better interpersonal relationships. Also, participation in group therapy and other peer support programs during and following treatment can help maintain abstinence.
7. **Medications are an important element of treatment for many patients, especially when combined with counseling and other behavioral therapies.** For example, methadone and buprenorphine are effective in helping individuals addicted to heroin or other opioids stabilize their lives and reduce their illicit drug use. Naltrexone is also an effective medication for some opioid-addicted individuals and some patients with alcohol dependence. Other medications for alcohol dependence include acamprosate, disulfiram, and topiramate. For persons addicted to nicotine, a nicotine replacement product (such as patches, gum, or lozenges) or an oral medication (such as bupropion or varenicline) can be an effective component of treatment when it is used as part of a comprehensive behavioral treatment program.
8. **An individual's treatment and services plan must be assessed continually and modified as necessary to ensure that it meets his or her changing needs.** A patient may require varying combinations of services and treatment components during the course of treatment and recovery. In addition to counseling or psychotherapy, a patient may require medication, medical services, family therapy, parenting instruction, vocational rehabilitation, and/or social and legal services. For many patients, a continuing care approach provides the best results, with the treatment intensity varying according to a person's changing needs.
9. **Many drug-addicted individuals also have other mental disorders.** Because drug abuse and addiction—both of which are mental disorders—are often concurrent with other mental illnesses, patients presenting with one

condition should be assessed for the other(s). And when these problems occur together, treatment should address both (or all), including the use of medications as appropriate.

10. **Medically assisted detoxification is only the first stage of addiction treatment and by itself does little to change long-term drug abuse.** Although medically assisted detoxification can safely manage the acute physical symptoms of withdrawal and, for some, can pave the way for effective long-term addiction treatment, detoxification alone is rarely sufficient to help addicted individuals achieve long-term abstinence. Thus, patients should be encouraged to continue drug treatment following detoxification. Motivational enhancement and incentive strategies, begun at initial patient intake, can improve treatment engagement.
11. **Treatment does not need to be voluntary to be effective.** Sanctions or enticements from family, employment settings, and/or the criminal justice system can significantly increase treatment entry, retention rates, and the ultimate success of drug treatment interventions.
12. **Drug use during treatment must be monitored continuously, as lapses during treatment do occur.** Knowing their drug use is being monitored can be a powerful incentive for patients and can help them withstand urges to use drugs. Monitoring also provides an early indication of a return to drug use, signaling a possible need to adjust an individual's treatment plan to better meet his or her needs.
13. **Treatment programs should assess patients for the presence of HIV/AIDS, hepatitis B and C, tuberculosis, and other infectious diseases, as well as provide targeted risk-reduction counseling to help patients modify or change behaviors that place them at risk of contracting or spreading infectious diseases.** Typically, drug abuse treatment addresses some of the drug-related behaviors that put people at risk of infectious diseases. Targeted counseling specifically focused on reducing infectious disease risk can help patients further reduce or avoid substance-related and high-risk behaviors. Counseling can also help those who are already infected to manage their illness. Moreover, engaging in substance abuse treatment can facilitate adherence to other medical treatments. Patients may be reluctant to accept screening for HIV (and other infectious diseases); therefore, it is incumbent upon treatment providers to encourage and support HIV screening and inform patients that highly active antiretroviral therapy has proven effective in combating HIV, including among drug abusing populations.

Effectiveness of Treatment[7]

According to several studies, drug treatment reduces drug use by 40-60 percent and significantly decreases criminal activity during and after treatment. Methadone treatment has been shown to decrease criminal behavior by as much as 50 percent. Research shows that drug addiction treatment reduces the risk of HIV infection and that interventions to prevent HIV are much less costly than treating HIV-related illnesses. Treatment can improve the prospects for employment, with gains of up to 40 percent after treatment.

Drug addiction treatment is cost-effective in reducing drug use and its associated health and social costs. Treatment is less expensive than alternatives, such as not treating or simply incarcerating addicts. According to several conservative estimates, every $1 invested in addiction treatment programs yields a return of between $4 and $7 in reduced drug-related crime, criminal justice costs, and theft alone. Major savings to the individual and to society also come from significant drops in interpersonal conflicts, improvements in workplace productivity, and reductions in drug-related accidents.

REFERENCES

1. National Institute on Alcohol Abuse and Alcoholism. (NIAAA). Getting Help, Alcoholics Anonymous, Al-Anon/Alateen, 2007. http://www.collegedrinkingprevention.gov/links/help.aspx
2. Principles of drug addiction treatment: a research based guide. NIDA. http://www.nida.nih.gov/podat/Evidence2.html. Accessed April 23, 2011.
3. Principles of drug addiction treatment: a research based guide. The National Institute on Drug Abuse (NIDA). 2009. http://www.drugabuse.gov/podat/TreatmentUS.html
4. Research Report series: Tobacco Addiction. NIDA. http://www.nida.nih.gov/researchreports/nicotine/treatment.html. Accessed April 23, 2011.
5. Principles of Drug Addiction Treatment: A Research Based Guide. Evidence-based approaches to drug addiction treatment. http://www.nida.nih.gov/podat/Evidence.html. Accessed April 23, 2011.
6. Principles of Drug Addiction Treatment: A Research-Based Guide. 2nd edition. NIDA. http://www.nida.nih.gov/PDF/PODAT/PODAT.pdf. Accessed April 23, 2011.
7. Understanding drug abuse and addiction: what science says. NIDA. http://www.nida.nih.gov/pubs/teaching/teaching3/teaching5.html. Accessed April 23, 2011.